BIG WAVES & WOODEN BENCHES

BIG WAVES
& WOODEN
BENCHES

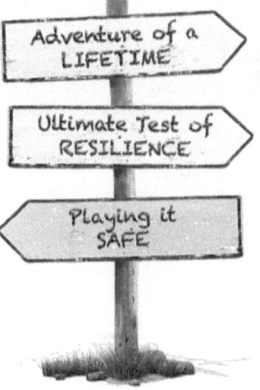

STEPHANIE WILSON

PENDY PRESS

PENDY PRESS

Library of Congress number: TX0009083507

Printed in the United States of America
First Printing, 2022

Hardcover ISBN: 979-8-9854389-2-5
Paperback ISBN: 979-8-9854389-3-2

Interior Design by Hudson Valley Book Design

For Rebecca, Amie, and Cody

This memoir is entirely true and based off the author's memory, which is probably wrong. The portrayal of each character is the author's perception and not necessarily factual. Some names and characteristics have been changed, some events have been compressed and some dialog recreated. Some conversations and characters may or may not be composite.

Trigger Warning:
This book has various triggers throughout. The greatest being chapter 39.

Photo & Video Collection

A chapter by chapter visual collection accompanies this book. If you would like to follow along during (or after) the read, you may do so here:

Instagram:
@BigWavesWoodenBenches

Facebook:
Facebook.com/BigWavesWoodenBenches

Or on my personal website:
www.TheStephanieWilson.com

PROLOGUE

START YOUR STORY WHERE EVERYTHING
CHANGED, THEY SAY.

Well, that's easy to do considering that within a four-week span, a series of events leveled my life as I knew it. A complete detonation, or so it felt. But before I go there—which don't worry, I will—I want to take a moment and start with an unusual suspect, one that looking back now, I believe was the catalyst in my life's unraveling. Let me explain.

It was always there. It slowly reared its head when I was seven, putting on roller-skating shows in the parking lot of our apartment complex. It grew more significant when I was ten and wrote plays for the neighborhood kids to perform on the playground. It continued at fourteen when I realized I would rather be in figure-skating shows impersonating Marilyn Monroe than competing to be the best.

I believed it was all childhood games, and something to let go of when it came time to work hard and focus on a full ride to college and a finance major. The fun Stephanie was replaced with a perfectionist and overly determined go-getter—all to make sure I didn't have the life of struggle I'd had growing up.

Then, during college, I was tasked with a huge class project. Since the assignment would be our only grade, the responsible choice was to make a standard, professional presentation. But that didn't happen. Something deep inside took hold of the steering wheel and there was no stopping it—I convinced my team to forego our plans for a formal presentation and create a film in the style of *Saturday Night Live.*

The film was a perfect dichotomy of hilarious stupid humor and the delivery of serious information from our research. On presentation day, we put in our VHS tape and sat back down with huge smiles on our faces. While the film played, the teacher laughed so hard, he was crying, which mesmerized me. I couldn't take my eyes off him. I sat there feeling different than ever before. Something inside me had come alive. A heartbeat of sorts I wouldn't feel again until a decade later.

Filming that movie was the most fun and enjoyable day of my entire college experience, a day that caused me to quickly become best friends with Caroline, one of my groupmates. Over the years, whenever we met for dinner and drinks, we often reminisced about making that film. Caroline's role had been to present how a company adapts to change. She'd put up an umbrella while the rest of us stood by with buckets of water; instead of pouring the water on top to simulate unexpected rain, we purposely tossed it underneath, choking her while she gave her presentation.

Every time she relived that moment, I would sit and watch her, wishing I could go back and relive that entire day, every day. To Caroline, it was simply a fun memory. She had since found love and had two beautiful children. She believed that a husband was key to my happiness and the missing piece to my successful career, custom home, and excessive shoe closet. However, for me, that memory brought a feeling of joy I had yet to recreate in my adult life. Sometimes when I couldn't sleep, I would research acting and filmmaking classes, wondering if taking one might make me feel that way again.

Ten years after the film, in 2010, during another reminiscing session with Caroline and a little too much wine, I bit the bullet and put myself on the waiting list of a local school called Art Sake Acting Studios. Weeks later, when I'd half-forgotten about doing so, I got a call offering me a last-minute spot in the Wednesday night class. I said yes before I could chicken out and hurried to get ready. Staring in the mirror at my petite, athletic frame and perfectly styled barrel curls, I didn't feel the part. I dunked my brown hair in the sink, letting my natural, puffy curls run wild. With a closet full of pencil skirts and button-down shirts, I wasn't sure if a Billy Joel concert tee, ripped jeans, and red high heels screamed "artist" the way I was hoping it would—but it was the best I had.

I walked into an old industrial building just outside of downtown Orlando, petrified, and after checking in sat down in one of fifty old, red, movie theater chairs. My excitement faded as I listened to the fifteen other students name-drop the schools where they'd gotten their acting degrees. *I don't belong here. What was I thinking? I'm some rookie who made a stupid film in college. These people are legit.*

Yvonne Suhor, the owner and teacher, walked out in harem pants and her blond hair in two buns like Princess Leia, but higher on her head. A former star on the show *Young Riders*, Yvonne gave up her budding acting career to honor her dream to teach.

Looking me up and down, she saw right through my facade. Her gaze landed on my red heels, and she commented how I "looked ready to party" before launching into the syllabus. Her huge brown eyes intimidated me at first, but within minutes, I could feel their warmth.

When my time came to perform our first assignment, I slowly walked onto the carpet and sat in the single plastic green chair placed directly center stage. The glare of the stage lights blocked my classmates' faces. I froze, unable to speak, then began to hyperventilate. Yvonne suggested I get some fresh air before returning to my seat, and encouraged me to try again next week. I had failed.

Despite my struggles, Yvonne taught me that acting is the ultimate exercise in being authentic, vulnerable and fully present—all while letting go of control. A foreign concept to me, and frankly, I hated it. The most intimidating challenge was to attempt those things while the other classmates sat and watched.

Each week, I would pray for Yvonne to shout, "Circle up, bitches," which signified the end of class. Relieved, I'd sit in a circle onstage with my classmates and do a gratitude exercise before heading home. I would walk out to my car raw and vulnerable, only to return the following week with my walls back up for Yvonne to knock back down. She refused to give up on me.

After a year of trying, it finally happened. I was doing a scene onstage and I entered this groove where I was harnessing real emotions from within and using them to make people feel. The scene ended, and the proud look in Yvonne's eyes told me everything I needed to know. I put my hand to my heart and smiled. That heartbeat I hadn't felt since college had returned.

Art Sake is also where I met David, my dearest friend and a fellow student. I remember us standing there, staring at each other, laughing hysterically—as if our souls were like, "There you are. Been looking for ya." Our friendship felt like it always existed. Together, we created a small group of fellow students that became like family—a tribe I was always meant to belong to.

My passion for storytelling ignited like a wildfire. Yvonne took me under her wing, teaching me not only how to act, but how to direct theater, entrusting me as one of her eight directors in her annual fall production of short plays called Play de Luna. Through it all, the two of us became close friends.

••

It all sounds amazing, right? So what's the problem?

You see, I wasn't like those people who had a fulfilling life and a unique side hobby that was fun to explore. The problem was, the more involved I became at Art Sake, the more detached I felt from the other me—a polished, goal-oriented career woman, unfazed by anything that stood in her way and obsessed with looking good on paper.

Yet this story isn't about my love for acting, but rather where that love led me. Inside those walls of that old industrial building, the parts of myself I'd never understood finally made sense. The people accepted me as I was, and I never had to explain myself. I no longer felt ashamed of my scars or my quirks, because at Art Sake, they were celebrated. I felt whole. I felt seen. I felt a sense of freedom that allowed me for the first time in my adult life to see a small glimpse of my authentic self.

So, while the series of events I am about to share feel like the obvious place to start, my soul will forever beg to differ. The safe, successful life I had created wasn't able to sustain even the smallest fraction of the real me, creating large cracks in the false foundations I had built for myself. And so it crumbled.

PART 1:

BIG WAVES

Adventure of a
LIFETIME

Playing it
SAFE

CHAPTER 1

SUMMER, 2013

I woke up drenched in sweat, screaming at the top of my lungs. It took only a few seconds to realize that I wasn't in my house in Orlando, Florida like in the dream, but rather in a hotel room in Mykonos on vacation. I sat up in bed and checked the time—3:00 a.m. Replaying what I could remember of my dream, I was shocked at how real it felt, as if mere minutes had passed since I stood at my bedroom window, peeking out through the blinds at a white van parked across the street with two men inside. My eyes locked with theirs. That was the last thing I remembered. I chalked the dream up to stress and forgot all about it—until it resurfaced two weeks later.

Returning home from my job at a model home sales center, I was looking forward to a quiet night with my rescue dog, Charlie. But when I opened the door, I immediately knew that something was wrong. Instead of waiting for me like always, Charlie was barking, running forward and back and behind me, jumping up, pushing his small paws on the back of my knees, forcing them to bend.

"Jesus, Charlie, what's going on with you?"

My heart raced as I walked into the living room—and froze. Next to where the TV had been, tiny bits of glass shone on the floor. A huge hole was gaping in the burglar-resistant glass in my terrace doors.

Running down my driveway I called 911, desperate to create distance between me and the house. I sat down with Charlie in my lap, and as I waited for the police to arrive, eyed the houses across the street, wondering if my neighbors were watching me. I buried my face in Charlie's fur and closed my eyes.

A mix of emotions whirled around in my body, abruptly interrupted by the sound of a patrol car coming to a halt. I stayed seated, clutching my dog like a frightened child clinging to a teddy bear. Despite my inability to sob, water flowed down my cheeks and onto his fur as two officers walked up the driveway.

"I'm Officer Ramirez. That's Officer Agrait. You reported a break-in?"

"Yes."

"Is there anyone still in the house?" he asked rather coldly.

I looked up at him with mascara-stained cheeks. *Yeah, pal, I searched the house. Tackled the perp down the stairs, hog-tied him, and read him his Miranda Rights. He's in there, waiting for you.*

"I don't know, sir. I was afraid to check," I whispered.

They continued walking toward the house, guns in hand. Twenty minutes later, the officers returned and reported the place clear. My home, though, had been thoroughly ransacked and my safe broken open.

"Anything vital in the safe, ma'am?" Officer Agrait asked, his voice soft and sympathetic.

"Um, everything important. I don't know…checks…credit cards. My passport was definitely in there. Oh God, all my passwords!" I moaned.

Officer Agrait sat down next to me and pulled out a bag of Swedish Fish. He popped a few in his mouth and then tilted the bag my way. His small gesture felt like a much-needed warm blanket.

"No, thanks," I said quietly as Charlie's nose perked up.

"You sure?" he pressed with a warm smile.

"I can't. I'm allergic to red dye #40. Makes me strung out and paranoid. Not something I need right now."

He put the fish away and slowly stood up to join his partner. Thirty minutes later, after dusting for fingerprints and interviewing neighbors, Officer Ramirez handed me a copy of the police report and debriefed me on his findings.

• •

I spent the night at a friend's house. Lying in her guest bed, I struggled to clear my head of the earlier events. Desperate, I forced myself to think of a happy memory at my home. The epic Halloween party I'd thrown the previous year came straight to mind.

I could still see how spooky the entire inside looked with all the red and orange light bulbs I'd put in the lamps. The smell of the catered food from the famous local barbecue joint hovered over my dark wood dining table. The music was so loud that at any moment, I expected the police to show up. I didn't care. Standing in my kitchen, I peered through the large, seamless piece of glass that overlooked the entire outdoor area. The setting sun made the lit tiki torches stand out in the background. I counted sixty people—my mountain-biking friends, my acting tribe, old friends from college, and coworkers—all dressed in Halloween costumes, having the time of their lives around the firepit. Best of all, sitting off to the side in the patio chairs, I saw three of my closest friends: Yanira, David, and Caroline, chatting together for the first time. Since each of them was from a different part of my life, that moment meant everything to me.

Without warning, the orange hue of my party melted into a dark gray, and the walls of my home began to crumble as Officer Ramirez's voice got louder and louder in my head.

Distracting myself was pointless; I couldn't shake his words. While interviewing neighbors, he'd confirmed a white van had indeed been parked across from my home several times. The fact that I had dreamt this shook me to my core and made me want to vomit. To make matters worse, Officer Ramirez warned that I needed to be careful because the burglars might wait for me to buy new things and strike again. Then, as if enjoying the torture, he added that Charlie most likely had hidden somewhere because cute, white, fluffy dogs were usually taken and sold to dogfighting rings as bait.

I don't remember if I set the alarm on the house this morning. If they took Charlie, I wouldn't be able to live with myself. Ever. How can I be so careless? I hugged my dog tightly but couldn't look him in the eye.

I wished I were home to see what they took and how the house had been left. There were only two places on earth that I could ever call "home": my house and Art Sake Acting Studio. Now one of them no longer felt safe.

The next morning, Yanira arrived with two coffees and a bagel sandwich she planned to force-feed me. Yanira and I met in my early twenties at a happy hour. After fifteen minutes of chatting, we agreed to go skiing together the following month. The next morning, she called to confirm it wasn't the wine talking and I said, "I'm game if you are." During that trip to Winter Park, Colorado, Yanira became my comrade for life. When one of us needed a copilot for a mission, the other came running.

We arrived at the bank the minute it opened. Yanira held my hand as I sat in the manager's office and was told my accounts had been emptied already by a woman who walked in the previous afternoon, pretending to be me. My mom had suggested I keep an "in the event of my death" folder in my safe, filled with every piece of information she would need in case something happened to me. Now, a strange woman had the packet containing my checkbook, my passport, spare credit cards, and every password to every login. I needed to see her face. I begged the bank to let me view the security footage; they assured me it would be sent to Officer Agrait.

The stolen money was replenished immediately by the bank— my first bit of positive news. Although it felt good, it didn't take away the feeling of violation in my gut. I hated the fact that someone was out there being me, while I was powerless to stop her.

I spent the afternoon alone, obsessively scrubbing the sticky black fingerprint dust out of the grout in my floor tiles, trying to rid the work-boot prints they showcased. My phone rang and as I went to answer, I noticed a blister had formed on my left index finger. I sent the call to voicemail, found a Band-Aid, and moved on to scrubbing the walls. I didn't want to talk. Besides, I knew why they were calling—that coming weekend, I was supposed to go with my old college friends on our eighth annual girls' trip down to Fort Lauderdale to see Dave Matthews Band.

When they finally got me on the phone, I insisted they give away my ticket, but they refused. I needed a break, they said. Charlie had gone to stay with my mom which gave me the freedom to go. Despite feeling like a zombie, I caved and agreed to join.

Dave Matthews' music has been a huge part of my life in good times and bad. On the worst of days, I would find the right deep-cut song that fit my emotions and play it on repeat. I would study every word, every beat, every inflection until it was ingrained in my head.

It didn't matter that I'd seen them twenty-two times already; the minute they walked out onto the stage, a sense of calm came over me, telling me everything would be okay. To add, it had rained all day causing a huge rainbow to arch over the amphitheater. I couldn't believe my eyes.

Dave began to play, and I surrendered to the beat of their music, swaying back and forth, singing at the top of my lungs. When the encore finished, Carter, the drummer, threw his drumsticks into the crowd, and I caught one in midair. Shocked, I looked at it in my left hand, then turned toward the sea of people cheering and applauding the concert behind me. I looked again at my hand. My first new possession not tainted by the burglary. A tan and yellow drumstick that to this day, stays close to my bedside.

CHAPTER 2

In the wake of the burglary, an onset of feelings and symptoms began to develop. Loud noises made me jump. Everywhere I went, I looked over my shoulder, petrified someone was following me. As I began to replace some of my possessions, I became convinced the men would return as Officer Ramirez had warned.

Frantically, I prepared. I researched things I could spray at my attacker and settled on wasp repellent and a fire extinguisher, placing them next to my nightstand, which now housed a four-inch knife. I planned an escape route through an upstairs window onto the roof and down the back part of my house, and installed a chain ladder to throw out of my bedroom window in case they cornered me.

My preparations didn't stop me from staying up all night in a state of panic, and my lack of sleep limited my ability to form a coherent thought during the day. I pressed on, deciding to return to work after one week. I believed the faster I could reclaim my old sense of normal, the sooner I would feel like myself again. Surviving my first day back felt like a small win—until I returned home to Charlie, that is.

When I walked into the kitchen, I freaked out. My heart pounded and my legs gave way, dropping me to the floor. Someone had been inside my home. By the time the 911 operator answered, I had collected myself enough to process and tell her: I had called by mistake.

On top of my kitchen island sat a dreamcatcher, some tea, and The Lord of the Rings DVD, courtesy of a few friends from Art Sake Studio who had a spare key—friends who knew that sci-fi/fantasy movies bored me straight to sleep. I calmed my breathing and stood up, walking over to the gifts. The words on the card wished me a good night's rest.

The mishap did bother me, but I was nowhere near ready to believe I needed help. *I was just caught off guard, that's all.*

I curbed the support of my friends. I couldn't handle any more sympathy or attention. Yanira pretended to believe me, but then proceeded to fill my fridge with homemade Puerto Rican cooking. Caroline, a natural "fixer," kept insisting there must be something she could do, but she had no idea what that could be. David used our craft as a way to pull my head above water, asking for my help with some preparations for our theater's fall production: Play de Luna.

Over and over, like a parrot repeating the same words, I assured everyone I was fine, despite sitting on a pile of feelings I couldn't identify. My symptoms were getting worse, bleeding into my already rocky work situation.

• •

The company I worked for built homes in large master-planned communities, and my job was to keep the loans from falling through—despite the fact that we were in the middle of the famous housing crisis. Oddly, I found it rather fun. My salary offered basic financial stability, but the more I observed the sales team, the more I craved their relatively large commission structure. After six years in management, I bit the bullet and transferred into sales.

I just about died when I got my first monthly commission check for $12,000. I had never before seen an amount that large with my name on it. As I improved and my sales numbers increased, I quickly socked away the down payment to fulfill the dream of building a home of my own.

I wasn't rich by any stretch, but compared to growing up in a family which occasionally had to rely on public assistance, I now felt flush. My financial status became the missing piece to feeling viable, respectable, and worthy. It also made up for every part of myself that I deemed unlovable.

Everything was going swimmingly until Bethany, another salesperson, was transferred to our community. Within ten minutes of her first day, she turned and addressed the four of us working alongside her, demanding that whoever had Saturdays off switch schedules with her. That person was me.

"Actually, Bethany," I said calmly, "I'm not in charge, but I waited a long time to get my desired schedule. I mountain bike, and races are on Saturdays."

"Well, *my* child plays soccer on Saturdays, which is more important than mountain biking."

My smile faded. "I think that's unfair. I am sorry, but I can't." I swiveled back around.

"Well, I highly suggest you rethink your decision," she warned.

After thirty days, Bethany got promoted to general sales manager. A week later, her high heels resounded her fury on the wood floor as she showed up unannounced in our sales center, transferring me to a slow community out in the middle of cow pastures—a direct threat to my cherished commissions.

Over dinner that evening, Caroline begged me not to quit. Being a stay-at-home mom, she didn't have a career but understood hard work, loyalty, and dedication. She urged me to work through the situation.

I stuck with my new assignment and worked my ass off, selling twenty-one homes in five months. But instead of praising me, Bethany created problems where they didn't exist, writing me up for a bad attitude and putting me on a ninety-day improvement plan.

The burglary occurred sixty days later, adding to my work struggles. At the end of the ninety days, Bethany sat smiling widely as the Vice President of Sales fired me.

Back home, I sunk into my couch, defeated. Eight years of loyalty flushed down the toilet. I never should have left my former team. *I put money first. And look where it got me.*

Then, a tornado of panic rushed through me: racing thoughts, physical pain, a pounding heart. I couldn't breathe. The room started to spin. Paranoia convinced me my dog and I were in danger. I grabbed Charlie and ran into the garage, making a beeline for a hidden closet I had designed for my bicycles, then slammed the door and crouched in the corner.

Through my panic, it took a moment to realize my mountain bike was there, safe and sound where I had left it last year. *They didn't take it.*

In the midst of hyperventilating, I stared at my old friend and the dirt still caked on her tires. I flashed back to my last ride, hearing the sound of high-pitched, squeaky brakes echoing down a mountain in Wyoming.   • •

In 2008, five years before the break-in, I wandered into a bike shop looking for a good deal. As I was eyeing a road bike, another customer approached me. He introduced himself as Shawn and began a sales pitch about how I should buy a mountain bike instead.

"They ride over things like curbs and logs," he said enthusiastically. *That sounds awful.*

"Besides, there's a group of us that meets every Tuesday night. We ride around town, then go eat and have some beers. You'll meet cool people. Learn some riding skills. It's great exercise."

Now he had my attention.

He motioned to a mountain bike in the corner.

"It's the color of Pepto-Bismol." I gagged.

"It's a great one to learn on. You could call it 'The Pink Panther.' We all name our bikes."

Shawn and I chatted a bit about the riding group he belonged to. I was still two years away from finding Art Sake and the tribe of people inside its doors, and craved belonging to a community. So much so that I agreed to buy an ugly-ass bike and show up the following night to ride it with complete strangers.

In the parking lot I paused and stared at my small, blue Audi A4 sedan, unsure how to fit the bike inside. I heard Shawn's voice again.

"Here, let me take it home with me. I'll tune it up for you and then bring it to the ride," he offered. I agreed…

I paid $550 for this thing and just let a complete stranger take it.

Lucky for me, he was an honest guy.

My inaugural group ride on The Pink Panther was painful. It took a week to stop limping from trying so hard to keep up. But sitting afterward at a table full of beer pitchers while I listened to the guys cheer my success made it worth it. I was now an accepted part of the group.

My abilities improved and I even dabbled in racing. But a few big crashes made me fearful of a sport I equally loved for the people it brought into my life. My constant bruises garnered a plea from my mother to quit and take up knitting instead.

The worst crash happened when my friend Derek dragged a few of us to a race that included fun challenges at various stopping points. The hipsters who hosted it stood next to their stylish bikes in their jean shorts and bright-colored shirts. Meanwhile we looked like a bunch of Ninja Turtles, with our dark baggy clothes, big backpacks, and muddy shins. They welcomed us anyway.

Thanks to a large stick in my wheel, I crashed within seconds of the race starting. Despite bloody legs and a huge blow to my head, I kept riding. By the third stop where we had to rap for ten seconds about our bike, the dizziness from my concussion became unbearable.

Derek noticed I was struggling to stand up straight. I insisted I was fine, found my physical balance, and looked up at the attendee recording me with a camera. I threw down the words in full-on rapper style as if I were Jay-Z.

"I might be dizzy, but I just rode up this hill,
'Cuz I got dope gadgets and a ton of skill.
Don't look at me like that;
I don't care what you think.
I'll leave you in the dust despite my bike being pink."

Everyone stared at me, stunned. We all started laughing. Later, while in the emergency room, I got a text from Derek. I had received the award for "best rapper" of the race. Derek was, and still is, most impressed by this.

My mountain-biking days came to an end during a trip to the Grand Tetons. While my two girlfriends hopped off the ski lift and barreled down the mountain, I stood frozen as all my recent crashes came flooding back. What I really wanted was to ride through canopied flat trails singing along to Dave Matthews from a portable speaker until I found the perfect place to sit and eat my packed lunch. By this time, I had already started Art Sake and could now discern the difference between trying something that scared me and putting myself in a situation I deemed dangerous for the sake of belonging. *I can't do this anymore.*

Unfortunately, there was only one way down. So, I leaned back into a standing position, squeezed the seat with my thighs, and pressed down on those brakes with my two hands like my life depended on it. The bike shook. It wanted to go faster, but I refused to let it. Every biking skill I had acquired over the years abandoned me. I lost control of my body and flopped around like a rag doll. A long "ahhhh" hiccupped out of me with every bump, harmonizing perfectly with the loud squeak of my brakes echoing down the mountain.

At the bottom I came to a full stop. My hands were throbbing from the death grip but I didn't care; I was just grateful to be alive.

• •

I came back to reality, sitting on the cement ground of my bike closet, holding Charlie. I blinked a few times, noticing my breathing had calmed and my panic attack had ended. Charlie started to squirm. I looked down at him, petting his cream and tan fur that reminded me of squiggly uncooked ramen noodles. I hugged him and whispered, "It's gonna be okay, baby boy."

Leaning my head back against the cement I exhaled. I knew I had to leave that toxic work environment. But I wasn't ready. The one thing I needed most now was a sense of control. Instead, I felt out of control. I ached with the loss of so many of my possessions and digital photos. I felt haunted with guilt because the burglars could have taken Charlie. I hated the fact that someone was walking around with my vital documents pretending to be me. *Within a matter of a month my life has imploded, and now, I am afraid I am losing my mind.*

I used the back tire to help me to my feet, then ran my hand over the bike frame and up to the left brake as I walked toward the door. Before I could let go I squeezed the lever tightly, realizing that once again, I was barreling out of control down a mountain, clutching the brakes for dear life.

Time to get some help.

CHAPTER 3

The sign on the door said, Psychologist and Life Coach.

Hold on a second. I'm here for a referral to a psychiatrist. I need a pill for my symptoms—not life coaching. I hope my chart specifies that.

I walked in, glancing around an overly bright and airy waiting room with motivational sayings everywhere one could fit. Yellow table lamps, flanking a muted green couch, rested on a shaggy, off-white carpet that made my nude high heels look an inch shorter as I sat down. I stared at two of the motivational posters hung above the sign-in table, mentally measuring the distance from their edges to the end of the wall, annoyed at how off-center they were hung.

I had seen a psychologist only once before—seven years ago at age twenty-six. Comments from old college friends about my personality made me suspect there was something wrong with me. Maybe I even had autism like my sister. So, I went and got tested. The doctor diagnosed me with "needing new friends"…and dyslexia.

My mother's nonchalant reaction to my news shocked me more than my diagnosis. She confessed that during my fourth-grade year at Blessed Sacrament Catholic School, my struggles became apparent to teachers who suggested I be placed in a special class. My mother protested the school's decision, explaining that my "I'll-figure-it-out" attitude would diminish if I knew about my challenges. Her unsuccessful plea made that year at Blessed Sacrament my last. Mom never shared the real reason I switched schools, leaving me to believe it had to do with me yelling at Father Gordon.

The incident occurred that same year when my mother bartended at the school's annual fundraiser, Casino Night—a volunteering commitment in exchange for free tuition. Infuriated by the hypocrisy, my nine-year-old self stormed into school the following Monday and announced that I needed to speak to Father Gordon immediately.

"Yes, Stephanie," he said softly, noticing my distress.

"Father, Mrs. Smith says that alcohol and gambling are bad and not what Jesus would do. You made my mom be the bartender at Casino Night. You are not following Jesus. You should be ashamed of yourself!" I said with my finger pointing at him.

I stared at Father Gordon and waited. He said nothing. But the expression on his face told me that he understood my message loud and clear. The following year, my mother switched me to a nearby Baptist school, and I grew up believing that I got kicked out of Blessed Sacrament because I had exposed the Catholic Church.

At my new school, I spent most of my time in class daydreaming. With each passing year, reading comprehension became increasingly challenging, but I didn't know why. Eventually, I found my secret to success: I transformed everything into a movie in my head, which enabled me to comprehend the teacher's lectures almost verbatim. With the added help of classmates who took the time to tell me what they read in our schoolbooks, I consistently made A's and B's. The episode taught me that with a little cleverness, I could accomplish anything I set my mind to.

The memory of my time in school reminded me of my strength and I questioned my decision to seek help. I reached down into the psychologist's shaggy rug and grabbed my purse strap. *Time to go. I will figure this out on my own. I don't want to be dissected by a "life coach."*

As luck would have it, the second I stood to leave, my name was called. I cursed under my breath and made my way into the therapist's office, walking as fast as my long, navy pencil skirt would allow.

If Oprah had a twin sister, she would be her. Sitting in a brown accent chair, Deborah was dressed like a crisp hundred-dollar bill, exuding a grounded, powerful essence that intimidated me. I set down my bag, sat on the couch, and observed her observing me.

Taking charge of the conversation, I told her about my evil boss firing me, my house being robbed, feeling guilty about Charlie, and how someone had stolen my identity. Then, I rapidly listed my symptoms on my fingers, like one doctor consulting another, and ended my speech by requesting a referral for a prescription, all in what felt like seconds. Deborah remained silent for a long moment, probably to let me take a breath.

"Stephanie, I believe you have PTSD. It's very normal after a traumatic event. How long ago was the burglary again?"

"Thirty days ago."

"That's very recent. Hang in there. The symptoms should subside within the next ninety days or so."

"I'd rather take something to speed it up," I insisted.

"I understand. But first, I'll need to ask you some questions. Get to know you a little more. Then, afterward, I can potentially refer you to a psychiatrist for a prescription." Her voice was calm but firm.

I looked at Deborah, defeated. To get what I wanted, I would have to share. Time to charm the gatekeeper.

"No problem," I said sweetly, crossing my legs and folding my hands.

She gathered her thoughts. "So, tell me something about how you've spent your time over the last five years."

"Well, I graduated with my MBA last December."

"Congratulations. From where?"

"Florida State University." Unable to resist the urge to impress her, I continued. "All while working full-time, studying acting, and building a custom home."

"Well done." She nodded, scribbling on her yellow legal pad.

Deborah sounded sincere, which softened my stance a bit. I could feel my shoulders relax.

"And the acting," she continued, "that's very interesting. How long have you been doing that?"

"Three years."

"How fun. Have you been in any TV shows?"

I laughed out loud at her question.

"No. I've directed a few short plays, but other than that, I just take classes."

She nodded and wrote down a few more comments. "So, was grad school fun for you?"

"Um, I had some fun, but it was pretty difficult for me, to be honest."

"Why was that?"

"I barely got in. I struggle with timed tests and couldn't pass the GMAT."

"If you didn't pass it, how did you get in?" she asked, leaning in toward me.

"I showed up at some talk the dean was giving, handed him my résumé, and made a deal with him to let me in on a probationary semester to prove that I could make good grades."

"Wow, that takes a lot of determination."

"Nah, just a bit of cleverness."

"And hard work."

"Oh, yeah. I worked hard…only to be forgotten at graduation." I laughed.

"You're kidding."

"Nope. There were only fifty of us to hood, but somehow the dean forgot me. I didn't know what to do. My family drove five hours to be there. I stared at them from the stage, confused. Eventually, the audience got the dean's attention and he scrambled to find my name on the list. He apologized and said, 'Without further delay, Sharon Williams, please come forward.' So then I had to tell him that was not my name. He leaned into the mic and corrected himself. The entire auditorium burst out laughing."

"That's horrible. I am so sorry that happened," Deborah replied. I shook my head.

"Nah, I love a good story. Besides, I got my revenge. I stole the hood they lent us to wear for the ceremony as a keepsake."

Deborah tried not to laugh but did anyway, which I immensely enjoyed. She looked down at the clipboard of paperwork I'd filled out prior to my appointment.

"So, it says here that you sold homes for a builder. You worked there for eight years. What about before that?"

"I was a loan officer at a mortgage company."

"And why did you change jobs?"

"Their rates were really high. I felt like I was taking advantage of people, and it stressed me out."

"I think it's wonderful that you were able to acknowledge the importance of your values and make a choice to change jobs."

"Thanks," I said, hoping to move the conversation along.

"Tell me about your family."

"Well, I'm the youngest of three. My oldest sister, Rebecca, has been married for fifteen years and has four kids. My middle sister, Amie, has special needs similar to Down Syndrome and lives with my mom and stepdad. Other than that, I have my grandmother, who lives in an assisted living facility. Ever since Pop died, my mom helps take care of her."

"What about your father?"

"He left before I was born. Met him when I was seven, but we don't have a relationship. I might even have a half-brother, but I don't know for sure."

"I'm sorry to hear that."

"It's no big deal. My Pop stepped up and was a better dad than I could have hoped for. We were insanely close."

"I bet it was hard to lose him," she said softly.

Without warning, and to my utter shock, tears fell down my face. She handed me a box of tissues, and I blew my nose loudly. "Sorry about that," I said, trying to hide my embarrassment.

"This is a safe space, Stephanie." She pointed to a trash can where I could discard the soggy tissues.

"Thank you. Losing my Pop still gets me choked up sometimes."

"I don't blame you. Are you okay with continuing our conversation?"

"Yeah, go ahead." I wadded my remaining tissues into a ball.

"Can you tell me what made your relationship with your Pop so special?"

I fought to stay composed, raising my voice an octave so that it didn't tremble.

"He was different. He loved a good story and a crazy adventure. He noticed I was into the outdoors, so he took me on long hikes. Taught me how to fall out of trees, wipe my knees, and keep having fun, ya know? He wasn't tough on me, but he challenged my abilities any chance he got. I spent my summers in his garage, helping him build boats and model train sets. He encouraged me to take a different road, try new things, experience the world and life. He hated living on a hamster wheel. There was no one like him. I trusted him. He was the father figure I needed…and then some."

I paused, expecting Deborah to say something. But she remained silent.

"When he passed I was holding his hand. I was only twenty-three."

I took a long moment, remembering how hard that day had been. How I felt his pulse in his left wrist slowly fade to nothing as a huge wind came into the room through the french doors at the hospice center. How I watched the wind swirl around the papers on the counter as if his soul was doing a victory lap around the room before leaving. How I told him it was okay to go as long as he showed me signs that he was still there, watching over me. I stared at my shredded tissue and then looked up at Deborah, realizing something I hadn't before.

"I think a part of me died too that day. I haven't been the same without him." I shook my head. "Please. I can't talk about him anymore."

"That must have been tough for your mom to raise three kids alone," Deborah said, honoring my request to change the subject.

"Yeah, money was a never-ending struggle. But she always figured out a way."

"Do you get along with your sisters?"

"Yeah. My oldest, Rebecca, helped raise us. She was more like a second mom. Amie is a blast. She is mentally still a kid. Still believes in Santa Claus. We have a lot of fun together."

"Growing up, was it hard to have a sister like Amie?"

"Of course, it was hard when people made fun of her. That and my mom could never work a normal job. Amie's needs were unpredictable. But we were close. Even with her delayed development, she was hell-bent on keeping up with me. She is three years older, but she walked when I walked, talked when I talked, et cetera. All beyond the doctor's expectations."

"And how does that make you feel?" she asked.

"I don't know. Good, I guess?"

"Valued?"

"Yeah, especially because I was deemed the 'one that would be trouble.' "

"Why is that?"

"I was full of energy and ideas. I was a lot to keep up with."

"Did you stay that way all through childhood?"

"No. By high school, I learned it was better not to make waves in an already hectic situation."

"How was your high school experience?"

"It was fine. I just wanted it to be over. I didn't really fit in."

"Did you date in high school?" she asked.

"Not really, no. I knew I needed a scholarship, so I was super focused. I had a serious boyfriend in college. Jed."

"How long were you together?"

"Almost four years. I saw the back of his head at a karaoke bar and told my friend that he was my future husband—without even seeing his face."

"That's a pretty strong connection," she said. "So what happened?"

"I wasn't ready for where it was going. I ended it and then three months later moved to France to study abroad for my final semester. Stayed a whole year. I came back, and we thought about rekindling, but I still wasn't ready to get married."

"Why do you think you weren't ready?"

"Marriage felt like a prison sentence."

"So, that was it?" she asked.

"Yep, he met someone else, married her, and now has two children and a white picket fence."

"You sound like you're relieved."

"I don't know if I would say I'm relieved. I just don't think I'm cut out for a traditional life."

"How does your family feel about that?"

I chuckled. " 'You'll find someone and fall in love and change your mind eventually,' " I said, using air quotes.

"Who says that?"

"Everyone," I replied curtly, letting her know we were done probing my past love life.

"How about socializing? Did you ever have a problem making friends?"

"Not really."

"Any drinking or drug struggles?" she asked.

"I love my wine, but no."

"Any other addictions or disorders we need to discuss?"

My posture stiffened, but I tried to play it off as readjusting. Of course, Deborah noticed and gave me a look that screamed, "Out with it." My head dropped. "I had some issues with bingeing and purging. I don't do it anymore, though."

I had never spoken these last words out loud before.

"Did you get treatment?" she asked.

"Well, my training at Art Sake helped greatly. That's where I study acting. But, no, I stopped on my own."

"That takes some strength."

Her response caught me off guard. "Thanks," I said.

"When did it begin?"

"About 2007. I felt like I didn't fit in with some of my old college friends, which sparked it, I suspect. But that's over now. The disorder, I mean."

"You have mentioned several times now about feeling like you didn't fit in. Was that always how you felt?"

"Pretty much. I was made fun of a lot in school, which was like, I dunno, whatever. I had plans, and I focused on those."

"But it still had to hurt a bit."

"Yeah, I guess. It hurt more in my adult life. I have some pretty tough friends."

"What do you mean by 'tough'?"

"Some of my old friends are very critical. When we get together with people who don't yet know me, they warn them that I am intense, weird, and super uptight. They don't know I know they do this."

"Why do you stay friends with them?"

"I figure they're just insecure, and I try to feel compassion for them. They joke with me about how good I am at everything and compliment me a lot—but I can feel their underlying annoyance with me."

"They have no idea how hurtful they are to you?"

"Probably not."

"And do they know you were struggling with a disorder?"

"No. No one did. And it will stay that way," I said firmly.

To my relief, Deborah set her notepad down. "Are you happy with your life?" she asked.

"Well, yeah. I've done everything I should have. I'm well-connected in my industry. I could get another job with a builder tomorrow if I wanted. I have a beautiful home, some money saved. I have my theater tribe, and I volunteer often. I have tons of great friends, even if some of the old ones are questionable. I have an active social life. Charlie, my Bichon mix, is the love of my life. What's not to be happy about?"

Deborah sat for a minute, looking at me intently. I could feel her warmth and compassion. At the same time, I could tell she was about to drop some kind of a hammer.

"Stephanie, I know you came here wanting to relieve your PTSD symptoms with a prescription. I'm sorry, I don't believe that is the solution. The symptoms will subside. Just give it time. But to be honest with you, I think there is something else going on here."

"Well, I'm not thrilled that you won't refer me, but I am curious what you think the issue is," I said, deflated.

"I see a bright young woman in front of me who loves her family, accomplishes goals, values community and adventure, but I couldn't help but wonder if there was something underneath it all that's wanting to surface," she said.

"What's that?"

"Freedom."

She looked steadily at me, waiting to see how that word landed.

"I'm free. I have no obligations weighing me down," I replied.

"You appear free, but I don't believe you truly are. Your achievements are great, and I'm sure you enjoyed most of them, but they were driven by either a need to belong or a fear of being poor. I also suspect that you've stayed away from marriage because that would solidify a life that you secretly aren't happy living."

I didn't know what to say.

"The life choices you've made seemed to have been in reaction to something, be it people's opinions, your lack of confidence, your father who abandoned you, or the world you think has rejected you. Your authentic self-expression is stifled, and I fear that if you continue to make decisions based on what you think you should be doing, you'll never have the freedom you subconsciously seek."

I stared at her, desperately wanting to get up and leave.

"Let me ask you something. When was the last time you took a risk that wasn't calculated?"

"I'm not sure what you mean," I replied softly.

"A risk where there is no agenda attached."

"I don't know," I said, defeated.

"I'm not shaming you."

My discomfort made me crave my old ways. My mind escaped, thinking of all the foods I wanted to binge on. I saw myself cooking Velveeta shells and cheese, snacking on Pringles in one hand and Oreos in another, with a freshly-made carrot cake waiting in the fridge.

"Stephanie," Deborah said, snapping me out of my fog. "At some key point in your life, I suspect after your Pop's death, that adventurous girl who was full of energy and ideas fell silent, and you've been carefully protecting her ever since. Maybe in the midst of everything that's happened recently, she is trying to tell you she is ready to come out."

"But she has come out. Doesn't my acting class count?"

"Stephanie." Deborah looked me square in the eyes. "I suspect those classes are just the tip of the iceberg."

I stared at the door, more fearful of her words than I wanted to admit.

"I'd like to coach you through this if you agree to us working together long-term. I think we can really peel back some layers and restore some freedom into your life."

"Can I think about it?"

"No problem. Regardless, I would like to see you again next week, and I have a small challenge for you to do beforehand. Think of a small risk that you want to take. Something that speaks to your heart versus something your brain thinks you need to do, something for the pure sake of the experience versus any form of agenda. It can be small, but nothing is off limits, okay?"

" 'Small challenge,' my ass!" I said, standing up.

She smiled. She knew I heard her loud and clear.

I unlocked my car door having already decided I wasn't going to complete the assignment.

CHAPTER 4

I spent the next four days dedicated to my couch, Charlie, takeout food, and romantic comedies. It felt good to relax, not think, and let my PTSD symptoms stay at bay as much as possible. On day four of my veg-out, I ordered my favorite Thai food and put on the movie *Pride and Prejudice*. Just as Mr. Darcy was confessing his love to Elizabeth for the first time, I pressed pause. Deborah had said something in our session that I couldn't shake, something about how the adventurous girl who'd fallen silent was trying to come out. Frankly, it was haunting me.

I grabbed a notebook and pen.

"Okay, younger Stephanie. What do you want? You tell me, and it's done."

I waited for something to write down. Nothing came.

"Fine. Have it your way." I tossed the notebook to the other side of the couch before pressing play again.

Sitting with my arms crossed I stared at the TV, half paying attention. As Mr. Darcy confessed his love to Elizabeth for the second time, I wandered back to the past, visualizing my younger, wide-eyed self. I was in Pop's garage, helping him shellac a boat he was building. He was telling me a story of how in Trinidad, his ship had been one of the first to sail through the jungle, and how the monkeys went nuts the first time they'd heard a ship's horn blare. He laughed, his face alive and full of excitement over his memory. I remembered feeling how badly I wished I was there, in his story, to see the monkeys. To be on that ship.

I grabbed my notebook and it took three seconds to write down: *I want to see the world.*

I wondered what it would be like on a ship, out in the middle of the ocean, hopping from country to country. *Does a trip like this even exist?* I grabbed my new laptop and googled: "see the world on a ship." The results shocked me. I found four trips offered from four different companies. *One hundred fifteen days on a small ship with the same people? These ships literally circle the globe. That's insane! I'll have to remember this for when I retire.* I closed my laptop and went to bed.

The following day, I couldn't resist the urge to play pretend. I canceled my planned veg-out and headed to Office Depot to buy a 3' x 5' map of the world, colored permanent markers, and some wine from the shop next door. Just for fun, I decided to plot the courses of those four trips to see which one I would go on if I won the lottery. Activities like this were not unusual for me. The last time I'd played this game, I spent two days researching small mountain towns with all four seasons and a great main street, planning every detail of a move I would never make.

I spread the map out on the floor and chose the red, black, blue, and green markers—one color for each ship. I selected one course and drew its path from country to country, then, using another color, began marking another course. Four ships, four courses, four colors.

Sitting back, I stared at the different lines swimming around each other like snakes circling the earth. Oddly, the black line seemed to float off the map and appear more prominent than the rest. *But why? Green is my favorite color.* I stared at the green line, waiting. Nothing. I returned to the black line. Again, it floated. Weirded out, I walked away.

For the rest of the evening I sat in silence with Charlie, watching the night roll in. The map, leaning against a nearby wall, stared at me. I felt as if that black line were imprinting itself in my mind like a mental tattoo. The pull it had on my heart was alarming. I wanted nothing more than to travel its course. To live out that line. *What has come over me?*

The next morning when Charlie needed his walk, I refused to look at the map on the way out the door. I feared making eye contact with it, petrified that I would look at it and still feel the need to go, and almost equally petrified that I would feel nothing.

Returning from Charlie's walk, I did it: I found the courage to look at the map. In two seconds, I knew I needed to call and get more information. I dialed the number from the website, ignoring the pounding in my heart. *It's just a call. Only information, no commitments. It's just a person, and you are only having a conversation. Calm down. Stop being so dramatic.*

"This is Diane. How may I assist you?"

"Hi, Diane, my name is Stephanie. I found Holland America's Grand World Voyage during an internet search and would like more information."

"Absolutely. The trip is one hundred fifteen days around the world. It departs from Fort Lauderdale, sails west, and then returns across the Atlantic back to Fort Lauderdale. It's like a cruise ship, but much smaller and more personalized—without the dance clubs, rock-climbing walls, things like that. It's an experience of a lifetime, but usually with a much older crowd. You sound young. Would that bother you?"

"Not at all. I figured I would be one of the youngest. I'm thirty-three, but I get along great with senior citizens." I felt stupid as soon as those words left my mouth.

"That's great! You might be the youngest, but if you can take time off and do something like this now, it's an experience you'll never forget. Have you looked at the pricing?"

The website said a ticket is twenty-two thousand dollars.

"I did, and I might be able to swing a ticket. But it's just me. Do you have a cabin for just one person?"

"We don't, unfortunately. You'll have to buy an entire room, which is two tickets at forty-four thousand dollars total. Excursions are not included, which can add up to be over ten thousand, not to mention alcoholic drinks and any incidentals. We can give a slight discount, but I won't be able to do much more."

Holy shit.

"Wow. Okay, how long do I have to come up with the money?" I asked, playing along.

"Well, our 2014 Grand World Voyage leaves in January. That's only about sixty days away, so we would need payment in full in thirty days."

"That's a bit quick," I said.

"Well, we could book you for 2015 if that works. That way, you have a year to pay the fare."

A voice in my head whispered, *Keep listening.*

"Well, that's something to consider," I said. "Can you give me more information?"

"Absolutely. But before I continue, I am curious what made you decide on this route? We are a travel agency, and I can book you on any of the voyages."

I decided not to tell her that this route had floated off the map. "It's the only one that goes to the pyramids. I can't imagine going around the world and not seeing them."

"Oh, I agree! You know, when researching excursions at each port, take note that you can leave the ship for a few days at a time and meet back up at the next port. So, in India, you can fly to see the Taj Mahal. In Greece, you can leave and go inland to see the monasteries. In Ecuador, you can fly up to see the actual equator."

As Diane recited all the places I could go, an imaginary cartoon came to life in my mind. There I was, hanging off the mast of a tiny brown wooden sailboat with a bright orange scarf around my neck, floating in the strong wind like the ship's flag. I was shouting to the captain at the helm to point in the direction of Tonga! Nuku Hiva! Myanmar! My directive orders changed as the names of these ports rolled off Diane's tongue. Remote places I would probably never see in this lifetime. I had to go. I needed to go. My soul had already left; she had set sail, and I needed to catch up to her.

"Does this sound like something you want to do? The deposit is refundable for ninety days, so if you change your mind, you can always call us."

She had me. Sweeping aside all concerns about logic or money, I shouted "YES!" into the phone.

"All right, Stephanie. Let's get a small deposit and locate your ideal cabin. May I suggest midship? It's the best area."

"Works for me!"

"Cabin 2152 on the starboard side is my recommendation."

"It's perfect." I closed my eyes and smiled.

"Great. I'm going to send you a packet of information. There are vaccines you will need, forms to sign, visas to obtain. Don't worry; we'll walk you through everything. For now, know that on January 5, 2015, you will set sail around the world. We are so happy to have you, Stephanie," she said before thanking me for my business and wishing me a great day.

"A great day"? Dude, I just booked a trip around the world…by phone…the same way you order pizza. Dear God!

I calmed myself down and picked up the phone again. I needed to cancel my appointment with Deborah.

The only person I would allow to talk me out of this would be me.

CHAPTER 5

I stared at the chandelier above my bed, wishing it was a fan, and wiped the sweat off my neck with my already drenched shirt. *No big deal. Just another night sweat—a gentle reminder that my PTSD still needs time to wear off.*

Sitting up, I remembered the decision I'd made yesterday, and a big smile spread across my face. I hopped out of bed and ran downstairs to make coffee, giddy over how much planning needed to be done. I took my coffee outside to the backyard, enjoying the overcast skies and post-rain breeze while Charlie stood at the edge of the patio's brick pavers, refusing to step foot in the wet grass. The side eye he gave me every time I told him to go pee made me laugh. Leaving him for 115 days would be tough on us both, a sobering thought that queued my sense of logic.

What if saying yes to this cruise was just a way to open me up more to other things already in my life that if I let them, could make me feel this same way? A catalyst of sorts versus something I am meant to follow through with.

My brain searched for anything it could think of to tempt my heart to cancel the reservation, leaving no stone unturned. The only thing that came remotely close to making me feel excited was the idea of leaving the safe confines of my acting class and trying to perform in front of a live audience. My heart leaped out of my chest at the thought, but then crippled itself with fear and insecurity. The last thing I wanted to do was make a fool out of myself, but this could be the answer. I needed to try. Not to mention that in perfect timing, Play de Luna auditions were the following week. While I would already be in attendance as one of the directors, I decided to put myself out there and audition for a role in the show. *Maybe this is the alternative.*

Two days later, I sat with Yvonne in the back lawn of Hillstone, a restaurant the two of us frequented often. The grassy lakefront area had little carved out alcoves covered in gray gravel, with Adirondack chairs and small wooden side tables. We enjoyed lounging and chatting about life over wine, grilled artichokes, and smoked salmon while the sun set over the water.

That evening, before I had a chance to bring up the subject myself, Yvonne suggested I audition for one of the plays. When I expressed my trepidation over performing outside the comforts of class, she said, "Why don't you try? Take a risk?"

The word *risk* hit me right in the gut. My mind wandered to Deborah and her challenge for me. I suspected a smaller, easier risk like acting in a short play leaned more toward what she had in mind compared to the trip I just booked. Oddly, taking the stage felt one hundred times scarier than circling the world out in the middle of the ocean.

The following Saturday, I showed up to the Play de Luna auditions feeling the exact same as I had my first day of class: petrified. Fitting, since I wore the same outfit—my Billy Joel concert tee, ripped jeans, but Converse instead of those infamous red heels—my way of honoring how far I had come and that win or lose, I would be better for trying.

To my surprise, I was cast as a lead in one of the plays, a story about a young woman who spoke her internal dialogue of self-criticism aloud while trying to cook dinner for a blind date who was about to arrive. I didn't know the director well, but thankfully he was nurturing enough to handle the neuroses I displayed over trying to get the role perfect. My need for control worked against me, and he finally had to sit me down and remind me to let go and feel the character's emotions. I tried, but couldn't. I practiced my lines alone in my living room for hours on end, but never found my groove. *This is going to be a bloody disaster.*

I invited no one to opening night. I wasn't going to fail in front of family or friends. As I sat in the theater's back office putting on makeup, I tried to keep the sweat in my armpits from showing through my costume. My nerves worsened the minute "places" was shouted as the lights dimmed. The silence that came over the theater made my heart sound like a bass drum. The house manager made a short curtain speech, causing cheers and applause that drowned out my pounding heart. The other actors backstage seemed to be energized by the cheering, but I sat even more frightened.

My fifteen-minute play was the sixth of eight in total, giving me over an hour of wait time in silence. Angela, a fellow student and the house manager, came and sat next to me. With her pale skin and dark hair she looked like Snow White, but as she grabbed my hand and squeezed it, the level of wisdom in her eyes made her seem like a wise old grandmother trapped in a twenty-seven-year-old's body. The warmth of her presence comforted me for only so long, and I wound up obsessively running my lines in my head like an overheated engine. Derek, the actor cast opposite me, came over right before we were set to take the stage.

"Here, bend your knees up and down. It will help get out the nervous energy." He began moving as if rowing a boat and ducking his head at the same time.

I stood unable to move until he put his hand on my back and said, "It's go time."

Derek didn't enter the scene until a few minutes in—lucky bastard—leaving me to walk out there in the dark alone. I took my place and prayed that my vocal cords would work, that I would remember my lines, and that I would somehow manage not to make a complete ass of myself.

The lights came up, brighter than they ever had in class, blinding me. Without warning, as if my brain left the building and my body and heart took over, I started to move and speak. I felt every emotion from every word, laughing, crying, and even having a meltdown onstage when the self-criticism my character outwardly spoke got out of hand, rendering an applause midperformance. It was a total blur and when the lights darkened, I felt Derek grab my hand and lead me offstage into the biggest embrace.

"Wow, Stephanie," he whispered.

"Wow, what?" I was too insecure to assume what he meant.

"You killed it. What were you even worried about?"

I knew the answer. My soul had everything to lose. I don't know if I "killed it" like he suggested, but I had never felt so alive and full of energy. So much so that it was nearly impossible to sit still and quietly wait for the two remaining short plays to finish.

• •

Over the course of our three-week run, each show became easier and easier and I couldn't wait for the weekend to arrive, knowing I would get to do it again. I walked into Art Sake feeling different about the place. It was no longer a school where I merely studied, did some directing, and made friends. I had officially earned my place. I belonged.

I invited Caroline, Yanira, and my mom and stepdad, Jim, to closing night. Peeking through the curtain I saw that Angela had seated them in the front row; a huge bouquet of roses rested on my mother's lap. Her loud laugh the entire first half of the show could be heard backstage. The entire cast loved her, as her contagious laughter fostered a more responsive, energetic audience for us to feed off of.

After the show, I changed and walked outside to load up my car. A man approached me.

"It's Stephanie, right?" he asked as he pointed to my name on the playbill. "I'm José. Super nice to meet you. This is my first time coming to something like this."

"That's funny cause this is also my first time doing something like this," I joked. "Did you enjoy it?"

"I loved it! I literally cried and laughed at the same time. I have to tell you though, I never realized how abusive the criticism in my head could be until I saw it right in front of my face during your play." His eyes glistened with tears, which surprised me more than his words.

"Yeah, I get it," I said. "I do it too. I think we all do, which is why that story spoke to me so strongly."

"Thank you for the reminder to be kinder to ourselves and for doing it in such a comedic yet truthful way," he said, then hugged me tightly and bid me a good night.

I stood there stunned until Caroline and my overly-proud parents walked up to chat before heading out. Yanira had zero intentions of calling it a night and insisted she celebrate with the cast at our theater's watering hole.

My brain was swirling too fast from the events of the night to drink. I sipped a soda water with lime as I watched Yvonne dancing with Angela and some of her other students, while David and Yanira sat laughing at a nearby table.

Art Sake had given me a tribe and a feeling of belonging. After that night, it also gave me a new sense of purpose. That should have been enough for me to stay. But even though it felt amazing, it wasn't enough. It didn't feel right to lean so far into this newly paved path as a way to save myself or to fill the emptiness aching deep within my core.

I need to go. And I know that on my deathbed I might have regrets, but going will never be one of them. The adventurer inside me has emerged and she has spoken. This trip will be a time for me, and me alone. Then, when I return, I will look to live a life of service to my art...and under no circumstances can I or will I go back to my old way of living.

I turned to the bartender and ordered a glass of champagne to celebrate my firm decision, lifting it into the air and toasting myself before turning to listen to the hilarious, but God-awful sound coming from the stage. I knew Yanira was drunk when she agreed to sing Ricky Martin karaoke with David. I leaned against the bar smiling, so happy at how quickly they'd become close. As I applauded the song, more so for it being over than for a job well done, Yanira locked eyes with me and came running over with her heels in her hand.

"Fef," she said, as she liked to call me.

"Yes, my love." I gave her a sip of my drink.

"I want to watch you every weekend onstage. Every single weekend. And on my TV. And read about you in *Us Weekly.*" She leaned in close to my face.

"Okay. I promise." I giggled.

"So get on it!" she shouted louder than she realized.

"Soon. I promise. There is just something I have to do first."

CHAPTER 6

For the remaining thirty days of 2013, I refused to think about how to pay for the cruise. Instead I committed to healing and rest. My symptoms subsided with the turn of the new year, just like Deborah predicted. I now had one year to make this trip happen. *It's go time. The countdown begins:*

12 MONTHS UNTIL DEPARTURE

I opened the packet the travel agency sent me and slid out the thick pile of paperwork for my visas and immunizations. A photo fell to the floor: my ship, the MS *Amsterdam*. I stuck it on my fridge like a proud parent displaying her child's art. She appeared tiny, but her small size allowed her to maneuver in and out of remote ports. To me, she looked perfect, and I couldn't wait for the day I got to officially meet her.

My usual overly optimistic, can-do self was back, and I needed a game plan. I began making a list of all the ways to generate income, putting the easiest option at the top of my list: selling homes for a builder. I had no intentions of staying in that industry upon my return, but if I could sell a bunch of homes for a year, then it would benefit everyone involved.

11 MONTHS UNTIL DEPARTURE. . .

Honesty isn't the best policy when you need a job and casually mention in your interviews that, oh-by-the-way, you will be leaving for 115 days in just under a year. My request didn't feel bold to me until I saw the look on the interviewer's face. After three unsuccessful attempts to work for a home builder I gave up, but was nowhere near ready to give in.

I went back to the list of options. Ironically, the next idea on my list had been suggested at one of my interviews when Jim, a Division President I had known for eight years, commented, "Stephanie, if you need a job for the year, go into general real estate. Hound your friends and family for referrals, and then go on your trip." So, I did just that.

8 MONTHS UNTIL DEPARTURE. . .

The results of my real estate efforts were sobering. I didn't earn enough to even cover my living expenses, and learned that it takes time to build up business. Time I didn't have.

I decided to stick with general real estate anyway, but also turned to the next item on my list of options: calling Fidelity Investments to cash in my 401(k). The brokerage agent's strong objection to my request embarrassed me. *What the hell am I doing?*

Mountain bikers have a set-in-stone rule. Whenever we needed to pass through a narrow space between two trees, we never, ever looked at the trees. No matter how scary it was, we had to stare solely at the space between which we needed to fit through. The second we looked at one of the trees, our bike headed straight into it. It took only one hard crash for me to learn that lesson, and I was not going to revisit it now. Worrying equaled looking at the trees and I knew I needed to stop.

I pressed my left wrist, feeling its pulse and pretending it was my Pop's. I knew the responsible thing would be to not spend the money, but thinking of him and the story-filled life he'd led ignited my own adventurous spirit. I could almost hear him saying, "You'll make more money. Now, go be free."

My heart needed this journey no matter the cost. Boarding this ship felt like my destiny—as if it was a decision made in the stars long before I was born. Even just the thought of walking away made me feel nauseous.

I whispered, "So be it," cashed in my retirement savings, and budgeted the income. With the addition of a few real estate deals, this money would support my daily living expenses until the end of the year, as well as cover a small portion of my trip. I was one step closer.

7 MONTHS UNTIL DEPARTURE. . .

Infuriated beyond measure, I walked up to the list on my counter and crossed off the second-to-last option. Without a steady job, I didn't qualify for a second mortgage despite my attempts to charm the loan officer. Without a loan, I couldn't access the equity in my home to pay for the rest of the trip. The past months, I'd thought of a million ways to try and make the money I needed, but to no avail. Frustrated, but refusing to give up, I stared at the last option lingering at the bottom of my list. The universe had me in a full on arm-wrestle, a test of determination I wished I didn't have to pass. *Have I not already sacrificed enough? I can't believe it has come to this.*

I looked around my beautiful Italian-themed kitchen and remembered how hard I had fought for this house.

••

A huge perk of working for a builder is the employee discount when building a home in one of their planned communities, something many employees took advantage of. Not me, of course. I wanted to live downtown, in the historic district, where my company did not own land.

I had called a friend who was a general contractor and began designing a historic-looking one-story bungalow with a big front porch with a swing. I found a triangular piece of land, difficult to fit a home on, at a bargain price. That didn't worry me at first. But after the city fought with me for nine months over my floor plan, what they finally agreed to looked nothing like a bungalow. Instead, in a neighborhood of one-story houses, they approved a two-story home with one large front window, not even centered. My home looked like it had lost an eye.

If I agreed to the city-approved design, we would be permitted to break ground immediately and be finished by my thirty-second birthday in May 2012. After some thought, I agreed to move forward—a decision that I paid for later with hate mail from opposing neighbors. It didn't matter. I fought hard to bring this home to life, and I was proud of my achievement.

Although my home morphed into something entirely different than what I designed, I put immense thought into how I could make the interior appealing. Two separate walk-in closets in the primary bedroom. A second sink on the other side of my bathroom, so no bumping elbows. Hardwood flooring throughout the entire upstairs. Chandeliers which added warmth to my high ceilings. A large outdoor area in the back, designed for entertaining. Docking stations in the walls where you could plug in your phone and play music through the ceiling speakers. These amenities, while enhancing my home's value, more importantly enhanced the cherished memories I created within its walls. Memories of Charlie and me being silly, quaint chats by the firepit with close friends, holiday gatherings, the graduation dinner for my MBA, and of course, the big Halloween party. The list felt endless.

Perhaps I was being overly sentimental. But growing up, I had always dreamed of living in a house—a place where I could literally run around the entire exterior instead of being hemmed in by the neighbors of an apartment building. I prayed every night to God to give my mom a house. A house with a nice backyard, my own room which I wouldn't have to share with Amie, and a huge dining room for Thanksgiving. My house—misshapen as it was—proved that I could create my own security. I had become my own hero. I'd made a home with a lovely yard, my own room, and a huge dining room where I proudly hosted my first Thanksgiving. This house held my heart. And now, after only two years, it was about to give me the biggest gift of all. *Look between the trees, Stephanie. There and only there.*

I took a deep breath, opened my laptop and logged in on my brokerage's website. I stared at the screen until it all became a blur. When I finally found the courage, I blinked away my tears and clicked the words, "List a Home for Sale," and started typing my address.

6 MONTHS UNTIL DEPARTURE. . .

Time to tell my family—or better said, time to drop a bomb. I arrived at my mom and stepdad's house in St. Petersburg, Florida, on a Friday evening in late June with Charlie in tow. Mom came running out to greet her "grand-fur-baby." Bringing my bags inside, I smelled my favorite dish cooking—chicken and potatoes. We sat down. I waited until my mom's wine glass emptied halfway.

"So, I have some news," I said casually.

Mom and Jim, were accustomed to my grand ideas, such as studying abroad in France and taking up mountain biking. But nothing I had ever thrown at them would top this.

"Well, I decided to go on a cruise around the world...on a ship! It literally circles the globe for one hundred fifteen days and stops at forty-four different places. How cool is that?" I began. I knew from experience not to dump all the information on them at once.

"Wow, okay, honey," Mom said slowly, but her big brown eyes looked like they were about to burst.

"What prompted this?" Jim asked, setting down his fork and folding his hands.

"I want to see the world, and I don't want to wait until I'm retired."

"When do you leave?" Mom asked.

"January fifth. But don't worry, Angela from Art Sake will watch Charlie," I said, knowing that would be her next question.

"If you need to do this, we support you," Jim said. "And I can drive to Orlando while you are gone and check on the house."
Here we go. . .

"Well, about that. I need to sell my house in order to go."

"Honey, you just built it! Are you sure this is something you want to do?" Mom asked.

"Yes. I need to do this. I can't explain it. It is what it is, Mom."
It is what it is? That's the best I've got?

Mom fell silent, but her look spoke a thousand words, stabbing me right in my heart.

I'd created security and provided for myself without worry, something she had yearned for at my age while raising us kids. I watched her struggle during those difficult years. After she'd put me to bed, I sometimes snuck out, sat by her bedroom door, and listened to her cry, wishing I could fix things and vowing to always have plenty of money when I grew up.

I get it. She can't help feeling that I am throwing my life away. A wave of guilt washed over me. I followed her cue and changed the subject.

5 MONTHS. . .

I intensely studied each port of call. Trying to do my research at home felt as if I were asking my ex-husband to help plan my wedding to my next spouse; I needed to find a workspace that wasn't so awkward. The Drunken Monkey Coffee Shop, just down the street, offered the perfect solution.

Every day, while eating an egg wrap on one of their mismatched plates, I dove into each port, reading and planning my tours. I often drifted off, wondering about my life on the ship, who the other passengers would be, and whether they would like me. I wanted answers that no amount of research could provide. Nevertheless, each day, as I walked out of the coffee shop, satisfied with my day's work, my soul felt both alive and at peace. Only one obstacle stood in my way: the sale of my house.

Despite its odd appearance, I expected it to sell quickly. Real estate agents brought potential buyers through, but no one would take the plunge. "Quirky" wasn't for everyone. I tried to let go, trust, and be the passenger in the car the universe was driving. But a part of me couldn't just sit back. I needed to lean over, put at least one hand on the steering wheel and do something to push things along.

One day, while en route to The Drunken Monkey, I passed a man with a sign that read: "Homeless. Need shoes. Veteran. Please help."

I pulled over and asked him his shoe size.

"Wow, big feet," I joked when he told me.

"They are super swollen, ma'am," he said.

I went straight to the mall and bought him a nice pair with extra arch support, along with a chicken sandwich, fries, and a sweet tea from Chick-fil-A.

It brought me so much joy to help that man, but I also couldn't help but think I'd earned at least a few karma points to help sell my home. I obsessively checked my email for offers from buyers.

Crickets.

I decided to switch from karma to faith. A friend suggested burying upside down a statue of St. Anthony—the Catholic patron saint of lost objects, people, and causes. They said it would help sell my home. I was on it.

I wasn't proficient in Catholic miracle practices. Instead of buying a statue that was blessed with holy water by a priest, I ordered one from Amazon, then found the specific prayer online and memorized it. In my yard I stood in a sundress with a black silk scarf covering my head, just like my Italian grandmother wore to church. I closed my eyes and prayed out loud while holding the plastic statue between my palms. "Dear Saint Anthony. Come around. There's something lost that can't be found. In this particular case, it's the buyers for my home. Amen." Then I buried the statue upside down next to the For Sale sign.

4 MONTHS...

A young couple came to view my house. At first, they seemed uninterested, but they came back twice to see it again. To my utter shock, they made an offer! I couldn't stop running around the house, screaming and jumping up and down, in total disbelief that this was happening. I was going to sail the world! I'd held on, kept the faith, and made it happen.

The only catch was that they needed to sell their home first to qualify for the mortgage. They asked to have sixty days to do so, or the contract would be void. With four months to go, I knew it was cutting it close, but I agreed to their terms in full faith it would work out.

The next day, I sat staring at my computer screen and the document I was about to sign. Reality set in. I pushed my excitement aside for a moment, and a somber feeling took its place. The minute

I signed the document, my beloved home would be legally in escrow, waiting to belong to someone else. I took a deep breath and dug deeply into the parts of my soul that were calling me to board this ship. To sail into the unknown. I closed my eyes and clicked the signature button, which automatically sent the signed document to all parties involved. It was done.

I went upstairs to run a bath, using excessive amounts of lavender Epsom salts. I sunk into the water slowly, inhaling the lavender to calm my emotions while allowing the salt to dehydrate my old life and the water to baptize my new one.

CHAPTER 7

3 1/2 MONTHS. . .

The sale of my home made my upcoming adventure finally feel real. I refused to dwell on any decision I had made thus far and focused my attention forward—which caused me to detach from my home completely. That broke my heart. I had no idea how often I would miss it or if I would ever regret selling it. Each time those thoughts entered my mind I rapidly shook my head, physically forcing them to dissipate.

Now that I had the means to pay for my voyage, I was ready to share my plans with close friends.

Yvonne was simple. I told her one night after class. She threw me her typical eye roll and lit a cigarette. She had only one question for me: "Will you be returning home to us?"

"Of course."

"Well, then have fun," she said with a half-smile.

David's reaction was my favorite. "Whoa, okay," he said, sipping a margarita. Our Art Sake tribe was waiting at a nearby table for us.

As we got up to join them, he smiled, hugged me, and whispered, "I'm not surprised."

Yanira took a deeper road, telling me that if God put this in my heart, and I could afford it, then I should go. That was, until I told her I was selling my home.

"Fef, are you absolutely sure you want to do that? You just built it. That was your dream and I would hate to see you regret it."

"I can't say I won't regret selling my home. But I will never regret going on this trip, and selling my home is the only way to do it. I have to trust."

"Well, I might be a little concerned, but I support you, Fef. I love you and am here for you. Whatever you need, okay?" I hugged her tightly, relieved.

While I pinned Caroline's response as the wild card of the bunch, I never imagined she would go rogue. We sat at Season's 52, a healthy restaurant twenty minutes outside of the downtown area. She didn't have much to say in response before changing the subject.

When we got into her car afterward, the look on her face told me we were on a mission. She normally drove like a maniac, but that night, it was excessive. We pulled into a plaza with three bars in a row, and she walked me into each one, immediately asking if I saw any cute guys I wanted to talk to. Each time I said no, she grabbed my arm and led me out. Caroline was six inches taller than I was, making me feel like her child. We got back in the car and she drove us to another part of town to do the exact same thing. We went to bar after bar, all across Orlando, for three hours, not staying more than five minutes in each. While I thought her antics to be condescending and annoying, in the end, I was highly amused.

Caroline was hell-bent on finding a solution to get me to reconsider my trip—finding me a husband. She cared about my dreams, I knew, but her actions told me she didn't fully understand why I was unraveling a life that seemed so close to being "happy" like hers. I just needed the right guy, she believed. Despite this disconnect, I loved her like family.

The rest of my friends and acquaintances heard the news via a video I posted on social media. Whether their comments were positive or negative, I didn't care. I focused on preparing for my departure, which included a long list of items not nearly as fun as researching ports: paperwork, vaccinations, currency exchanges, prepping my house for its sale, and what felt like a million little things. Like a tornado, I was whirling around too quickly to notice even the slightest hint of negativity.

3 MONTHS...

Our annual Play de Luna with Art Sake was back. I couldn't believe it had already been a year. Above the weekly classes I was still taking with Yvonne, I craved an additional creative outlet that would ground me through the massive changes in my life. So, I decided to once again direct one of the eight one-act plays. The play I was given had a large cast and fight scenes with swords that required detailed choreography, keeping me busy and in such a fabulous mood.

Over the past year, I had questioned if preparing to leave would dilute my love for the craft. It did not—not even a tiny bit. I stuck this piece of knowledge in my back pocket for when I returned.

45 DAYS...

While prepping the turkey with my mom the night before Thanksgiving, my buyer's real estate agent called and informed me their house didn't sell. They were canceling the contract. I couldn't breathe. *Universe, what is this? A cruel joke?* I ran into the bathroom and stared at myself in the mirror.

"Don't you dare cry. Don't. You. Dare."

I knew if I sank into the soul-crushing feeling of defeat for even five seconds, I would give up and cancel my trip. Instead, a deep-rooted stubbornness surfaced. I forced myself to enjoy the holiday, and then the following day, I relisted my home for sale at a lower price.

30 DAYS...

December 1. One month left. The time came to pay for the cruise in full. I called American Express and they agreed to put the large, outstanding balance on my card and extend the balloon payment until March—providing I got a sales contract on my house before I left. If I didn't, I would have to enact my travel insurance and cancel the trip. I agreed. *I'm still in the game.*

Sternly, I reminded myself that over the next thirty days, my mindset was going to matter most. Fear and negativity were the two trees, and I refused to look at them.

23 DAYS...

I scooped up my last box of belongings from upstairs and set it down near the patio furniture now sitting in my driveway, ready to be sold. Yanira had arrived, and she was already hard at work.

Yanira and I were the kind of friends who showed up for each other without question, hesitation, or judgment, and always with the necessary supplies in tow. Today's operation: a Saturday garage sale to sell off the rest of my life in thirty-five degree weather, bone-chilling for us Floridians. Yanira was bundled up with a knit beanie on her head, cursing the cold while redisplaying my items after insisting I'd done it all wrong. I knew that her frenetic energy was for my benefit. If she noticed my welled-up eyes, she didn't let on. Instead, she opened a cooler to unpack the supplies she deemed necessary to get through the day: mimosas.

I tried to stay present but couldn't keep the nostalgia at bay. I already missed the days of snuggling in bed with Charlie and looking out the windows of my second-floor master suite, slowly watching the treetops turn from black to green as the sun rose. He loved our home as much as I did and behaved as if he owned it. This house was his first real sanctuary. Mine too.

"I'm gonna light the firepit until it sells," Yanira announced.

Rubbing my numb hands, I watched her arrange pieces of wood into a perfect pile, which reminded me of the last time I'd lit it, the night Angela and I made s'mores and talked until dawn about life and boys.

Yanira's voice yanked me back.

"Fef! What the hell is this doing in the grill?"

"You have to be kidding me!" I said, standing up. I ran over to the portable grill that was about to be purchased and grabbed Charlie's favorite stuffed whale that had been hidden in there all this time. I turned to Yanira to explain.

"So last year, David and I had an after-hours nineties dance party in the living room. Alanis Morissette came on, and he went nuts singing. He used the whale toy as his microphone."

"So, how did it end up in the grill?" she asked.

"Well, Charlie wasn't very happy about it, and the next day it disappeared forever." I shook my head.

"So he hid his toy in protest." Yanira laughed.

"He is a smart, sneaky little thing. I'm not surprised he was able to slide off the lid and put it back on perfectly. Wait till David hears." I turned to Yanira, forcing a smile.

Even after ten years of friendship, I stood in awe of her natural beauty. A frozen, red, swollen nose dripping snot did nothing to ruin her caramel skin; long, dark brown, wavy hair; and a face to stop traffic. But her loyal and generous heart is what made Yanira truly gorgeous. I needed someone who supported my crazy, unorthodox decision, despite the uncertainty I faced—and that day, she didn't disappoint. My ship set sail in two weeks, and I still didn't have the money I needed or a sales contract on my house. She knew this weighed on me deep underneath the steadfast faith and determination I had been showing the world.

"Finish your mimosa; I am ready for another round," she said, maneuvering me toward a much-needed buzz.

As I sat in my driveway freezing my butt off, drinking mimosas, and watching Yanira negotiate the sale of everything I owned (except the bare necessities left inside), I began to think of all the events that had led me to this moment, from the robbery right up to the phone call I made to Yanira, asking her to help me sell my belongings. All week I had pretended that everything was a "go" for my departure. I called my car dealership and informed them I was turning in my lease on January 2. I booked a rental car for my drive south to meet the ship. And now, I was watching one of my closest friends load the still smoking firepit into the back of a pickup truck.

"That's it," Yanira said. "My work here is done. How much did we make?"

"About fifteen hundred dollars." I smiled, grateful for her hustle and negotiating skills.

"I'm off. Call me later," she said, grabbing her purse.

"You have no idea how much today means to me. I needed you."

"Fef, I believe in you. You are a force, and I have your back." She looked at me as if her eyes were an arrow and mine a bull's-eye, holding my gaze until she knew that I believed her.

"Hey!" I shouted as she was unlocking her car door. "Can you help me with one more thing?"

"Of course."

"I want to plan a going-away party the night before I leave. Will you help me plan it?"

She smiled her yes, then slammed her car door shut.

14 DAYS. . .

I repeatedly reminded myself that I would NOT exercise my cancellation insurance until the morning of the ship's departure from Fort Lauderdale. *I will watch this ship leave whether I am on it or not.*

Time was running out. Real estate agents continued bringing potential buyers to view my home, but there were still no offers. I needed a miracle. Instead of freaking out, I sent invitations to almost everyone I knew for my going-away party. Yanira and I decided on a night of karaoke and drinks at the theater's watering hole. It was the perfect venue for what I hoped would be the bash of the year.

4 DAYS. . .

The time came to say goodbye to Charlie. Angela waited patiently with his bags while I hugged him tightly, whispering words I hoped he understood. "Please don't feel abandoned. I'll be back sooner than you know. I know you'll miss me, and I'm gonna miss you terribly."

Angela hugged me, assuring me he would be fine. I believed her, but seeing Charlie drive off was the only moment that entire year when I wanted to cancel my trip. I could have sworn my heart was physically on fire. The only slight comfort was knowing that Angela would take amazing care of him.

3 DAYS. . .

Angela and two other Art Sake tribe members came to my house to help me move my essential things into Yanira's spare room. As if to signal all that I was now shedding, a sudden, raging menstrual period took hold of my body. It was unprecedented and scary, leaving me visibly pale and weak.

Nobody would let me lift a finger. Instead, I watched them work hard at packing the truck. I—a girl who took taxicabs to her surgeries—was allowing people to help me while I sat and did nothing. I sighed at the enormity of this step. As soon as my stuff was moved, all menstrual distress miraculously ended. My body's message was clear: something bigger was going on within me.

My haven stood empty, unsold. Next to my feet were my prize purchases—three orange and silver hardshell suitcases that stopped me in my tracks when I saw them in the store. They were the exact orange of the scarf that cartoon-Stephanie wore the day I booked the trip, a sign to keep going when I needed a boost. I loaded them up in the rental car and made my way downtown. David surprised me with two nights at a hotel as my going-away gift. Swimming in uncertainty, I deeply needed to feel loved and treated like a queen. David gave me both.

I declined all social offers and ate alone at the hotel restaurant, needing to regroup and process my game plan. Pushing this trip back a year felt wrong. If I didn't go now, the trip would have to be pushed off indefinitely for at least a few years so I could go back to work and reestablish myself financially. Another option would be to screw over American Express and not honor my balloon payment due date of March 30. That felt just as wrong as going back to my old life. The only thing that felt right was selling my home and boarding this ship. But it was out of my control.

1 DAY. . .

My going away party began at 7:00 p.m. I wore the perfect pink dress, with a thick row of black velvet at the bottom. After eighteen months of fighting like an Amazon warrior, it made me feel unbelievably feminine.

Walking in from the parking lot, I spotted three people sitting at a table with two glasses of wine and a non-alcoholic Shirley Temple. There sat my mom, Jim, and Amie, whom I hadn't expected, only because they lived so far away. I laughed as Amie patted her cheeks with her hands repeatedly, something she did when excited. Tonight

I needed their love and support most of all, and they delivered. I also knew that if my other sister and her family weren't all the way in Pittsburgh, they would have been there too.

I was overjoyed to finally introduce my family to Yvonne, who left shortly after, hugging me and telling me to have fun and that she couldn't wait for me to be back home. So many people showed up, it looked as if my farewell were a wedding. The only disappointment was Caroline, who couldn't come because her son wasn't feeling well.

Standing next to my mom I watched my friends having a blast, until she nudged me to go join in on the fun. Every drink, every dance, every picture, and every word of encouragement was a prayer to every god in every religion. Despite those prayers, I refused to let myself feel desperate. Whether or not I could pull off this trip was out of my hands. I had to let it go. I didn't know how things would turn out, but I was going to have the best night of my life and live as if tomorrow wasn't promised. And that I did. So much so that I barely remember passing out right outside the hotel room door as Angela went and got us a working key.

THE BIG DAY...

We woke up around eight and ordered waffles as we lay in bed and giggled.

"So, you're going to really drive down there?" Angela asked.

"Yes. I want to see the ship up close. I have a hotel room booked because the ship pulls away tomorrow. Passengers arrive tonight for orientation. On the way down I'll call Amex and see if there's something we could work out. It just doesn't feel right to go with a huge debt hanging over my head."

"There is always next year."

"No. That feels off. I can't describe it, but when I watch that ship pull away, something in me is going to die. I'll go back to my old life, stay involved in Art Sake, but...I...I can't explain it, Angela."

"No, I get it. Regardless of what happens, I want you to know how much I admire you for following your heart like you have this year."

"Thank you. Having you here with me means the world. I know we just became close, but it's like you have always been around. I'm going to miss you."

She hugged me before I threw another huge bite of waffle in my mouth and we went back to giggling. There was a knock at the door and a familiar voice calling my name. *Caroline.*

"Whoa!" Caroline said as I flung my arms around her. "You almost knocked me into the wall."

"Sorry, I am just so happy to see you! David and Yanira are meeting us down in the lobby for an extended farewell. Come join us!"

I closed and zipped my suitcases and went downstairs. For an hour we sat, laughing and telling stories. *Just a few more minutes. I need more time with them before I cancel the trip. More laughs.*

"Hey David," I said, "I can't believe I never told you this. Do you remember the night you used Charlie's whale toy as a microphone?"

Everyone began teasing David.

"Hey, you need a prop when you belt Alanis Morissette, okay?"

Before I could continue, my phone rang. I didn't recognize the number, but decided to take it.

"Yanira, tell him where we found it," I said as I walked away from the group.

"Hi, is this Stephanie?"

"Yes. This is she," I said through the echoing noise and laughter.

"My name is Jane with Epic Realty. I brought my client in a month ago to see your home."

"Yes, I remember," I said.

"She wants to put in an offer."

CHAPTER 8

My whole world was now spinning. I held onto the wall, not knowing if I wanted to throw up or pass out.

The offer was less than I wanted, but enough for me to go on the trip and come home with money to restart my life. I said yes to the lower price on two conditions: I would get to keep the chandelier from my bedroom, and we would have to get everything signed that day because I was leaving the country for four months. The buyer's agent agreed, stating the paperwork would be in my email within the next few hours.

I went back to the group and screamed, "Circle up, bitches," just like in class, and then told them the news. I jumped up and down as everyone cheered. David opened his arms, and I hugged him a bit too tightly, which turned into a group hug. I didn't want to let go of the perfect combination of people I'd waited so long to have in my life. I knew the goodbye wasn't permanent, but my heart ached like it was. Everyone let go, but I clung to David for one lingering moment.

"You did it, Stephanie. You. Did. It. Now, go. I'll be here when you return." He broke our embrace and gave me a slight push toward the door.

I heard a mix of—

"I love you, Fef."

"We'll miss you, Stephanie."

"You did it! Go get 'em."

"Meet a hot guy."

"I'm proud of you"—all at once as I walked out of the lobby doors.

I stopped back at my house to slap a Sold sticker on my For Sale sign, and Angela came along to videotape the event. I gave a brief speech to the camera, choking up. Afterward, Angela tried not to cry as she made her way to her car, and I walked into my home. I looked around, taking in the fact that I was standing in my creation for the very last time.

Here stood my beautiful house, tall and strong. Quirky, yet inviting; fun, yet misunderstood. She fought hard to come to be, despite all that she endured.

Then it hit me. *I built me.*

I whispered, "Thank you," then locked the door for the final time, letting my hand rest on the handle for a few extra moments before turning toward my car.

I don't remember driving to the ship. Did I sing the entire way there? Probably. Three hours later, I pulled into the hotel and couldn't get onto the Wi-Fi fast enough. The document, already signed by the buyer, was waiting in my email. I signed it. Exhaled. Looked into the mirror hanging above the desk. I stared at myself for a while, liking the person looking back at me.

The next morning, I boarded the bus that would take me to the ship. As the MS *Amsterdam* slowly came into view, I imagined everyone else securely locking the doors of their houses for 115 days, then returning home. *That was my plan, but now this ship I am staring at is all I have.*

I crossed the gangway to be greeted by Captain Mercer and Henk, the Head of Hotel. I'd taken a few short cruises before, but this felt so different. So formal and grandiose. I noticed their intrigued looks as I greeted them hello. It was as if they already knew who I was. *Maybe I'm just imagining things.*

I found my stateroom and sat on the edge of my new bed, observing the perfectly laid out, compact space with a small couch, a window, and more closet room than I expected. Aside from a kitchen, everything I needed existed within less than two hundred square feet, perfectly arranged like a game of Tetris.

After unpacking my suitcases, I opened my carry-on and took out a framed picture of Pop, taken when he'd traveled through Europe. He had no set plans, no hotels booked, and just one change of clothes. The look on his face was the perfect mix of mischief and adventure. I set it on my nightstand.

The last item to be set in its new place was my Dave Matthews drumstick. I picked it up, clenching it in my hand like on the night I'd caught it. This drumstick found me when my world turned upside down, and it only felt right to bring it along for the ride. I squeezed it before setting it down in its new home just to the left of my alarm clock.

Needing some air, I decided to take a tour of the ship. As I made my way upward from deck 2, I said hello to every person I passed as if I were the big-shot mayor of a small town. Passengers responded to my greeting almost instantly by asking for help with finding something or with setting up internet access. I had to repeatedly tell them, "I don't work here. I'm a guest just like you." No matter what they said in reply, each of their faces gave me the same shocked look, which I wished I could have captured on camera.

The ship was full of deep blue and red tones, gold accents, and beautifully varnished wood. Deck 3, the promenade deck, was made of natural teak; another passenger made sure I knew that as I held the door for him. I took a lap admiring the deck before wandering into the main atrium. There stood a gold and crystal sculpture three stories tall with two different clocks and a tribute to the planets and constellations. I stood still, staring at it breathless.

I found a piano bar, a library with more books than I could have imagined, and multiple sitting areas with various artwork on the walls. I marveled at how some areas were bright and airy, while others were dark and sultry. So many ambiances for such a small ship. I stuck to the main areas, not venturing too far off the atrium in fear of getting lost. My ego didn't want to have to ask for directions.

After an emergency drill for all passengers, I climbed the stairs to the top deck to sit and feel the breeze. I watched a stunning woman in her fifties gliding across the deck despite a bit of a limp. She had on a blue-and-white striped dress and sailor hat with a red scarf tied around her neck as if she were at a costume party. The unapologetic confidence she exuded made me feel even more nervous than when I first stepped on board.

Blowing horns and tugboats rearing their engines snapped me out of my stare. Another set of horns blared, and two seconds later, we began to move. I smiled, ran to the railing, and peered at the water below. The gap was increasing between the ship and the dock, wider and wider. I raised my right hand high into the air, giving an exaggerated farewell wave, like someone signaling a rescue plane.

I erupted into a fit of laughter as tears flew off my face. I looked left in the direction we were heading and saw nothing but ocean. The sun was setting, and the sky filled with a rosy glow, as pink as the dress I wore to my going-away party the night before.

I had fought like hell to sail on this ship. The adventure I had dreamed about for so long was finally real. Something for me and only me.

HERE WE GO!

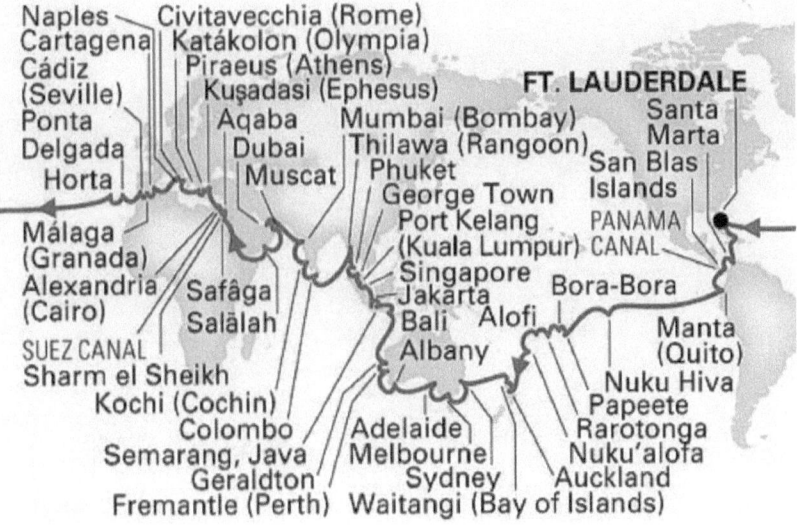

Naples — Civitavecchia (Rome)
Cartagena — Katákolon (Olympia)
Cádiz — Piraeus (Athens)
(Seville) — Kuşadasi (Ephesus)   **FT. LAUDERDALE**
Ponta — Aqaba — Mumbai (Bombay)   Santa
Delgada — Dubai — Thilawa (Rangoon)   Marta
Horta — Muscat — Phuket   San Blas
George Town   Islands
Málaga — Port Kelang   PANAMA
(Granada) — (Kuala Lumpur) CANAL
Alexandria — Safâga — Singapore   Bora-Bora
(Cairo) — Jakarta
Salâlah — Bali Alofi   Manta
SUEZ CANAL — Albany   (Quito)
Sharm el Sheikh   Nuku Hiva
Kochi (Cochin)   Papeete
Colombo — Adelaide   Rarotonga
Semarang, Java — Melbourne   Nuku'alofa
Geraldton — Sydney   Auckland
Fremantle (Perth) Waitangi (Bay of Islands)

CHAPTER 9

I stared out at the rhythmic waves, hypnotized until darkness forced me to turn around and engage with my new life. My pulse raced in a fit of excitement. I observed the deck in one slow-moving panoramic glance, noticing passengers settling into comfortable familiarity: places, people, and activities they perhaps knew from previous years. I envied their ease.

Deciding to dive in, I walked over to an area of tables and sat down.

"You play bridge, honey?" a woman holding a clipboard asked.

"No, I don't."

"Well, this is the meeting for the bridge players. You might want to move. Or, you can stay and learn to play, but it's quite competitive." Her tone made it clear I should decline the offer.

I got up from the table feeling like an unwelcome guest at someone else's party. The freedom I longed to feel was overshadowed by self-consciousness and anxiety. I stood back against the railing, unsure of what to do or where to go next.

I returned to my cabin avoiding all common areas, grazing my shoulder against the outermost passageway wall as I walked, trying to blend into the wall like a gecko. I set down my camera on the blue two-seater couch and noticed that my bed had been turned down for the night. Perched neatly at the edge was a trifold pamphlet detailing the ship's schedule, the weather, and any potential port information for the following day. It reminded us that we had three days at sea before reaching Santa Marta, Colombia. Setting the paper down on my small desk, which, with its lit mirror behind it, doubled as my vanity, I noticed an envelope I hadn't seen earlier. I unfolded it rapidly, slicing my finger. *Why can't things just be easy?* I put on a Band-Aid and then read:

> "Please join us for our first of many singles' events on 2015's Grand Voyage. Meet us tonight at eight thirty in The Crow's Nest. For our newcomers, that's the lounge above the captain's bridge and the highest point on the ship. Take the forward most elevator to deck 10 and then through the door to your left. Come introduce yourself, mingle, and enjoy some live jazz."

Dear God, no. I don't want to go to a singles' event. Almost everyone on the ship could be my grandfather.

Not wanting to leave a bad impression on night one, I opened my closet door and eyed two options before selecting the longer, more uninviting black skirt. With a quick look in the mirror and a shrug of surrender, I reluctantly made my way upstairs to deck 10.

A black-and-gold metal sign at the front of The Crow's Nest welcomed singles, and was followed by a more enticing handmade sign which proclaimed, "Free Champagne and Hors d'Oeuvres." *Well, I'll be damned. If I had known there would be free drinks, I would have been the first here.*

I navigated my way through the group, smiling and nodding as I picked up the pace, making a beeline to the table holding glasses of champagne. Fearful the table would not be replenished, I took one in each hand, telling the server behind the table that the second one was "for a friend."

That extra drink came in handy to find the third-degree questioning the other attendees freely unleashed on me amusing. I moved around, appeasing their inquisition over and over until I sounded like a broken record.

"Yes, I am traveling alone."

"Yes, I am single."

"No, I have never married."

"No, I don't have any kids."

"Yes, I paid for this cruise myself."

"No, I am not twenty-five, but wow, thanks for the compliment."

"Yes, I am on for the entire duration."

And for the grand finale: "Well, to be frank, traveling with people my age just isn't as fun." This line won them over. Every. Single. Time.

I filtered my story, explaining that I wanted to take a mid-thirties "mini-retirement"—a strategically selected word they could relate to; a word I hoped would help them see me as a potential friend. To my surprise, by the end of each conversation, the suspicious joined the intrigued.

Spoons started to clink against glasses. A female officer standing at the front waited to address the crowd.

"Welcome to all of the single travelers. Congratulations on having the courage to come solo on such a voyage. We hope you are excited about the friendships you will soon forge, as traveling alone opens up opportunities for connection that don't always happen otherwise."

Everyone started clapping and cheering.

Oh. "Singles' gathering"…as in single traveler, not single-and-ready-
to-mingle. How did I miss that? The announcement persuaded me
to remove my sweater and reveal my bare shoulders in the overly
warm room. I glanced at the drink table and saw one lone glass of
champagne remaining, waiting to rescue me.

I scooped up the drink without making eye contact with the
server. As I turned away, a short, brunette woman entered, looking
somewhat lost and disheveled, panting as if she couldn't find the
elevator and had just climbed all ten flights of stairs. She stared sadly
at the empty champagne table. I quickly took a sip. *Too late to offer*
it to her now.

Through her panting, I learned that her name was Tara, and this
trip was a retirement gift to herself. From what she shared, unlike me,
she was definitely here to "mingle." Feeling guilty, I offered to buy
her a glass of champagne before excusing myself to take a brief walk
outside on the pool deck to cool off.

The strong, cool breeze was exactly what I needed, but I wasn't
expecting the rocking that came with it. After almost falling, I took
off my heels and walked barefoot to the pool bar, lured in by two
lively people laughing as if they were at a stand-up comedy show.
They looked younger than the average passenger. The woman was
tall, blond, and dressed to kill in a floral sheath dress. Her husband
was dressed in a floral shirt and shorts as if he were on his way to a
Jimmy Buffet concert.

"Well, hello! Have a seat, lady!" they said in strong Australian
accents, almost in unison.

We exchanged introductions. Kel was retired from the film
business in Australia, and Julie was a former flight attendant. Kel
offered to buy me another glass of champagne.

"Sure," I replied with a smile.

"What is it with Americans and that damn word? Surrrrrre," he
mocked, elongating the word while trying to mimic my accent. "It

sounds so funny, but also sounds as if you are really UN-surrrrrre."
He turned beet red, laughing at his own joke. I was dying to make a
snarky comment about his mismatched Hawaiian-themed outfit, but
I decided to refrain and let him be the comedian.

"So, what's your story?" he asked.

"I don't have one. Just decided to take a break and come travel," I
replied, looking them both straight in the eye as a large swell surged,
almost knocking me off my stool. Julie grabbed my arm to help stop
my fall.

"You are so short you can't reach the footrests to hold on. I give it
one more glass before a swell puts you on your ass," Kel said, making Julie
laugh. I rolled my eyes and smiled. *He's probably right.* Kel continued his
interrogation.

"So, you just booked a trip around the world for a hundred
fifteen days by yourself because you wanted to take a break and come
travel."

"Sure did," I said, before realizing I'd used *that* word again.

"What sparked this? Something had to have put this idea into you
head."

"Nothing sparked it. I wanted to see the world, and this seemed
like a great way."

Our eyes met, and I knew he could see right through me—and
I, him. He knew that I was hiding something, and I knew that under
his jovial but abrasive demeanor, he was a big softy.

After an hour of laughter and small talk, Kel offered another
round of drinks, signaling to me that he was not going to give up
his pursuit to get me to divulge. Reluctantly I agreed, knowing one
more would cause me to cave. Then I looked around: not one other
soul in sight.

"Where did everyone go?" I asked Julie.

"This ship retires by eleven most nights," she replied, sounding
annoyed.

My inner night owl felt a sliver of disappointment, although on that particular night my tired body favored the masses. I canceled my drink order, said good night, and got off the stool with Kel's help. As I walked away, he shouted my name. On his face was a daring look paired with a huge, warm grin.

"I'm not buying it. We have one hundred and fifteen days, and believe me when I say, I'll buy enough champagne to get it out of you."

I gave him a shrug that implied, *I have no idea what you're talking about.*

A comforting warmth spread through my body as I walked away. Julie and Kel were the first people I met who beat out the voice in my head screaming I didn't belong on board. I wanted to be open and share my story with them. *I'm just not ready.*

DAY 2 - AT SEA

Announcements coming from the intercom system in the hallway infiltrated my cabin, pulling me slowly from sleep. After tossing and turning much of the night, I was savoring the comfortable position I had finally found and didn't want to get up. But it was already past nine. Once I showered and readied for my first full day on board, I looked in the mirror, approving of the cream-and-brown striped linen pants and navy shirt I had chosen, then headed for the door.

I wrapped my fingers around the brushed nickel handle, but could not make myself turn it. *Everything I came for is on the other side of that door. Come on, get out there.* I forced myself to open it halfway and peer out. Three people were at the far end of the hallway, walking toward the elevators. My heart pounded so hard I could hear it. I shut the door, sat down on my small navy couch, and took off my shoes. I stared at the wall, trying to breathe and make sense of my hesitation. Remembering how prior to booking the trip I had written in a notebook that I wanted to see the world, I walked up to my desk and picked up a pen and a small white pad with the ship's logo on it. I sat back down on the couch and silently asked myself what I needed. Without hesitation, I wrote down: *to process.*

Often after we mountain biked over something really difficult, passed through narrow spaces between trees, or had any kind of a close call, we would pull over and look back, marveling over how well it all worked out, letting the adrenaline wear off before continuing. I had moved so quickly and steadfastly this past year. I never took that moment. *I need that moment.*

I stayed on the small couch, replaying the many events that had taken place. The painful moments, the excitement, conversations, and especially the unbelievable last-minute miracle. After what felt like hours, I felt mentally exhausted, but peaceful. Except for the weird feeling deep within my core—unknown emotions I feared wanted to surface.

Refusing to comply, I diverted my attention toward the old box TV hanging in the corner. I turned it on, wishing I could watch *Pride and Prejudice* like I always did on days I needed self-soothe. There were no outside channels. My only options were created on board: cooking shows, a ship tour, shopping, and a movie channel. Thankfully, that day's lineup consisted of a romantic comedy marathon. *It's not Mr. Darcy, but I'll take it!* As *You've Got Mail* began, I threw my pajamas back on and ordered a delivery of buttermilk pancakes and bacon for lunch, then indulged in bite after delicious bite as I watched Meg Ryan fight to the bitter end to save her bookstore.

• •

Hours later, I woke from a nap to see nothing but pitch blackness outside my window. I turned off the alarm telling me it was time to shower. The first of my nightly sit-down dinners began at 8:00 p.m., and all I knew was that I would be dining at an assigned table with five people I had never met. Desperate to make a good impression so that I didn't end up eating at the buffet alone every night, I chose my outfit carefully: a coral skirt, a blue floral shirt, and soft gold heels—a bright and bold outfit to match the Caribbean we were now sailing through on our way to South America.

I looked at the ship map to get my bearings. My cabin was on deck 2, and the dining room appeared to be on both decks 4 and 5. Deciding to try deck 5, I walked crookedly down the dark blue carpeted passageway. The ship rocked more than my high heels could handle. I approached a man standing at the entrance dressed in a white officer's attire. I smiled, trying not to fidget.

"Miss Wilson. Good evening and welcome. Your table awaits you on deck four. Head down the main stairs and it will be right at the bottom. Enjoy your dinner."

The fact that he knew my name made me blush. I tried to respond, but stuttered.

Just smile back and walk inside toward the stairs. You've got this.

The only stairway leading me to the deck below was a massive, curved staircase in the center of the dining room. As if I had just walked out onto a stage, those dining upstairs along the balcony stopped chatting and stared at me. I tried my best to smile and somehow appear graceful while peeking down at the steps to avoid falling. I was ten minutes late, making five sets of staring eyes assume I was their missing person as I headed down. They smiled and waved. I exhaled.

"Well, hello! You must be Stephanie," one of the women said.

"I am. Hello, everyone." I sat down and introductions and pleasantries flew rapidly across the table in every direction.

Two personalities jumped to life right away: Detta and Pete. Detta, a widow from Arizona, had perfectly styled, chin-length, light brown hair and a wide, warm smile. She had owned Captain Kirk's chair from the original *Star Trek* series, as announced out of the gate by Pete, followed by how he wished he could have sat in it before she sold it. Pete, also widowed but residing in Tennessee, had quite the saucy spirit. His overly emphatic way of talking and bold facial expressions completed his tried-and-true, old Southern gentleman look.

Sally and Ken were the two other major players. Sally, who was from Montana and never married, had a very formal sense about her. She took the cruise quite seriously and showed a social etiquette that I would expect from someone traveling first class on the QE2. Every time she spoke, she tilted her head down, but looked up at me like she was telling me the biggest secret in the history of the world. Ken, whose lean, athletic build and great skin made him look way younger than his suspected age, lived in Michigan. He was quieter than the others, but friendly, and loved to laugh at the shenanigans. Sally, the more discerning one, did not seem to be an outward jokester, but rather made small, intelligent, and hilarious comments under her breath.

Don, new to this group like me, was quite shy, a trait given away by how he blushed anytime something slightly above bland was said. He appeared to be a normal, gray-haired, casual, nice guy, compared to the uniqueness of the rest of the bunch. He didn't reveal much about himself, making me want to know more. Everyone except Don had met on the 2013 World Cruise on this same ship, and all decided to return as friends this go-round.

After ten minutes of introductions, the group proceeded to launch into the exact same line of questioning I'd endured the night before at the singles' party. Like reading a script, I gave the exact same answers, which seemed to satisfy them.

"Do you like escargot?" Sally asked. Her short, white hair glistened like metallic strands, framing her face perfectly. The look in her eyes told me this was an important question, which she confirmed in her next remark. "Whenever we request it, the cook makes it just for our table on nights that others don't get escargot." Her pride in receiving this special treatment was evident.

"You are being interviewed to see if you can stay at our table," Pete announced as he slowly tilted his head downward, which made his large eyes appear even bigger. Despite his sincerity, to my ears his Southern accent made him sound comedic. I stared at him longer than what felt polite, struggling to figure out who he reminded me of.

"Sure, I like escargot," I said.

I lied. I had never had it, nor did I want to.

If eating snails means that I'll be an accepted member of this table, it'll be a gross but necessary sacrifice.

"We prefer not to talk about politics or religion as a social rule of thumb," Ken said politely, hinting at past tensions.

"Two topics I avoid at all costs, so that's not an issue," I replied, taking a gulp of my pinot grigio.

"Well, on a good note, you bring the median age of our table down substantially," Pete said. The table laughed.

"I hope you like to eat because our table selects the full three courses, and we enjoy staying the entire two hours until the ten o'clock show starts," Detta said as she took off her glasses to clean them with her napkin.

"Yes, we do," Sally confirmed, sending me a look that said not joining in was a deal-breaker. My eyes widened, but I nodded in agreement.

"And you absolutely cannot bring someone to the table for dinner unless we all approve beforehand," Pete announced, pointing to the two extra chairs that completed our round table. "And guests can only come one night. Don't let anyone get any ideas that they can be a part of our group."

"On formal nights, we meet in the piano lounge beforehand so we can be seen," Sally interjected, sounding like she had time-traveled from the nineteenth century. Her comment sparked a moment of silence.

I stared at my new nightly dinner crew, one by one, looking them in the eye, plotting my response to all of this. I couldn't tell how serious they were about these rules, but I had a strong urge to have some fun of my own. I set down my knife and fork, pushing my appetizer plate toward the center of the table.

"So, it seems like there is a bit of a rule book to sit here," I said as Detta's smile slowly faded. "I do have one question for you all, collectively. If you all don't answer this correctly, I am afraid I will have to find another table to eat at."

I had them right where I wanted them. All ten ears tuned in, eagerly awaiting my next sentence.

"It's a yes or no question. Feel free to answer in any order you wish."

"Dear God, what is it?" Pete said. His voice carried across the dining room.

"My question is: Did I pass the test?"

"YES!" they all shouted in a fit of cheers and laughter. Detta put her hand over her heart while Ken lifted his glass.

"To Don and Stephanie, our newest members!" We all cheered and clinked glasses.

"I will admit though, I am not used to this. I normally watch TV while eating alone next to my dog."

"We all do," Detta said with a warm smile while Sally and Pete nodded. Don blushed, while Ken seemed unfazed. I had a feeling he kept a busy social life back home. As excited as I assumed they were about seeing the world again, I gathered it was their time here at this table they looked forward to the most.

Two hours of what felt like endless conversation and laughter passed. I felt stuffed and officially accepted. Content, I looked around the dining room, realizing there wasn't another table I would rather sit at.

After dinner concluded we slowly waddled over to the ten o'clock show. The performers were talented, but after ten minutes I realized I was not going to come again; I simply couldn't stuff my face and then stay awake for an hour in a dark theater. I wasn't the only one. Across the aisle to my left, I spotted a man shamelessly passed out cold in his robe and slippers.

Following the show, I bid farewell to my new friends as we slowly started walking in the direction of our respective staterooms. Detta walked alongside me and we continued to chat. Right before we reached my stateroom, she whispered, "This is me."

"Detta. I'm next door!" I pointed.

"Who would have guessed that!" She gave me the warmest hug good night and closed the door behind her.

I crawled into bed feeling content, which was amazing progress from needing to self-soothe all day. The foreign felt a tiny bit less so, and I drifted off to sleep, smiling.

CHAPTER 10

DAY 3 - AT SEA

I woke up at eleven to the comforting feeling of being rocked like a baby, mixed with the stabbing pain of needing to puke. We had reached deep waters, and as much as I wanted to blame my nausea on the well-crafted three-course meal from the previous night, I was seasick.

"Ma'am Wilson," Reny, my stateroom attendant, called as he knocked.

I opened the door halfway, hunched over.

"Are you okay, ma'am? You haven't left your room today."

He looked at my face and gasped. "Oh no, ma'am! You are sick. You can't be down here. It will make it worse."

Reny called someone on his radio and a female officer escorted me to the upper deck, where I was met with ginger ale, a small white pill, green apples, saltine crackers, and a boatload of embarrassment.

"Watch the ocean and stay above deck until it subsides," she instructed.

I sat, holding onto the round bronze railing attached to the edge of the bar, shocked to see how the pool water slammed back and forth. Even more shocking was the lack of reaction from other passengers each time I covered my mouth and ran to the bathroom.

An hour later, I felt a tap on my back. I lifted my head off the bar to see Detta and Pete.

"Forgot to pack your sea legs?" Pete asked.

"I don't think I'm cut out to be a sailor," I moaned.

"Did you take the white pill?" Pete inquired as Detta gathered the rest of my uneaten crackers into her hands. I nodded.

"If this is how it's gonna be every day, I am getting off the ship and flying home."

"You need to sleep. Once you do, it should go away. Come on," Pete instructed.

Detta helped me into the room, set the crackers on my nightstand, and tucked me into bed while Pete waited outside.

"I'll check on you before it's time for dinner," Detta whispered while a blurry Pete waved from the hallway.

I stared at a small circular water stain on the ceiling, wondering what had caused it. My eyes got heavy, and the sounds from the hallway became a distant echo. Beneath the noise, I could hear the voice of my mother telling a funny story about me to my stepdad last Christmas.

"When Stephanie was a kid, she loved the Etch A Sketch. She'd sit next to her Pop watching him make all kinds of pictures on it. Right before he was done, she'd grab it and shake it to smithereens. She'd laugh and laugh as she erased his drawing. Pop would act like it was a big deal, and then he would start over. Stephanie would patiently wait until he was almost done, then she'd grab it and erase it again."

The sound of my mother's voice morphed into my own, whispering, *You Etch A Sketched your entire life. What were you thinking?*

Then silence as my entire world faded away.

••

Three hours later I woke up starving, feeling as if I'd never been sick. An envelope had been slipped under the door: an invitation to meet the captain at a private happy hour before dinner.

Beyond excited, I rushed to the closet, choosing a purple sheath dress and black pumps. I ran into the bathroom leaving a mess in my wake, trying desperately to be on time.

Minutes later, still catching my breath, I stood in the receiving line to enter. I held my head high and shoulders back, hoping I looked sophisticated. When my turn came I walked up, smiled, and confidently shook both Captain Mercer's and his wife's hand. They welcomed me before turning to the next guest behind me.

The event was held in an intimate, dark blue room, with small display windows in the wall which I suspected were used to showcase art or to have an exhibit of sorts. Stark white cocktail tables had been brought in and placed throughout the room. I chose an empty one and smiled as I stood there alone. Unlike at the singles' gathering, no one approached me. My insides clenched. A bartender with a tray of champagne handed me a glass and I grasped it in both hands, while sipping nervously.

Slow down on the sipping. Stop fidgeting. Smile. This is so awkward. Maybe I look too anxious and uptight like my old friends always said. Come on, relax.

My thoughts were interrupted when a woman with white curly hair regally walked in. Short, petite, and decked out like she'd prepped all day for this very moment, she reminded me of Queen Elizabeth.

Everyone stopped and gaped. Some even dared to say hello. Others merely nodded from afar as if knowing better than to approach her. The woman, holding on to the arm of a young male officer, walked toward me. She looked me up and down, letting me know I was being weighed and measured. Our eyes met; the spark between us ignited my curiosity. I gave her a small side smile, hoping that would intrigue her to come say hi. It didn't.

The captain made a welcoming speech. He was older yet handsome, stoic yet captivating—the perfect combination of a ship's captain and the exact person I would want in charge should pirates raid the ship. I blushed with pride as I clapped and raised my glass to his eloquent toast. Just as I relaxed enough to make my way into a conversation, the captain and his wife made their way toward me. I straightened my back and smiled.

"You're Stephanie, the *Eat, Pray, Love* girl!" the captain's wife said.

"Pardon me?" I asked.

"You are going around the world alone like Julia Roberts did."

"Yes, I am the '*Eat, Pray, Love* girl.' " I'm not a fan of comparison, but my improv training at Art Sake kicked in, telling me to just go with it. It was her attempt to connect, and I didn't want to discourage her.

"Do you knit?" she asked.

"Who, me? No, I'm afraid not."

"Well, you should join the knitting group. We're making blankets for kids in hospitals. We'll teach you."

"Sure," I said reluctantly.

She smiled, and recognizing another familiar face, she and the captain excused themselves, while I decided I was ready to leave.

I found my tablemates in the lounge where Debbie, one of the ship's entertainers, was killing it on the piano, singing songs by Carole King. They each had a glass of wine, except Pete, who had a Bloody Mary that he clearly ordered ages ago and hadn't touched. Anne Marie, a server on the ship whom I was slowly getting to know, approached.

"Ma'am Wilson, a pinot grigio?" she asked, having already memorized my drink preference.

"Yes. Thank you, Anne Marie. And let me treat Pete to whatever he wants. I don't think he likes his drink."

"I like it just fine. Why you rushin' me?" he snapped back.

Anne Marie looked at his watered down drink, giggled, and nodded before leaving to get my order.

"How was the Captain's event?" Sally asked.

"It was nice to be in one of the first groups to go, but no one talked to me."

"Honey, you must get used to standing out," Detta replied.

"Never you mind any of them. You've got us," Pete said, patting my back.

Ken leaned in. "You will know the entire ship soon enough. Give it time." He had a way of speaking that made me believe anything that came out of his mouth.

I softened my stiff shoulders and leaned back into my chair with a big smile.

"Oh, and there was this lady there who they treated like royalty."

"Dolly," they all said nearly in unison.

"She lives on the ship," Sally said.

"Like, all year round?" I was shocked—and now even more intrigued.

"She bought a cabin for the remainder of her life for a set amount," Ken explained. "She never leaves the ship unless she is visiting her family."

"Did she speak to you?" Pete asked.

"I wanted her to, but no."

"Well, don't expect her to. She is rather picky," Sally chimed in. Her tone suggested she had tried and failed.

"Yeah, you are a guest on *her* ship," Pete said.

We'll see about that.

"So, the captain and his wife referred to me as the '*Eat, Pray, Love* girl,'" I said.

The table erupted in laughter and comments until Sally raised her hand, capturing our attention. "Oh, I've heard that a few times. You are quite the talk of the ship."

The color drained from my face.

Pete jumped in before she could elaborate. "Well, you do look like Julia Roberts."

I rolled my eyes.

"Besides, it's better than being called 'the ship's gold digger,' " Pete added. We both began laughing uncontrollably while the rest of the table just stared, unsure what was so funny.

"Thanks, Pete," I said. "Way to put it in perspective."

DAY 4 - AT SEA

If three days at sea taught me anything, it was that I could push as hard as I wanted, but the wide-eyed state of shock I had felt since upending my life would not wear off until it was ready. My brain wanted to feel settled. To feel the comforts of familiarity instead of having to process newness everywhere I turned. I needed to let it go and stop forcing it.

To add to this deer-in-the-headlights feeling, the unidentified emotions that had started pushing upward during my movie marathon on my first day hadn't subsided. I just didn't know what they were, nor did I want to find out.

In an effort to have a plan, I hung on to the belief that the minute my feet touched land the following day in Colombia, everything would be better. *The ship will take some getting used to. These ports are what I came for.*

I got into bed feeling like I had when I believed in Santa, tossing and turning all night knowing that if I could just fall asleep, I'd wake up and it would be Christmas.

DAY 5 - SANTA MARTA, COLOMBIA

I skipped off the ship, moving so fast I almost missed the captain standing in the gangway waving goodbye. I had an hour before my tour began. Upon first glance at the luxurious sailboats to the right, I drifted off toward them, enamored with how the morning sun made them glisten as if they had glitter on their masts. The closer I got, though, the more the sparkle subsided, and I saw mostly fishing boats, some even preparing to depart. I waved hello, practicing my minimal Spanish before moving on.

Meandering along the streets of this coastal town, I was trying to decide if it looked more like an island town or a European village. Most of the stores were still closed, but I managed to find a place to order a Colombian coffee. Walking back toward the port, sipping my coffee, I felt like I was now somehow a local..

For my first excursion, the choices were either to stay in the harbor town, or head out to Tyrona National Park for hiking and then relaxing on the adjacent beach. I chose the latter, hoping the bus ride would cover more ground for sightseeing.

It took only ten minutes after leaving Santa Marta for my eyes to widen. Shacks. Kids with no shoes and ripped up clothing. Living conditions I was prepared to see on this trip, but still hit hard to witness in person. This made me even more frustrated that my choices had been two tours that stayed in the pretty parts. I wanted to walk around and truly see what life was like here in Colombia.

I observed as much as I could, but anytime we came to a stop, I looked down, ashamed to make eye contact with the people hanging around outside. *I gave up things I suspect they would kill to have, just so I could have an adventure.*

The bus arrived at the most beautiful, lush park with walking paths winding through abundant green foliage. It felt tropical, like I had transported myself to Hawaii. I ventured away from the group toward the beach, noticing huge round rocks randomly piled up as if the cosmos were playing a game of marbles. I sat on one, alone, admiring the gorgeous blue sea. Unsure of the source of my discomfort, I did know that for whatever reason, I was anxious for the day to end. But before it did, we were led into a large hut surrounded by forest and colorful plants to enjoy an amazing meal of tostones, chicken, rice, and beans. As I sat there eating a dish that Yanira had cooked many times, I somehow felt extremely nourished.

Back at the ship, I sat at dinner, staring down at my appetizer: a bowl of butternut squash soup with a drizzle of pesto oil on top in the shape of a heart. I drifted back to earlier in the day. I still couldn't shake the horrible living conditions I'd observed from my air-conditioned bus. I sat disgusted with myself. I'd disembarked the ship wanting something from this port, this country. I expected it to snap me out of my mental struggles. *God, I'm so selfish.*

"Your soup's getting cold," Detta said, breaking me out of my daze.

"Oh, I was just letting it cool a bit. I burnt my tongue at lunch, so I have to be careful," I replied quickly. I grabbed my glass of wine and raised it to toast the table with a wide, upbeat smile. "To our first port!" I said as we all clinked glasses.

DAY 6 - SAN BLAS ISLANDS, PANAMA

One passenger had already fallen while getting onto the tender boat bobbing around in four-foot waves, and I was certain I would be next. As I stepped down, regretting wearing flip-flops, a hand grabbed mine.

"Thanks," I said as a woman helped me sit down on one of the benches.

"Of course, Miss Wilson," she said with a heavy Greek accent. We looked about the same age, and her small frame matched mine, but her voluminous brown hair rivaled that of mermaids.

"You know my name."

"We try to learn everyone's, but you stand out," she said, laughing. "I'm Kiki, the manager of shore excursions. I come along to make sure the tours go smoothly."

"That is one hell of a job to have, Kiki."

"I can't complain. Are you excited for San Blas?" she asked.

"Yep. Did a ton of research on the Kuna Indians. I am dying to see how they make their Mola fabric or even just admire their way of life. I wish we could see more than one of the islands they live on."

"Well, they don't actually live on this particular island. They come here when a ship arrives. It's set up as an example." Disappointment flooded my body as Kiki stood to help me up onto the dock and then turned to assist the others.

I walked around the makeshift village, painted in bright primary colors with the Kuna standing around in their native costumes. I tried to venture to parts that weren't as populated, to peek behind the hanging sheets used as privacy curtains. On an island that looked as if it had no power, I saw kids wearing street clothes, watching TV, and eating Snickers bars. The oldest boy gave me quite the dirty look, so I quickly turned the corner to find a young girl, no older than three, having a hissy fit over being forced to walk around in her costume.

Back near the common area, I noticed one of the grandmothers of the tribe sitting in an orange plastic chair smoking a pipe. I asked to take her picture by pointing at my camera, and she responded by rubbing her hands together to signify money. I gave her a few dollars, took my shot, and nodded in thanks. She stayed frozen, and her face, unchanging, gave no hint of her thoughts. I couldn't tell what she was feeling. Peeking into my camera, I saw a woman whose loud clothing didn't match her Mona Lisa expression.

After an hour I returned to the ship. I walked through the gangway and swiped my ID card, then heard a familiar Greek accent. Kiki was chatting with one of the officers. She paused and looked at me as I walked by.

"An example, huh?" I said, shaking my head.

"I know…It's not my favorite port."

"I feel like I was just on a Disney ride."

"I'm sorry, Miss Wilson."

"It's Stephanie, and honestly, I'm not sure what to make of the ship. The ports. Any of it."

Kiki wasted no time. She excused herself, had me follow her to her office to drop off some paperwork, then led me up to the Lido deck for an early lunch.

"The Kuna don't want us ruining their islands. They are protective of them. Our ship pays to come to their port, and they rely on that money."

"I was dying to see the real way they lived, but now that you say that, I actually agree with their decision."

Kiki smiled as she picked up a plate.

"We are allowed to eat together?" I asked, unsure if she was breaking the rules.

"Oh, yes. Well, we eat up here for all our meals unless invited to join a guest's table in the dining room." I wanted to invite her to dinner later on, but remembered my table's rules about bringing guests.

Kiki and I chatted and laughed for two hours over chicken stir-fry, and I learned that she works on a ship for nine months straight before returning home to rest for three months. Despite her more proper way of speaking English, Kiki exuded a childlike excitement which I adored. She even managed to raise my hopes for both the upcoming ports and the culture on board.

Even though I loved spending time with an older generation, having someone my age with whom to connect felt like a nice reprieve. I got up to leave, thankful for how the afternoon turned out.

DAY 7 - THE PANAMA CANAL

The ship was in an uproar. A big day: we were passing through the Panama Canal. An announcement came over the speaker inviting us to The Crow's Nest to hear a guest lecturer give a presentation on water transportation. The words "water transportation" sounded eerily familiar.

Then I remembered. In seventh grade, I'd participated in a team project during our study of the industrial revolution. Oddly enough, my group had decided to make a comedic film for our presentation, just like I did in college, a memory I had totally forgotten about until now. Our film was titled *Water Transportation Day,* and it was a story about how we needed a holiday to celebrate the Panama Canal. *Now here I am. Time to celebrate.*

I raced around the ship in search of the best view until I learned the captain was opening the bow, a place that was normally restricted. I walked out, shamelessly turning in circles with my arms out. The panoramic view was perfect. It took the entire day for a ship to move through three sets of locks, or gates: getting raised to eighty-five feet over sea level, sailing through Gatun Lake, and then slowly being lowered back down to sea level. People who were on land came to the Canal to watch as we were lifted and then sent into the next lock. My arms got tired of waving, but I didn't care. This was exactly what I'd come for, to feel invigorated and alive. To get to experience something so iconic that overwhelmed me in the best of ways. I decided to take all my photos for the event in black and white. It felt fitting. After all, at the risk of sounding cheesy, I was sailing through history.

• •

Later at dinner, while eating Beef Wellington, Sally and I were in a full-on debate over whether Detta looked like Sally Fields, when Pete leaned over and whispered, "I think I need to upgrade my cabin to a large suite so we can have a Suez Canal party!"

"Pete! The Suez Canal is on the other side of the world. We just went through this canal. What's the rush?"

"Aw geez, now who is Pete saying I look like?" Detta asked from the other side of the table.

"No, no. Pete said he refuses to watch the Suez Canal from a public area. Quite the canal snob," I joked. "But, I will admit, viewing it from a private balcony does sound amazing."

"I to-o-ld you," Pete said with a mischievous wink.

Not long after our conversation, Pete managed to snag a gorgeous, spacious suite on the luxury deck.

DAY 8 - AT SEA

I spent the afternoon on the Lido deck taking in the fresh air and the endless sea, happy to not be seasick or hiding out in my room. I brought a book with me and sat with my legs kicked up, too engulfed in the story to care about being social. I wanted the ship to know I was rejecting getting to know them as much as they were me.

Within minutes, a woman sat down, introduced herself, and began chatting with me. Soon after she left, a couple stopped by. It was like a conga line developed, and I spent the entire day talking with several people. I'd believed up until this point that I had failed at trying to look approachable. Now, in the flip of a switch, I got to know what felt like the entire ship.

The day got away from me and I showed up at dinner in a pair of jeans, having not showered and looking rather disheveled. The only comment made about my appearance was a unified demand to know why I was smiling so wide.

As I filled them in on my day and all the people I'd met, Ken nodded contently, and I remembered his words from after the captain's happy hour.

Our server interrupted my storytelling to take our order. Pete requested shrimp cocktail as his appetizer for the fourth night in a row.

"You live on the wild side, Pete," I said.

"You haven't seen me dance," he retorted. "Just wait. One day, we will."

"I don't know any of the steps."

"Oh, don't you worry."

I shook my head, chuckling.

"So, we cross the equator tomorrow," Sally said.

"I know! I am flying up to Quito for the day to see it. I'm super excited." I noticed the entire table was staring at me.

"What?" I asked.

"It's your rite of passage," Sally announced.

"You're going to kiss a fish!" Pete shouted so loudly and with one arm extended that I thought he was addressing the entire dining room. Ken put down his glass, knowing Pete was the last person who should explain it to me.

"It's a tradition that I believe goes back to the royal navy," Ken said. "If you've never crossed the equator by sea, you are called a Polliwog. Once you cross it, you become a Shellback. It's a ritual consisting of challenges and ridicule before you finally earn your new title. In the past, it was a way of testing the endurance of sailors to make sure they could survive long, challenging stretches at sea."

"You get hazed!" Pete inserted.

"Pete, don't scare her," Detta interrupted as if she were scolding her child. "They won't do that here."

"The ship has a big event on the Lido Deck and all Polliwogs do kiss a fish, but not until the second crossing in March. We'll know each other better by then, and the jokes will be funnier," Ken said matter-of-factly.

"Our cruise director will dress up like King Neptune, who is in charge of the initiation," Detta added.

"Sounds fun," I lied. *I am NOT kissing a fish. This is one rite of passage I plan to skip.*

DAY 9 - QUITO, ECUADOR

I had a flight at dawn from an airport near our port to Quito, Ecuador—a quick day trip before we sailed across the Pacific Ocean. The ship's 4:15 a.m. courtesy breakfast delivered straight to my cabin had been a sweet gesture, but now it stood at the center of my regret as fear-induced nausea consumed me. I gathered my nerves and reasoned with myself. *The plane doesn't look that makeshift. You aren't going to die.*

As the plane took off, my reasoning didn't hold. I gripped the seat, praying for the forty-five-minute flight to be over and envying the relaxed passengers, all of them oblivious to the dangers that haunted me. I hated my fear but hated, even more, the gentleman across the tiny aisle who thought it was funny that I was more worried about the plane than our destination, a town known for its active volcanoes and earthquakes.

After a day of golden churches, conversations with street vendors, amazing food, and people-watching, I made it to the place I'd left port to come see: the equator. I chuckled, because it was just a long, yellow stripe. Quickly I took a picture, but the eight-year-old deep inside of me started to get restless. *Oh, SHE is the one who planned this excursion.*

The certainty of that arrived minutes later when I lost all adult-like composure, handing complete strangers my camera and asking them to film me. I skipped over to the line and started shouting, straining my voice as I began to jump back and forth across the equator with my hands waving in the air.

"Look, I'm in the Northern Hemisphere, now I'm in the Southern…Oh no! I am falling back into the north!"

My performance elicited laughter, but of course my inner adult didn't find it humorous. Instead, I spent the entire ride back to the airport justifying my desire to see the equator. I thought of how I always see both sides of things and can never make up my mind.

Or how I often feel like two completely different people. On and on it went, taking me down a rabbit hole as I compared myself to the equator in any way possible. Finally, my inner child urged me to replay the video. I watched myself act like a buffoon and laughed out loud, feeling the excitement I'd longed for at the previous two ports. Eight-year-old Stephanie was right. I didn't need a reason. It was a line that divided the planet, and dammit, I just wanted to go straddle it!

CHAPTER 11

DAY 11 - AT SEA

Our second of eight days on the Pacific Ocean brought perfect sunshine as the ship headed toward the French Polynesian Islands. As we traveled farther from land, the weak internet signals completely diminished, making it impossible to communicate with the outside. The ship became my cocoon, and I fully disconnected from the magnetism of the world and its seven billion other people—a cherished encapsulation that forced me to simply exist and just be. No to-do list. No goals. No stress. I didn't want this stretch of time at sea to end.

I spent the afternoon journaling while enjoying the calm seas on the back deck. From a distance, I heard someone mention that we had a weak internet signal. Even though I wanted to stay in my bubble, something in my gut told me I needed to check my email. After smiling through a few messages from friends, I read one from an agent at the brokerage who had agreed to handle any lingering items from the clients I'd served this past year. She informed me of

an error I'd made; now the client might have to pay a few thousand
dollars for the home's necessary pipe repairs. She assured me that it
would be handled, and to enjoy my trip, but the tone of the email
clearly revealed the frustration of everyone involved. Before I could
respond, the internet signal was lost, as if somehow, its sole goal
that day was to come alive for ten minutes to undo my stress-free
existence. I slammed my laptop shut. Those stuffed-down emotions
I'd been suppressing broke free, revealing an inner rage I couldn't
control. I knew I needed to get out of sight, and fast. I sprinted across
the deck toward the stairs and down to my cabin.

The door slammed shut behind me and I lost control, tipping
over the chair. It wasn't enough. With one swift swipe the papers flew
off my desk and scattered onto the floor. I opened my closet and one
by one threw my shoes hard against the window. Anything I could
grab in my hands I launched into the air, destroying my entire cabin.
With nothing left to throw, I stood breathless. Turning toward my
mirror, I looked at my pitiful self, panting with mascara-stained eyes.
I hated who I saw. *A fuck-up.*

"You loser!" I screamed so hard my vocal cords cracked. "You
can't do anything right! You can't keep a job…you're a phony…
why can't you function like a normal human being? You are an ugly
monster, and I HATE you. I FUCKING HATE YOU," I shouted,
gasping.

I collapsed in bed and bawled, believing every word I'd said.
Hidden beneath my so-called success was a self-hatred as deep as the
Pacific Ocean. I wanted off of planet Earth. I prayed that God would
let me die. My shame and pain weighed more than anything I had
ever experienced. Within this tornado of dark rage, a small part of
myself sat in the corner watching, shocked. For the first time in my
life, I had lost all self-control.

• •

Later on, I stared in the mirror at my swollen eyes. Two hours of crying had made me look like I'd gotten into a fistfight. I smeared hemorrhoid cream on my face—an old actor's trick for under-eye bags—and robotically got in the shower, refusing to further acknowledge what had happened. I dressed in a short, asymmetrical black dress with one huge sheer sleeve, and applied my makeup heavily to hide the evidence. Then I pasted on a wide smile and walked out of my cabin.

Upstairs at The Crow's Nest, happy hour was in full swing. I sat down like a fragile bird, wanting something strong to numb the pain of a broken wing. As I cleared my throat from the burn of the gin and soda, I heard a familiar voice.

"Surrrrrrre," Kel said, approaching with Julie. I smiled and invited them to sit. Julie looked absolutely stunning with her blond hair and black formfitting dress. I wasn't surprised to see Kel sporting a black shirt and white tie, rebelling against the recommended tuxedo.

"We would be honored if you would join us for dinner," Julie said.

I knew my table was dying to see me on our first formal night, and I wanted to see them, too. But I also knew my smile wasn't going to fool them. The thought of sharing about my afternoon made me feel way too vulnerable. I looked at Kel and smiled. "Absolutely," I said, avoiding "sure" at all costs.

We made our way to their table, located on the deck above mine in a quaint, intimate section. Kel ordered special wine and treated me like a guest in their own home. I saw a serious side to them both that was new to me. Julie ordered for the table and kept it light and healthy, even refraining from dessert.

"Let me guess...you are here to find yourself," Kel said, wasting no time.

I shrugged. "What's to find?"

"You tell me."

"Kel, is it okay that she came on this trip for no particular reason?" Julie asked.

Her protective nature felt soothing, especially after the day I'd had.

I turned to Kel. "My close friend and acting coach, Yvonne, believes that there is nothing to find, only walls to break down and layers to peel back."

"Wise woman. I might have mentioned this, but I was in the film industry before I retired," he replied.

"You did. I think that's so awesome!" I said. I didn't want to ask further about his work for fear of appearing opportunistic. "Storytelling is very powerful."

"I agree," he said as the waiter brought our main course.

"How is the lobster?" Julie asked, reminding me she was the softer host of the two.

"Fantastic! It's the only seafood I like."

Kel opened his mouth to say what I assumed would be a joke but closed it and continued eating. Within the lengthy stillness, I slowly began to feel the urge to share. To let them in. I set down my fork and took a deep breath. "I'm not here to find myself. I'm here because I question the choices I've made in my life before beginning this trip."

Julie was about to chime in, but Kel put his hand up to proactively silence her.

"I guess I confused success with truth. So, I undid my life. All of it. Now, I've set out to see the world. A trip I will never regret or wish to undo. Then, when I return home in May, I'll start over and make different choices."

Kel's empathetic look further dropped my defenses. For the first time since arriving on the ship, I shared my full story.

DAY 13 - AT SEA

Life on the MS *Amsterdam* was becoming routine, a new word in my vocabulary. My schedule was vastly different from that of other travelers, as I seemed to rise and shine much later than most. I often joked with Ken and Sally, the early birds of our group, that by the time I woke at eight, it was nearing their lunchtime.

Each morning, I enjoyed some time to myself before heading to breakfast alone on the Lido Deck, which was perfect, considering I was no good at conversation before I had my coffee. Afterward, I would head to the outside tables to enjoy the fresh air. Without fail, I would walk past Julie and Kel doing the daily puzzle, or spot Pete and Detta giggling over a post-breakfast snack. Sea days were a time of rest, something I was warned I would gravely miss when our days became back-to-back stops at one port after another.

No matter how many times I went to the Lido Deck, I was awestruck by the vast sea. I had never bonded with the ocean when sitting on a sandy beach, but now, somehow, being in the middle of it, staring at the deep blue, endless horizon felt like home. Each day I would consciously breathe it in before finding an empty table and opening my book, which would eventually wind up closed as I chatted nonstop, bonding with the other passengers.

This particular day as I sat reading, "The Queen" herself started walking toward me. Dolly, the woman from the captain's happy hour was coming to chat! I wanted to know everything: why she walked with such tightly held shoulders. Why her face looked so stern, as if she had battled in a long war. Though her delicate steps showed her age, she exuded a powerful essence that I wanted to unpack.

I waved, welcoming her to sit at my small table. I had hoped for this moment, but never expected it to happen. She stopped three feet away and I looked up at her in silence.

"You are in my seat," she announced without emotion.

"I am so sorry." I jumped up, frantically looking around for another table but finding none available. I was the loser in a game of musical chairs. Embarrassed, I made a beeline for my cabin to hide for the rest of the afternoon.

• •

Later at dinner, like a woman carrying a hot gossip story, I arrived a few minutes early, eager to tell all about my Dolly encounter. To my surprise, I found everyone already seated, staring at me without their usual smiles.

What on earth is going on? I have no idea how to behave right now.

We sat in silence as our server came and took our orders. Everyone chose shrimp cocktail to start. Wondering if I was the reason they were mad, I pandered and ordered it too. *I hate shrimp. Why did I just do that?*

The sound of our knives hitting the butter dish almost echoed. I eagerly waited for someone to speak. Finally, Sally broke the silence.

"What happened to you last night?" she asked with a look in her eyes I couldn't interpret.

"Last night?" I said, choosing the ditzy route.

"Yes, it was Formal Night, and you were not here at dinner," Detta said softly. "We wanted to see you in your gown."

"You missed our special order of escargot," Sally said. I tried to hide my relief.

"I was invited to join Julie and Kel. I'm not sure if you know them, but they eat upstairs," I said in the same way I would explain to my mother why I missed curfew.

I noticed the men staying silent. Ken watched everyone else with an amused look, while Pete eyed me like a bird of prey.

"I'm sorry," I said sheepishly.

"We didn't even get to see what you looked like all dressed up," Sally echoed, her sharp look softening to appear more disappointed than angry.

The appetizers arrived, which paused the lecture. I took my first bite of shrimp, instantly regretting my choice to fit in.

Pete finally began to speak, and I grabbed the seat with my hands to hold on.

"You do *not* eat at other tables. You eat here with us," he said.

"Unless you are off the ship, of course," Detta said with a smile.

Don kept his head down, eating slowly, while Ken kept looking around at everyone but me, trying not to laugh.

I looked at Detta, Sally, and Pete, hating how betrayed they looked. Hurt by my rejection on a night they'd really looked forward to.

"Okay," I said in a small voice. I grabbed the third shrimp and took a bite to find it wasn't fresh. I gagged, took it out of my mouth, and plopped it on the dish without apology, praying for dinner to be over.

I went to The Crow's Nest straight after. I ordered coffee and sat listening to a conversation about an a cappella group that performed earlier in the evening, until I heard a bang and turned to see Pete's watered-down drink hit the bar. He sat down and elbowed me. "You didn't even wait for me."

"I didn't eat with you last night. I didn't wait for you. I'm breaking all kinds of rules, huh. Maybe tomorrow I'll bring an unapproved guest to dinner."

"We were disappointed and giving you a hard time."

"Your southern accent and deep voice made it sound worse than you realize."

"Oh, toughen up, princess," he said with such an enormous smile I began to chuckle. I looked away as my eyes began to glass over.

"I was having a bad day and thought it best I stay away. I didn't want to bring the mood down."

He gave me a warm hug.

"Nonsense," he whispered. "We want you there rain or shine." He squeezed me tighter.

"I honestly thought no one would care," I whispered back. He pulled away, but kept his hands on my shoulders.

"Well, you thought wrong. You have become part of our family."

I looked at Pete, wanting to lighten the mood.

"Ya know, I came to dinner with some Dolly gossip." His face lit up.

DAY 14 - AT SEA

I entered the Lido Deck and found Dolly already enthroned on her self-appointed chair for the day. There was an open seat near her, but I chickened out and decided to admire the view indoors up in The Crow's Nest.

Walking in, I found trivia was about to begin. In the crowd, I spotted a huge mane of red, curly hair which I knew belonged to Victoria, a college graduate who was on board with her mom just until New Zealand, where she would be studying wine in grad school.

Victoria invited me to join. I warned her I wasn't very good, but she didn't care; her calm, grounded nature wasn't the competitive type. As we sat chatting, the most obnoxious ruckus barged into the room.

"Who are those four idiots?" I asked.

"They're singers on board for the week. An a cappella group called The Alleycats," Victoria replied.

The Alleycats were feeling no pain, despite the fact that it was only 3:00 p.m.

I am no stranger to afternoon happy hour, but come on, this isn't a frat party.

Before I could say anything else, Victoria jumped to their defense. "I've already befriended them. They are really sweet guys… just maybe having a little too much fun."

Her comment made me suspect that she liked one of them.

The trivia host entered carrying a box full of stationery, some pencils, and a microphone. Upon first glance, I lost my breath. He was the most gorgeous blond-haired, blue-eyed man I had seen in a long time. *Dear God! Who is that, and where has he been this past week-and-a-half!*

"Will you come with me to their final show two nights from now? I want you to watch them perform," Victoria said.

"Who?" I asked, refusing to break my stare.

"The Alleycats."

I snapped out of my lustful trance and smiled. "For you? Of course!"

• •

Later at dinner, I arrived having no idea what to expect, but found everyone in a great mood. Relieved, I sat down and began our normal ritual of passing bread rolls and talking about the events of the day. I wanted to kill two birds with one stone—to spend more time with my table, and to see that man again.

"So guys, anyone want to play trivia when we are at sea?" I asked the group.

"Sounds fun!" Detta responded instantly as everyone else but Don agreed to join.

Mission accomplished.

DAY 15 - AT SEA

I hadn't planned on developing a workout routine while on this trip, but the day after I lost my shit, I felt a sudden need to go to the gym. Refusing to spend my trip of a lifetime worrying about my figure, I'd pushed away the thought. However, after twenty minutes of inner debate, I got up, dressed, and decided to succumb to my urge—just this once. So, I walked up the six flights of stairs, regretting the rule I made of only taking the elevator when wearing heels. The gym was alive with activity, and everyone seemed to know what they were doing, which felt intimidating.

I had gotten up onto one of the ellipticals and begun pedaling, getting into a rhythm. After twenty minutes or so, I felt this strange, stagnant energy release itself from my body. One by one, things I needed to feel, acknowledge, and then say goodbye to came forward. My mind pictured each clearly, as if I were wearing virtual reality goggles. People who had hurt me, situations I didn't need, things I had done that I felt ashamed of. A part of me wanted to stop pedaling, to get off the elliptical and never return. But I knew I needed to stay and face my feelings versus destroying my cabin again. An hour later, I left the gym emotionally drained, but feeling lighter than I ever had. Strangely, I couldn't wait to do it again and vowed to add workouts to my routine every morning we were at sea for the remainder of the trip.

Now, here I am on the fourth straight day, releasing stuff I had no idea I needed to let go of.

The elliptical sessions made me cry every single time while I was still pedaling. Forgiveness isn't easy, but I also knew that everyone else in my life had had their battles, and when I stopped taking their actions personally, I saw them for who they were—as broken as I was and doing the best they could. Sometimes, I saw my own face, and shuddered at the thought of how horribly I had treated myself. I found it easier to forgive the other faces than to forgive my own.

Eventually, the releases began to dwindle, and it wasn't long before part of my focus turned outward and forward, to the vast, empty sea ahead.

DAY 17 - AT SEA

On our final day crossing the Pacific, a heaviness enveloped me. I rode the elliptical twice but there was nothing to release. Instead,

I felt vacant. Within me was a giant hole of regret over the time I'd wasted on my former life. Time I desperately wanted back.

I spent one of the most beautiful days at sea judging every step I had taken in life, angry I hadn't chosen a different path or found Art Sake sooner. The optimist within me knew that I would return home and create a new way of life, with new passions, new experiences, new accomplishments, and even a new home! But my inner critic's judgment of lost time lingered, raining on that parade. *Why couldn't I have gone through this ten years ago?*

• •

Later at dinner, Detta gave me a concerned look. "You are eating like a bird," she said.

"I promised Victoria I'd see the Alleycats sing tonight, and I need to stay awake," I explained.

All eyes at the table turned to me with surprise.

"Yes, I am actually going to a show," I said, pushing away my dessert as everyone poked fun at me by clapping, which caused the entire dining room to stare. I shook my head and stood up.

"Do I have everyone's permission to leave ten minutes early to find Victoria in the theater?" I asked sarcastically.

"Permission granted," Pete shouted as we all laughed.

• •

I was surprised to see the theater so packed. I sat next to Victoria and her mother, dumbfounded at how anxious they were for the start of the show.

The lights dimmed, and chatter fell silent. Four guys in white tuxedos with vests in various colors entered the stage. I rolled my eyes and tried not to snicker. Then they opened their mouths to sing mashup after mashup of Smokey Robinson, Michael Jackson, and assorted artists across the decades. Their harmony made it sound like there were twenty of them onstage, and their angelic tone blew my mind. They weren't just singing, either; they were playing off each other, having a blast. Their contagious fun-loving energy caused something inside me to shift. To feel it too.

The Alleycats reminded me that this trip was meant to be fun. My life before this day couldn't be changed or undone, and judging it was a waste of the gift of being here on board. Those four a cappella singers gave me the most beautiful message—and like most amazing performers, they'll never know.

CHAPTER 12

DAY 18 - NUKU HIVA, FRENCH POLYNESIA

After eight days at sea, I could still feel the rocking of the ship as I took my first steps onto the solid ground of the remote island of Nuku Hiva. I walked down the wooden dock wide-legged in order to keep my balance as a forewarned infestation of hammerhead sharks splashed around underneath.

"Hey, Pollywog!"

"Hey!" I answered before realizing I had just ratted myself out.

The head chef of our ship's specialty restaurant stood holding two large, freshly-caught fish which I suspected would be part of that evening's menu.

"Time to kiss the fish!" he said.

A group of witnesses appeared behind me, ready to be entertained. *No getting out of this one.*

I stepped closer, trying not to gag, then quickly gave the fish a peck and dramatically wiped my mouth to get rid of the foul taste and smell. The crowd laughed and clapped, and my inner performer took a bow.

An hour later my dizziness wore off, and I could properly explore the island. I mingled with the locals, practiced rusty French, and tried exotic fruit I had never seen before, but which tasted like heaven. I even made my way to the very top of the island's mountainous terrain. The view down below looked almost fake, as did our teeny tiny ship anchored in the harbor. It reminded me of the model train sets Pop and I would make in his garage. I smiled at the memory, then headed back to sea level and wandered into the quaint village where I ran into Ken, Detta, and Pete, joining them for a late lunch.

With stomachs full of a local dish that seemed to be a mix of Puerto Rican and Hawaiian cuisine, we wandered into a stone church the size of a small house, with huge wooden doors and stained glass. There, we spotted Victoria, the Alleycats, and two other passengers, Larry and his husband, Bill. Larry asked the Alleycats to sing for us one last time. I expected them to perform something fun like before. Not that day.

They chose a song I knew from Catholic school: "Let there be peace on earth, and let it begin with me…" Their voices echoed off the stone walls and straight into my bones. The combination of their harmony, their sweet voices, and the ancient stone church made my entire world stand still. I returned to the peaceful feeling of having no thoughts, no concerns, nothing to do or be, and stood there fully immersed in the sound of this timeless moment.

• •

Later that evening as the sun set, I found Victoria at the back of the ship, watching Nuku Hiva get smaller with distance. She looked sad, which was unusual for her.

"They became my friends so quickly, and I already miss them," she whispered.

"At least it's a lot easier to stay in touch now with social media."

"Yeah, but I will never see them again. Ever."

I stayed silent, allowing her to process her thoughts.

"I just said goodbye to our home, my car, and all my friends in San Diego. My whole life. I don't know what's ahead for me in New Zealand, and that's really scary," she finally confessed.

I listened to Victoria's story about the courageous decision she'd made to leave everything behind, wanting so badly to tell her I had done something very similar. To share in her fears and vulnerabilities. But I couldn't. Being fifteen years older than her, I was just too embarrassed.

DAY 22 - BORA BORA

It's true. The water is as clear as the photos.

The last few days in Tahiti we had been met with nonstop rain, making my time in Bora Bora special. I was tempted to relax under the sun in an over-the-water tiki hut with a straw hat and a piña colada in hand, but the adventurer within had other plans. Hell-bent on having fun, I booked a trip that seemed like a great idea at first. But, when it came time to leave the safety of a boat and submerse myself among sharks, I wished I had opted for the tiki hut after all. My GoPro captured the sounds of me hyperventilating far more than it captured the sharks.

As if the gods of Bora Bora heard my plea, our boat moved a few hundred meters away to an area which I was assured was shark-free. Believing the guide, I relaxed and swirled around underwater, observing the coral and taking pictures. The terror I'd experienced moments ago heightened how serene the ocean now felt, making me so happy I'd had the courage to try. Someone had made a sign on the ocean floor with stones that said, "Love Bora Bora." And that, I did.

The chartered boat docked near a restaurant and bar where I knew my table would be hanging out at. I hustled over, excited to tell them some big fish tale of how I was almost attacked by a shark.

Feeling no pain, Ken, Pete, and Detta erupted in applause when I walked into Bloody Mary's, the famous bar in Bora Bora. They had visited this island on their last world cruise, making their day more about drinking the "best Bloody Marys on earth" versus sightseeing.

"Sit down and have one!" Detta said, almost shouting. I signaled the server that I wanted what they were having.

"What did you do today?" Ken asked. He was the most coherent of the group.

"I narrowly escaped death!"

"You what?" Detta asked.

"I swam with sharks," I clarified, realizing they were too tipsy to prank.

"You mean the kind with no teeth?" Pete said.

"They had teeth, Pete. But apparently, they are totally harmless."

"Seeeee?"

"Pete, it doesn't matter. When a shark is swimming straight towards your face and waits until it is inches from you before turning away, you don't breathe. I tried to touch one, but kept imagining them opening their mouth and biting my hand off."

The server set down my Bloody Mary. Taking a sip, I exaggerated my reaction to how good it was, making everyone laugh.

Detta elbowed Pete. "Send Stephanie to the bathroom," she shouted.

"She's too young."

"Too young for what? I am thirty-four years old, Pete," I pushed back.

"Fine. Go into the men's bathroom and wash your hands," he dared.

Ken turned red, and Detta giggled uncontrollably.

"I'll get in trouble," I protested.

"Not here. Trust us. Just go and wash your hands in the men's room," Pete urged.

I gulped down my drink, got up from the table, and gave them all a suspicious look before heading to the men's room, where an annoyed man was waiting outside as a woman walked out, laughing. He looked at me and rolled his eyes before telling me to go ahead. I walked inside and faced the sink. Reflected back at me in the mirror was a regular bathroom. I put some soap in my hand and then looked for the handle to turn on the water. There wasn't one. Not even a lever at my feet. *How am I supposed to turn on the sink?* Being five foot two, I seldom thought to look up. When I finally did, I was greeted by a gigantic, twenty-inch, wooden penis hanging from a chain suspended above. Shaking my head I pulled it, which caused water to stream into the sink.

As I walked back to the group, they burst into laughter and more applause.

I had officially fallen in love with my possessive, loud, hilarious, and sometimes dysfunctional dinner family.

DAY 25 - AT SEA

January 30 came and went in the blink of an eye, literally; we skipped right over that day when we crossed the International Date Line. Fascinated by this phenomenon, I wished the ship could have anchored so I could dance on this line, just as I had at the equator. I would have jumped back and forth, singing, "It's Thursday, now Saturday, now Thursday, now Saturday." Then, knowing me, I would have tried to be only on that line, insisting I had found Friday.

Perhaps I was already there, in my own version of Friday, dancing in the space between. I now had enough distance from the past that I no longer mourned what was. Gone were the days of crying fits and rage. At the same time, the end of my trip was too far away for future decisions to appear on the horizon. I felt fully present, fully in between.

To add to the absurdity of time, I stopped looking at the calendar. I slowly started living to a rhythm of three days at sea, followed by one day at port, then four days at sea and two days at port. That was all I needed to know. This timelessness was incomprehensible to the Stephanie who'd boarded this ship—the girl who wanted to take on the world yet needed control, the girl who had nonstop goals and deadlines for her life, all in a rush to create wealth and be successful. That Stephanie would have never allowed herself to be so disconnected to time. Now that same woman couldn't even tell you what day it was.

DAY 27 - TONGA, A POLYNESIAN KINGDOM IN THE SOUTH PACIFIC

After a night out on the town, I woke up early to a hot, muggy day in Tonga. We'd pulled into port ahead of schedule due to a storm that prevented us from anchoring at both Alofi and Rarotonga. As unfortunate as that was, we now had extra time to spend on this island.

Since it was a Sunday, Ken, Pete, and I were on a mission to find the Tongan king and queen's church and "mingle with royalty," as Pete kept joking. We walked to the gangway and saw a new face. He was tall, brown-haired, about my age, and rather handsome. His head was down, staring at a map.

"Sir, you look lost," Pete said.

"I heard the king and queen attend a local church. I want to check it out but need to find out where it is." He smiled warmly.

"You can join us. We're heading there now," I said while trying to ignore Pete's winks.

"I would love that. I'm Sam. I'm here with my mom, who's a guest chef on board for a few days. Just until we reach New Zealand."

The air was thick, making me wish we didn't have to cover up our shoulders and knees to honor Sunday dress code on the island. Drenched in sweat, we entered a white church that looked like it could hold two hundred people, max. The service had already started, so we sat in the back.

While Sam and Ken paid full attention, Pete and I did not; we sat staring at the king and queen sitting to the left. Halfway through, the novelty wore off, leaving us bored and loudly whispering a plan of escape. After a few glares from neighboring churchgoers, which embarrassed Sam and Ken, Pete and I decided to leave early.

"Hey, Stephanie," Sam whispered.

Pete and I both leaned in toward Sam. "What's up?" I whispered back.

"I'm busy tomorrow, but would you like to go snorkeling with me on Tuesday?"

"She sure would," Pete said before I could decline.

I rolled my eyes at Sam and smiled. "Yes, that sounds fun."

"Great. Meet me at the gangway at nine a.m.?"

"Okay," I said as Pete and I swiftly got up and left.

Running down the front steps of the church, I thought our rudeness had ended until I heard Pete shout at the top of his lungs, "We are going to hell!"

DAY 28 - TONGA

Day two in Tonga started with a tour of local traditions. After a Kava tea ceremony which left me feeling slightly buzzed, I was led to a woman sitting cross-legged among a pile of nutshells and palm leaves. My guide shared that Tonga boasts the most amazing skin exfoliation treatment, made by grinding together specific nutshells and leaves native to the island. "Put out your hand," he said. I looked around and saw no sign of any exfoliation balm. The woman sitting in front of me opened her mouth and spit out a perfectly rounded ball of leaves and nutshells she'd ground together with her teeth. She placed it in my left hand.

"Now rub it up and down both your arms," my guide directed.

I looked at him quizzically before peering down at the chewed substance in my hand. Noticing the Tongan woman staring directly at me, I gave in, rubbing it up and down my arms while trying not to wince.

"Do you have a cloth to clean off my hands?" I asked my guide.

"Oh, no, that's the best part!"

"It is?"

"Yeah! Just rub it all over your hands, and your dry skin will disappear. Be sure to let it dry and naturally fall off," he said enthusiastically before ushering me along.

As I walked toward my van with my arms out like a zombie, I spotted Don off in the distance watching a cultural dance. We locked eyes, then he looked at my arms and chuckled. I looked at his arms—nothing. I searched arm after arm to see zero muck. *Was I the only sucker who said yes to this?* I laughed at myself as a passenger helped me into the van so that I wouldn't get it on anyone.

We drove across the island to the last portion of our tour: the blowholes. While I snapped pictures and enjoyed the misty spray, using it to wash my arms, I let out a loud, "Huh!" over how soft my skin felt. I dried my arms on my shirt as a woman came from behind me.

"Ma'am, smell this," she said in a heavy accent. I turned around to find a small vial stretched out to meet my nose. While pulling back, I was caught by the scent, and the most magnificent and intoxicating smell filled my lungs.

"Wow, what is that?" I asked, shocked and intrigued.

"Magic oil," the woman said with a smile.

"How so?" I played along.

"It makes you a magnet to all you desire."

"Wow, that's some serious magic. So, what do I do with it?"

"Wear it like perfume. A small bit. No more."

After learning it was only ten dollars, I couldn't resist. I bought the oil and returned to the ship to get ready for dinner.

••

Back in my cabin, I accessorized my black sheath dress with small diamond earrings from my grandmother. And the magic oil. Placing my index finger over the top of the vial, I tipped it upside down, then dabbed a small drop of oil on both my wrists and neck before heading out to happy hour.

Taking a shortcut through the tiny casino, I found Ken with two of his friends at the blackjack table. I hadn't yet gambled on board, so I sat down and asked for forty dollars' worth of chips, while teasing Ken that I was going to take all his money.

"What is that smell?" Ken's friend said as I placed my first bet.

I looked back and forth between them before realizing they were referring to me.

"Oh, my God, it's this oil I put on, isn't it? It was just a dab."

"Honey, the whole casino can smell it. Are you sure you didn't bathe in it?" Ken's friend said.

With each passing second, the odor grew stronger as if the oil had come alive and taken over. I started coughing. Mortified, I looked at Ken.

"I bought this oil on the island. I don't know what's happening. I'm going to go wash it off."

As soon as I turned to stand up, Pete approached us with his token watered-down Bloody Mary in hand. "Good God, almighty! What on earth is that?"

"I know, I reek," I said.

"It's so strong, it's cutting off my air supply."

I wanted to tell Pete to stop being so dramatic, but he wasn't.

I ran to my cabin and in a panic, scrubbed my wrists in the bathroom sink like a surgeon prepping for an operation. The scent had now engulfed my entire room. After soaking in the tub for twenty minutes, I was on the verge of being late to dinner, but the smell hadn't faded enough. I arrived at our table to tell everyone I couldn't stay. With one sniff, they readily agreed to send me to the buffet alone.

I dashed upstairs, taking the least populated route. Turning the last corner too quickly I ran smack into the hot officer who had run the trivia game a few days before.

"Hey, Stephanie," he said in a Dutch accent.

"Hey!" I said, backing up, desperate to keep him from smelling me. I looked at his name tag. Hendrik.

"Did you enjoy trivia the other day?" he asked. My awkwardness seemed to have sparked his own.

"Kinda. Not sure it's my thing."

"That's a shame."

I backed up even farther. My temperature was rising, and I knew that could only mean bad things for the magic oil. I tried to keep walking, but he kept trying to engage me.

"Want to join me at the buffet?" he asked.

Quick, change your plans.

"Oh, no, I'm not hungry. I am actually heading off-ship," I replied as I turned and changed directions back toward the gangway.

"Okay. Well, I am taking a ferry tomorrow to a neighboring island to do some snorkeling if you want to join me."

"Oh, I can't," I said, remembering my plans to snorkel with Sam, courtesy of Pete.

"Well, if you change your mind, I'm leaving at nine."

"Okay," I said as I ran to the gangway, hoping some fresh air would do the trick. Or, maybe I would find a smelly dive bar and offer my services.

I walked off the ship and noticed a circle of fifty people sitting in the grass. As I got closer, I recognized some of our Indonesian and Filipino crew members.

They waved me over to join, and I sat down. By now, my nose was numb to the smell, so I waited to see if anyone noticed. Not a word. A guy with a guitar and a girl with a bongo played a Beatles song as everyone sang along. Feeling relieved that my oil debacle was over, I relaxed and joined in singing. It took belting just one song at the top of my lungs for me to get lost in the moment. It was simple, it was beautiful, and it was better than any bar I could have ventured into. An hour later, between songs, a familiar voice shouted from all the way across the circle. It was Reny, my stateroom attendant.

"Ma'am Wilson, you smell niicccce."

DAY 29 - TONGA

While piling raisins and brown sugar onto my oatmeal on the Lido Deck, I heard a voice I recognized. *Sam.* He was inviting me to eat with him before we headed out. Too chicken to cancel on him for Hendrik's invitation, I agreed.

After discarding our dishes we headed for the gangway, and while laughing at an officer's joke as we scanned our badges, I noticed Hendrik standing just outside, looking at me and Sam. Turning away as I passed, I glimpsed him shaking his head.

A woman waited at the end of the port, offering to drive us around for the day in exchange for some cash, a side job she had when a ship came in. The island was so small, her tour felt intimate, as if she were showing us her house.

We didn't know we had to bring our own snorkeling gear, but the owner of a quaint hotel offered us her personal stash if we agreed to eat at her restaurant. The beach was beautiful, but the shallow water made the visibility not as clear as in Bora Bora. We fought the strong current for an hour before we were exhausted and starving.

Back at the hotel restaurant, we ordered a cold beer and the chef's special. Sam made minimal talk, reminding me of Don. I did everything I could to make him laugh, and when I finally did, his head flew back and his whole body committed to it, making me want to lean in and kiss him.

His loud laugh somehow granted him permission to relax, as we wound up sitting at that table for hours laughing and talking each other's ears off, completely forgetting our plans to go back out snorkeling.

We headed back to the ship, smiling like two kids. I'd had great fun in Tonga, even though it had had its fun with me.

I walked up the gangway and scanned my badge. The officer on duty looked at me and made a comment that changed my entire mood.

"One month down, Miss Wilson. Can you believe it?"

• •

Later at dinner, I sat thrilled to be reunited with everyone after my night in exile. My cabin still smelled like the magic oil, which they all found hilarious. As I listened to Ken and Detta fail to refrain from making opposing political comments despite our rules, I ate slowly, haunted by the officer's words. *One month down.* I looked around the table, making a mental note to memorize every detail and savor every moment while I prayed for time to slow.

CHAPTER 13

DAY 31 - AUCKLAND, NEW ZEALAND

I was up and at 'em well before dawn at the gangway, eager to be the first off the ship. I had heard so much about New Zealand from a friend I'd made back in 2002 while studying abroad in France. Paul had extensively described how picturesque and safe his country was, and how nice the people were, making it sound as if someone losing their wallet would be their front-page news. He called it, "the last paradise on earth." With every story he told, my eyes would widen, mesmerized by his tales of this mystical land.

Paul himself was gorgeous, as was his accent, making his sales pitch on New Zealand even more alluring. Ever since my time in France, I'd longed to see what he was talking about. To hear people call me "Steee-pheh-nee" like he had. To see if the images in my mind matched reality.

Judy, another New Zealander, was meeting me at the ship with her son Chris to spend two days showing me North Island. Back when she lived in the States, she was a certified companion for my sister Amie, and would take her places like the movies and bowling as a way of giving her social interaction without our mom around. I didn't know her that well, but my family adored her. The second she heard I was coming to New Zealand, she insisted on being my tour guide. I felt a bit nervous to accept such generosity with nothing to offer in return, but knowing how Amie felt about Judy made me excited to spend time with her.

Judy and Chris wouldn't arrive for a few more hours, leaving me time to roam around Auckland. Paul was right. New Zealand felt like a hidden wonder, tucked away from the rest of the world. I walked up and down the streets, and even though it looked like a normal city, it somehow felt simple and uncomplicated. *These people are so calm for being in a city. So odd, yet intriguing.* The place was squeaky clean and everyone immensely friendly. No matter where I wandered, the ocean wasn't far. I could hear Paul in my ear whispering, "Told you so."

Every shop I walked into had a gorgeous man working there, greeting me with his hot accent and wide smile. The local coffee shop. An organic tea stand. The athletic store. Even the women's boutique! As if all the "Pauls" of Auckland had conspired to greet me. After purchasing two beverages, tennis shoes, and a floral shirt, I had become an out-of-control flirtatious schoolgirl. Men aside, I swear the coffee tasted better, the clothes fit nicer, and the sun simply shone brighter, to the point where I almost started skipping down the street.

Just in time, Judy and her son arrived to rescue me from myself. We piled into Chris' small hatchback car and headed out of Auckland. Much of our traveling took place on a small narrow road that dipped and climbed like a roller coaster. Chris drove like a maniac. Judy flew around in the back seat laughing while screaming his name to slow down. *I swear he's speeding up every time she screams.* I laughed so hard my stomach hurt. We finally hit a highway that would lead us southeast to Tauranga, and Chris pulled over to the shoulder of the road. I suspected it was so we could all catch our breath. Wrong. He and Judy looked at each other, grinning.

"Steee-pheh-nee, it is your turn to drive on the left side of the road!" Judy shouted.

"There's no way. Guys, I am directionally challenged. This is not a good idea."

"Oh, come on, what's the worst that could happen?" she said.

"Do you really want me to answer that?"

"Just give it a go. I'll help you," Chris offered.

I moved into the driver's seat and looked down at the gears. *Thank God I know how to drive stick.*

I kept repeating to myself, *Keep my side of the car on the inside of the road, keep my side of the car on the inside of the road.* I slowly crept forward and entered traffic, screaming like a wild banshee. *Oh, God, I have two people's lives in my hands! On second thought, after Chris's erratic driving, I shouldn't feel bad. We are all daredevils here.*

I started shifting. *Second gear, third gear, fourth gear… I am doing great! Fiffffffitttthhhhhhh… Shit.* For some reason, my left arm would not shift to the left and upward to get the car in fifth gear. Chris laughed and helped me from the passenger side, after which I promptly hired him for every upcoming fifth gear change.

I am on the opposite side of the earth, in the Southern Hemisphere where even the toilet water rotates the opposite way, sitting on the opposite side of a car, driving on the opposite side of the road. I love it!

"Take a picture, Chris!" I shouted. "No, wait. Shift me into fifth!"

Chris didn't know which to do first, but I could tell from his wide grin that he found the experience amusing. He snapped a photo, and I gave a thumbs-up. *This is life! More, please!*

We arrived in Tauranga and saw a large cruise ship out to sea; due to the strong waves, it was not able to bring passengers to shore in the small tender boats. I sat on a bench gazing at it anchored in the ocean, feeling so grateful that we had pulled into Auckland. I would have died if I had to skip this port.

New Zealand coastal winds were no joke, but they didn't take away from the joy of our hike around the coast. I kept stopping, trying to capture its beauty, both in my mind and on film. The rocks, the trees, the coastline. The goats wandering around the shoreline. Every piece of nature glistened and seemed untouched. Judy and Chris, chuckling at my over-the-top enthusiasm, started taking pictures of me taking pictures. Normally, I curb my photography to avoid becoming so snap-happy that I miss the experience of being in the moment. But I couldn't help myself. It was the prettiest place I had ever seen, and I couldn't put the camera down.

We stopped for a late lunch at a diner. I noticed the ungodly amount of cream on top of the pastries in the display case. *How have they all not had heart attacks?*

"Try them all, they are amazing," Judy said.

Hearing my arteries protesting, I declined. "I'll get the roast beef sandwich."

"You mean, a sammie?" Judy teased.

I gave my sammie order to the waitress, who chuckled, reminding me I was the foreigner with the funny accent, not them.

DAY 32 - COROMANDEL PENINSULA, NEW ZEALAND

We woke up early and headed out to a place called Hot Water Beach. Chris parked the car in what seemed like the entrance to hiking trails, then led us through a walking path of thick green vegetation before climbing over several large boulders. As we crested the top, I looked down to see a tucked-away beach in the shape of a half-moon.

We slowly walked along the sand, seeing few people. I strolled to the edge of the water and put my toes in. *Nope, not hot. So why the name?*

"Start digging," Chris instructed.

"Go on, make a hole with your feet," Judy said. About eighteen inches into the sand, piping hot water erupted from the ground like a volcano.

"Fissures under the ground make the water hot," Chris explained.

"People dig massive holes for their group of friends, so it becomes a natural hot tub to hang out in by the beach," Judy said.

Running around like an enthusiastic Golden Retriever, I dug holes all over the beach with my hands and feet, creating little hot tubs.

I exhausted myself before we headed to a nearby town with a restaurant and some cute shops. It was thirty-one days into the trip, and I bought my first souvenir—a bracelet. Two separate leather bands, one brown, the other black, were held together by a little silver bead, imprinted with the word "love."

I decided that the bracelet's two colors represented the past and the future, and I was the silver piece holding both together. Being there in New Zealand, standing in a little town, I could tell this country would one day mean something more to me. How? I wasn't sure. What I did know for certain was that every goodbye I had said while sweating on the ship's elliptical made space in my heart for something new and something aligned with my genuine self. I believed more feelings like this would come and fill in the empty space on the blank canvas I had created.

I hugged Chris and Judy tightly as I said goodbye. Judy hung around to watch the ship pull away, and every thirty seconds or so, she waved. I stood on the top deck and waved back as if we were in an old black-and-white movie. She had felt like a distant family member to me during the years she was Amie's companion, but now that I'd bonded with her, I realized she was an angel on earth. Her heart held so much love for everyone, particularly those with special needs. I finally understood why she was so special to my family.

Coming to New Zealand felt like a thirteen-year cycle completing itself. Remembering again Paul's stories, I recalled how badly I had wanted to travel to his homeland, but planning a trip to this faraway place always seemed so impractical. *Now, here I am.*

We had one more port left in New Zealand, but I already knew I had surrendered my heart to this country. I hadn't even left yet, and I already longed to know when I could return.

DAY 33 - WAITANGI BAY, NEW ZEALAND

New Zealand, an already perfect show, provided an encore: Waitangi Bay, a small harbor town on the northern part of the island. Eager to set foot again on the country's soil, I took one of the first tender boats into town. The stunning scenery was like something in a model train set. Above the smooth-as-glass water, the town rose, appearing like the side of a small mountain. As I made my way down the wooden boardwalk I glanced at the name of each boat parked in the harbor. "Carpe Diem." *So unoriginal.* "Serendipity." *Oh, come on.* "Forsail me not." *Clever. I see what you did there!* "Highest Parasailing." *Wait, that's not a name.*

I spotted a neon pink sign next to the boat that said, "Highest parasailing in the southern hemisphere." I had paused a few seconds too long, causing the captain to turn around.

"You want to go up?" he said. His swaggering, confident demeanor suggested he thought I was an easy sale.

"I'm afraid of flying. Parasailing kind of belongs in that bucket," I pointed out.

But the captain had heard it all before and saw right though me. A moment later, I pushed aside my fear and handed him the necessary cash and took his hand to be guided on board. I sat down, joining three other people I didn't know, and agreed to partner with the quieter gentleman.

The boat accelerated and the parachute inflated, lifting us into the air. My heart raced as the town started shrinking, and I screamed as we continued to be lifted higher. I focused on the rope that fastened the parachute to the boat. *If that rope snaps, we're dead.* But the higher we got, the less I seemed to care. Our boat diminished into a pushpin. We reached our altitude and it felt like we were floating. I couldn't hear a thing from down below.

Later, I got off the boat with tears in my eyes, unsure if it was the wind or the immense pride I felt for having the courage to surrender my sense of control.

• •

Hours after returning to the ship I headed to dinner, anxious to see everyone. It had been three days and I missed them, terribly.

It took that time away to realize how much eating dinner with them meant to me. From our two table attendants making us laugh with humorous props and dances to the night they lifted Pete's dish cover to reveal his dinner: a rubber chicken—not to mention how funny it was when one of us had a bit too much at happy hour, and the entire table helped guide the conversation around their drunken tangents on the most obscure topics.

Yet other times, our dinners were quiet, and we simply enjoyed each other's presence while eating. I'd expected to hate those nights, but I was wrong.

"We thought you ran off and got married," Pete said.

"I did, to a hot New Zealander. He's on board, resting in my cabin. I can't wait for you to meet him."

"I told you, you can't bring guests to the table unless we approve, so tell him to enjoy the buffet," he replied, daring me to engage.

"I'll just take my new husband and go eat with Julie and Kel."

"Don't you dare!" he said as we all laughed.

"I've missed you all so much. I need to hear everything you did without me."

Don, our quiet loner, gave a few comments before looking at Pete to take over. Pete, of course, gave a dramatic monologue of his time in New Zealand with Ken and Detta. Any chance Detta could get a word in, she would clarify his embellishments.

While we always told stories of our time apart during dinner, I wondered why everyone was sharing such details about Auckland, since they'd already been there on the previous cruise. Then I noticed most of the eye contact was directed at Sally, who couldn't venture out of port due to her bad knees. *This is how they include her.* I smiled, then joined in. After we all exhausted ourselves of storytelling, we contently listened to Sally's update on what we'd missed on her prized ship.

Midmeal, a commotion by the window alerted us that the sunset was in rare form. We left the table and the dining room's dark tinted glass to go upstairs to see for ourselves what was happening.

We found the sky painted with the brightest shades of pink, purple, orange, and red. The clouds, small and round, were scattered across the sky in an arc like a rainbow of bright gold. I'd uttered the words, "This is the most beautiful sunset I have ever seen" before, many times. But I was wrong. *This* was the most surreal sunset I had ever witnessed.

I turned to go fetch my camera—only to stop dead in my tracks. I knew that this sunset and this moment couldn't be captured on film. Instead, I tried hard to memorize every detail, so that fifty years from then I could close my eyes and relive it. Unfazed by the wind, I let my dinner get cold while the sun-soaked golden sky draped over me like a blanket. Thank you, New Zealand, for the farewell gift. *I promise you I'll be back. I just need some time.*

CHAPTER 14

DAY 36 - SYDNEY, AUSTRALIA

After my time in New Zealand, Australia had big shoes to fill.

The "Sail-in" to Sydney, as they called it, was the buzz at both my dinner table and around the ship. I was up in The Crow's Nest at sunrise, watching as we pulled into a long stretch of breathtaking waterway that sat next to the Sydney Opera House. By now I knew that every port had some form of a welcoming event out on the dock, be it a display of local dance, costumes, or even just a cool welcome sign with live music. But Sydney chose to give us the most unique welcome so far: the police.

The captain came over the loudspeaker. "All guests, crew, and officers. Please go directly to the gangway. Everyone must exit the ship immediately, and then wait where you are told. You will be allowed back on, so don't worry about gathering your personal effects."

I made my way through the gangway in sweatpants, a tank top, flip-flops, and a messy ponytail. No sooner did the fresh air of Sydney hit my face than Henk, the head of hotel, approached me with two Sydney police officers.

"The police have requested to search your room," he stated after greeting me.

"Uh, okay. Should I be worried?"

"No, it is routine, considering the circumstances."

Circumstances? What circumstances? I asked other passengers if their rooms were getting searched. *Nope. Just mine.*

Waiting at the end of the dock, I listened to the sounds of hundreds of people whispering, but I couldn't bring myself to talk to anyone. I wanted to vomit. *I don't care if they are officers. Two strange men are going through my stuff. AGAIN!*

I sat on a curb trying to breathe. The sound of squeaky mountain bike brakes started screeching in my ears as if I were back in my garage closet. A montage of chaos from the past year erupted in my head. Echoes of the police officers talking to me while I sat in my driveway and my therapist's voice fought to overpower the squeaking. No matter how hard I tried, I couldn't tune it out. I turned my back from the crowd as everything began to spin, then put my head between my legs and tried to breathe, hoping no one would notice.

About twenty minutes later, I heard a commotion and turned around to see a woman with short black hair being escorted off the ship in handcuffs. I recognized her as a passenger, but we had never met. Her head was down as she complied with the officers' directions. Her submissiveness made me believe she was guilty of whatever they accused her of.

Immediately after she was put into the squad car, we were allowed back on board. I sat at the edge of my bed, surveying the room, trying to notice if anything was out of place, wondering what belongings they'd gone through. Sweating profusely, I grabbed my purse. *I have to get out of here. Now.*

I tried to shake it off by heading into the busy streets of Sydney, but soon found myself leaning against a wall, watching people walk by. Everyone was dressed impeccably and had an air of confidence to them that looked almost cold. Each time I made eye contact, I swore they were judging me. The burning in my chest raged while my mind continued to spiral.

Like a panicked zombie, I ran into Guess, the first store I recognized. The purchase of cute jeans, a hot top, and heels, as well as a quick stop at a makeup counter, had my ass prancing right alongside the beautiful people of Sydney. Thirsty, I stopped in a trendy tea shop and ordered a peppermint tea, spinning the mug each time I took a sip, creating a circle of dark red lipstick marks on the ivory rim.

The tea gave me a chance to breathe and settle my mind, snapping me out of my PTSD relapse. I realized the paranoia over my appearance was all in my head; I'd simply needed something to obsess over to distract me from my feelings.

I squeezed my left wrist's pulse and could hear my Pop whisper, "Take it easy on yourself." He was right. There was no point in feeling ashamed or embarrassed by my episode, but I did long to return to the version of me that had walked off the ship. Deciding to change out of my new clothes, I stood up to find the bathroom, but instead came face to face with the very young wife of one of the ship's officers.

"Well, hello, Stephanie," she said with a fake smile. Lisa was one of those wives who had been taken on cruises, when she was husband-hunting, so her family could marry her off to an officer—a fact she had proudly shared with me the day we were introduced on the Lido Deck. Now safely married, she strutted around the ship like she was the First Lady, wearing way too much makeup and outfits that weren't appropriate for the casual activities to which she wore them.

"Let me show you around the city. I used to come here all the time to shop," she said, as if she felt it was her duty as an officer's wife to play tour guide.

Say no. Say no. Say no.

"Sure," I mumbled.

I fought to keep up with her fast pace as I followed her across the city.

"This place is fantastic. I ate here for my twenty-first birthday. We sat next to the Baldwin brothers. Oh, and that dessert place over there, we know the owner. But of course, I rarely eat sweets. You should try it sometime."

Ugh, please make this stop. If this girl tells me one more bougie "fun fact" about Sydney, I might explode.

"That clothing line is amazing. I attend their preseason fashion events to buy ahead of the trends. Soooo worth the long flight."

Just when I thought my poor feet couldn't walk another step, Lisa decided we should eat lunch. We sat outside in wicker chairs at a small table with a pretty red umbrella which shaded us from the hot sun. My curiosity about the earlier events started to fester. *She's an officer's wife. She has intel.*

"What was that all about this morning?"

"I'm not supposed to say," she said before leaning in closely, "but I'll just say this. That woman, Wendy, used money that wasn't hers to buy a ticket for this cruise. Since she's Australian and back on home soil, she was arrested. I am not surprised. I mean, did you see her tattoos?"

"That's nuts," I said, ignoring her last comment. "I hadn't gotten a chance to meet her yet."

"It's a good thing you didn't. I heard they searched another passenger's cabin, thinking they might be an accomplice or somehow be associated with her."

Holy shit.

"It wasn't you, was it?" she said, looking at me directly. *Wait, does she know?*

I focused on her forehead, watching her sweat bead up on top of her extremely thick makeup. "No. It wasn't me," I said dismissively as the waiter served our lunch.

"So, are you married?" she inquired.

"Nope."

"Engaged?"

"Nope."

"How old are you?"

"Thirty-four."

"Wow. I'm twenty-six, and this was my fifth engagement."

"I've dated a bunch," I mumbled.

"Well, I guess I just skipped dating and went straight to engagement every time!"

She let out a hideous, loud laugh. I laughed along, trying to harmonize with her pitch to make it less painful to those sitting around us.

As Lisa rambled on, I could feel her condescension. I tuned her out, fantasizing about flipping the table over and watching her go flying off her chair.

"Well, that was a great lunch," she said, putting her napkin on the table.

Uh, I'm glad YOU think so.

She proceeded to pay the bill, which made me feel a tad guilty for my thoughts.

"What should we do next?" she continued.

"I actually need to go meet someone back at the ship," I lied.

"Oh, you must be going to the opera tonight with everyone. We got tickets as well, but Peter doesn't get off duty 'til later, so I'm going to stay here to raid some boutiques."

Standing up, I grabbed my purse and shopping bag and channeled my inner snob, unaware that my snob apparently had a slight hint of an English accent. "Lisa, you have been a fantastic tour guide. I learned so much about this city today. How will I ever thank you for such hospitality? Have a splendid rest of your afternoon at the boutiques. Oh, and thank you for lunch!"

I made my way to the nearest public restroom to finally change my clothes. I took off my blouse and grabbed the tank top I had on earlier. *Look at me and my boutiques and my five fiancés. Oh, really? Well, look at me and my MBA, bitch.* I kicked off my heels, sending them flying into the wall. *You think you're so awesome? I'm the one who is taking this trip. As. A. Paying. Passenger.* I pulled up my sweatpants and threw my hair back into a ponytail. *Who the hell acts like that? Are her parents proud?* I took a paper towel and wiped off my makeup. *They were probably relieved to pawn her off on someone else. Nah, they're probably just like her.* I slid into my flip-flops and grabbed my shopping bag, now filled with all the clothes I had bought. *Why the hell didn't I just say NO to her? Come on, let it go. It's not worth it.* I looked in the mirror before walking out. My scruffy look somehow made everything better.

• •

That evening, I attended a sunset piano concert on the top deck of the ship. I saw Sally sitting alone and joined her as a chance to spend some time with her and fill her in on Sydney. We chatted until Debbie began to play, then I drifted into a state of relaxation as the soft harmonic melodies of her classical songs filled the night air. The lit Sydney Opera House behind her looked like a hung poster. In a few hours, *Madame Butterfly* would begin in the iconic venue, just a football field away. *It feels like the entire ship—except me—has opera tickets.*

I stared at the building's majestic beauty. She looked like a bunch of clam shells stuck together, which I found fitting since three sides of her face the water. I felt a pressure in my head to attend the opera. But a soft voice in my heart whispered, "Next time." *But who knows if there will be a next time? How can you come to Sydney and not see an opera at the Sydney Opera House? Are you crazy? Come on, it isn't too late to go.*

"You seem lost in the music," Kiki whispered, sitting down next to me. "Are you seeing the opera tonight?"

"I can't decide. I didn't have an entirely good day in the city, and I really want to experience more of it."

"If you want more of Sydney, Mark and I have really cool plans," she said, referring to her coworker.

With nervous excitement, I made a final decision to abandon the opera house for some blind faith in what Kiki and Mark had in store.

We walked for what felt like miles. Mark, a soft-spoken but understatedly hilarious Canadian, led us down the back alleys of Sydney until we reached a nondescript door no higher than five feet. Ducking inside, we descended narrow cement stairs into an underground cave that could fit about forty people. *Might not be worth skipping the opera for, but I like it.* To the left, on a small platform, sat the drummer, guitarist, and a female singer. Tan plaster walls with black trim and gold lighting gave off a relaxed, yet still engaging ambiance.

"This place looks like something from the time of Christ," I said to Mark as we chose two of the few available stools. Kiki opted to make her way directly to the dance floor, falling quickly into the rhythm of the music. I watched her freely dancing and swaying. She seemed not to care one bit who was watching.

My inner control freak started to feel threatened by her every move. I wanted so badly to join her—not because I felt like dancing, but because I wanted to feel free of self-restriction and judgement.

"You should go join her," I said to Mark.

He quickly shook his head no. Clearly he was not leaving his stool.

The singer finished an original song and broke into a cover of Florence and the Machine. "Shake it out," she sang. "It's hard to dance with a devil on your back, so shake him off."

The lyrics lifted me off my stool. Three seconds later, my floor-length black maxi dress, wedges, and I and were on the dance floor with Kiki. No one else was there. Just us. I began bobbing back and forth awkwardly.

The singer continued:

"And I'm damned if I do and I'm damned if I don't
So here's to drinks in the dark at the end of my road
And I'm ready to suffer and I'm ready to hope
It's a shot in the dark and right at my throat
'Cause looking for heaven, found the devil in me
Looking for heaven, for the devil in me.
Well what the hell I'm gonna let it happen to me."

I started to lose myself and my surroundings, melting into the lyrics. I closed my eyes, listening deeply as the singer belted out the song. My mind no longer had to think of what to do next. My body simply moved. I looked over at Kiki and smiled, feeling an unspoken bond develop as we synced rhythm.

That night, Kiki and I became lifelong friends—a gift the opera could have never given me.

CHAPTER 15

DAY 37 - BONDI BEACH, AUSTRALIA

Just after dawn, my cabin phone woke me out of a sound sleep. Kiki was calling to see if I wanted to spend the day with her at Bondi Beach.

"The ferry leaves in an hour. Hendrik wants to surf, so he will be joining us if that's okay."

"Yeah, I'll come," I said nonchalantly before jumping out of bed at the speed of light.

I walked off the ship to find Hendrik waiting in blue shorts and a white T-shirt. His loose blond curls blew in the wind.

"Hey," I said.

"Hey," he said back.

The more I searched in my head for something interesting to say, the more paralyzed I became. We stood in an awkward silence for what felt like an eternity. The tension was finally broken by Kiki skipping down the dock like a six-year-old who'd been just let out for recess.

Still mute, I spent the entire ferry ride listening to Kiki and Hendrik talk about every topic under the sun. I promised myself I would find something interesting to say once we got to the beach. As luck would have it, Hendrik left us the second we docked to get wax for his board and to go surf.

The awkwardness continued when Kiki and I saw a sign for a surf competition starting on February 10. We wanted to check it out, but we had no clue what the date was that day. We ended up scaring a poor guy running a hot dog stand by asking him not only for the date, but also what day of the week it was. So much for smooth sailing.

• •

Later at dinner, I begged them to let me out of it, but no dice. My table was forcing me to sing. It was karaoke night.

We sat gathered together in The Crow's Nest as Hendrik approached us to collect our song cards. "Really? This is what you're going with?" he said to me sarcastically.

"Yep. It gets great results," I said, nervous as hell about my choice. It was a huge risk for a girl who cannot sing, but it worked the last time I tried it.

• •

Two years ago I'd sat in a karaoke bar as my last resort. I had just taken Yanira to finalize her divorce and she refused to let me take her home until I made her laugh. We went to brunch, shopping, then dinner. No joke or witty comment worked. Her face was long, and her energy deflated. She had been there for me so many times; I was not going to fail her.

Desperate to succeed, I selected the most obnoxious song I could think of. When "Bohemian Rhapsody" came onto the TV screens, the eight other patrons groaned, inspiring me to worsen my already bad singing voice. I sounded like a dying dog. I even added in every theatrical body movement I could think of before taking a dramatic bow to zero claps.

When I sat back down in my seat attempting to keep a straight face, Yanira looked at me, trying to catch her breath from laughing. "Fef, you can take me home now."

• •

I hoped my repeat performance would elicit the same laughter on the MS *Amsterdam.*

It did not. Rising above the polite claps was the raspy voice of a woman, who had to be more than a hundred years old, saying loudly to her husband, "Wow, she was horrible."

Mortified, I brought the microphone back to Hendrik, who was laughing and shaking his head. I could tell by the spark in his eyes that the ice had broken between us. I floated back to my table in disbelief.

The song worked again.

DAY 40 - AT SEA

I woke up to a ship full of pink and red for Valentine's Day—a holiday I had only celebrated a handful of times in my adult life. The ship had planned a formal party later that evening, so I set out my black-and-pink dress from my going-away party.

After an hour on the elliptical, I decided to change my routine for the day. I made my way up to the level above my cabin and out to the gorgeous teak Promenade Deck, where I relaxed under a beach towel in a tucked-away, out-of-sight lounge chair. I watched the deep navy blue waves as we made our way around Australia.

At the start of the cruise I would have used this hidden alone time to feel sad or angry about some portion of my life or my past, but in the month since, all of that had changed. I felt so connected to the ship. The people there, my table family, Kiki, Julie and Kel, and the friends I had made on board. Every moment made my heart smile. *I took a break from life to live, and I have never felt as alive as I do now.*

I managed to lie there all afternoon, smiling, hypnotically watching the waves before realizing trivia was about to begin. With no time to shower, I would grace my team with messy hair and smelly workout clothes. *They won't care.*

As I pushed through the double doors to enter the common area of deck 3, I ran into Hendrik, also on his way to trivia.

"Hello, Stephanie," he said, blushing.

"Hello, happy Valentine's Day!" I said. *God, when was the last time I wished a guy that?*

"Are you coming to the party tonight?" he asked.

"I sure am. How about you?"

"I'm working it. I'm done at eleven. You want to maybe hang out after?"

Wait, what?

"Sure," I said in my best offhand voice.

"Cool. Say 11:15?" He took a pencil out from his trivia box and wrote down his cabin number. "When you come, do not let anyone see you. It's against the rules to have guests in our cabins and vice versa."

Walking behind him to trivia, I was shocked at what just happened—and absolutely petrified of what might happen later.

I put my 11:15 plans firmly out of mind while getting ready for the party. *It's just a hangout. Do not obsess over it.* I slipped on my dress and picked up the same plain black shoes I'd worn the last time, but then set them down and instead opened a box of shoes I had under my bed. I had brought them just in case there was a themed party that needed something over the top. They were entirely covered in gold, silver, and soft blue beads of glitter. I slipped them on and walked around my room while looking in the mirror at their intense sparkle. *Funny how some glitter can make me feel so unrestricted and free.*

The party was packed, and everywhere I turned, I was met with an effusive, "Happy Valentine's Day," or a comment about how great I looked. Even Bill and Larry, whom I'd met in the stone church when the Alleycats sang in Nuku Hiva, came to find me. They heard word of my glitter shoes and had to get a photo with me, making me feel like a celebrity.

I spotted my entire table—even Don!—over by the bar. Pete immediately stepped forward as I walked toward them and lightly took my arm.

"Young lady, cha-cha with me," he said, leading us onto the dance floor.

"Pete, I don't know how."

"Nonsense."

"People are going to talk."

"Let them." He pulled me into formal dance position. I tried to follow his steps but struggled.

"You know, Stephanie, it's more fun to be talked about than to be the one doing the talking." He laughed.

My thoughts quieted, and my body fell into a rhythm of steps that somehow it already knew. *What's happening? How do I know this?* As we moved to the beat of the live band, forgotten memories came flooding in. I was transported back to my Pop's living room. I could hear the scratchy sound of his record player blaring a classical tune he hummed while purposely bouncing through the steps to help me follow the beat. His firm hands softly guided me. I could smell my grandma cooking in the kitchen while Amie watched us from the couch, determined to try herself. Joy radiated off Pop's face as I caught on. Now here I was decades later, feeling the same guidance of a hand on my back and the same bouncing that helped me catch a beat. I looked up at Pete and smiled. *It feels like I have my Pop back.*

• •

Later at dinner, we laughed at how perfectly coordinated we were, all of us wearing white, black, red, or pink, as if the photographer who snapped our group picture had given us these outfits. The photo became a new favorite.

I was enjoying myself until escargot was served, made special for our table. I had managed to escape it when dining with Julie and Kel, as well as when I was off the ship in New Zealand. But fate had caught up with me. I watched Sally's face light up before staring down at the plate of snails, covered in butter and garlic. Uncertain how to eat them, I sipped my wine while watching Ken take a bite first before I followed suit. Grabbing the tiny fork provided just for this dish, I pierced a snail and lifted it out of the butter. *I think it's too big to swallow whole. Just commit and get it over with.*

I put it in my mouth and began to chew, surprised at how good it tasted. I tried to hide my shock as I looked at Sally, who was smiling. "They are good, right?" she said.

"Absolutely! The ship knows how to make them. I have never had them this good before," I said confidently.

Sally's look of satisfaction was worth its price in gold.

After dinner, Pete joined me at The Crow's Nest. Usually, we chatted about casual topics and things we found funny, but that night, he shared his life story about two previous marriages and then his third and deep love, Colleen, who had died a few years before.

"Have you really never been married?" he asked.

"Nope, never."

"Good, stay that way. And when you meet him—and you will— don't ruin your amazing relationship by marrying the guy." Pete laughed, but I knew he wasn't joking. "Marriage ruined my first two relationships, and not marrying Colleen saved my third, despite its tragic end."

"You sound like you loved her so much. I can see it in your eyes when you talk about her. Marrying her couldn't have changed that."

He shook his head. "We are not meant to be caged. Married people act like they own each other. It smothers the flame. It isn't about loyalty. It just flat out messes with your head."

I had never seen him look so serious. He did have eighty-one years on this earth and multiple marriages under his belt. Maybe he had a point. But at the same time, I knew I could try a little harder and actually give men a chance.

Pete changed the subject, pulling me out of my head. He told me about a woman who walked up to him earlier in the day, warning him about me. "She told me you are trying to get in my will!"

Our laughter spilled over, filling the empty Crow's Nest.

"The crazy part, Pete, is that it doesn't make any sense. If I were looking for a sugar daddy, I would not have spent a fortune to come on this ship. I would have found an old rich guy before the cruise began and made him pay for my ticket. Actually, I had to buy two tickets! I could have brought someone along and been their sugar mama!"

After downing the last bit of my wine, I bid Pete a good night. It was just after eleven.

I lurked outside Hendrik's cabin door, my heart pounding. At this hour, no one was around. I took a deep breath and knocked. The door opened swiftly, and I darted inside.

Hendrik's room had stuff everywhere, and surfer décor hanging on the walls. He motioned for me to sit next to him on the bed. I pretended I didn't see his gesture and sat in a chair a few feet away instead. Every muscle in my body was tense, made even more evident by my hands, which were pressed firmly between my knees. He seemed as uncomfortable as I was. Nothing flowed easily or felt effortless.

"So, your cabin is on deck two?" he asked.

"Yeah, almost directly below you."

"Is it this size?"

"Actually, it's bigger," I said.

"How so?"

Why are you asking me about my cabin? You work on the ship. You probably already know this.

"A little bigger sitting area. I think these cabins are shorter to make room for the Promenade Deck," I said.

"Do you like your cabin?" he asked.

Really? That's what you want to know about me? If I like my cabin? "Yeah, it's great. I had no idea I could feel so at home in such a small space," I replied.

Crickets.

"I heard Pete upgraded his cabin to a suite," he said.

REALLY? Now Pete's cabin? What's going on? Am I messing this up? I mean, what does he even want? He is barely trying to get to know me. His questions are so meaningless. And what was that pat on the bed for? Is this just sex? Is that really all he wants?

I looked around the room trying to find things to ask about to keep our bland conversation going. "So where did you get that surf sign? Is there a fun story behind it?" I asked.

"I honestly don't remember. I've had it forever," he replied.

UGHHHHH!

He looks almost defeated. Wait, am I the one that's not interesting? Does he no longer find me pretty? I feel like I need to be less guarded, but what am I being open to? Sex? A relationship? I can't have a one-night stand on Valentine's Day. Not after the amazing day I had. That would feel horrible. I have no idea what to do. Oh, God, he is getting up. He is coming towards me. He is leaning in. I closed my eyes and felt a kiss on the forehead.

"Good night, Stephanie. Thanks for stopping by to hang." He peeked out the door. "It's safe to go."

"Good night, Hendrik," I said as I slipped out of his cabin. *I have no idea what that was, but I'm certain it was my doing.*

I entered my cabin to find a light blue Tiffany box on my bed, a Valentine's gift from the ship: a round, sterling silver, velvet-lined box with our ship's image engraved on top of it. I suspected it was designed to hold intimate jewelry, perhaps wedding bands. I laughed. It was gorgeous, but after Pete's warning about marriage and my complete inability to flirt, it probably would only ever hold my earrings.

DAY 48 - FREMANTLE, AUSTRALIA

After Sydney, I spent every Australian port with Ken, Detta, and Pete, from our artsy tour of Melbourne to the kangaroos and koalas in Adelaide. Oh, and poor Albany, a one-horse town, might never be the same after the loud ruckus we made walking through the shops. Now in Fremantle, Detta and I sat outside at lunch, enjoying the charm of the small city. Pete and Ken had wandered off, giving us some girl time.

"I cannot believe today is our last day in Australia," I said.

"Are you glad you came on this trip?" Detta asked.

"Yes. I have no regrets," I said. We had become so close that I decided to tell her more about my past.

"I wish I had been there with you all in 2013, but as you now know, I was living through my own personal hell."

"But look at where it got you! I lived through my own. My second husband was the love of my life. He was my equivalent of Pete's Colleen. I miss him every day."

"I am so sorry, Detta."

"He worked in the TV industry, which is how I got Captain Kirk's chair. Selling it enabled me to experience the world with such wonderful people."

I looked at her somber face. I knew without a doubt she would trade in the Star Trek chair and all of this adventure for one more day with her husband. She grabbed both my hands and gave me her wide smile which lit up her entire face.

"You have no idea how much you have added to our table, Stephanie. We just adore you."

"I feel the same way about you guys. To be honest, at first, I wasn't sure about two-hour dinners. Now I can't imagine life without them! And I didn't get why you wanted me there every night, but now I couldn't bring myself to eat with anyone else. You all have taught me so much already about family, friendship, and community. It's been the best part of this trip."

Detta smiled. "Honey, you also teach us so much. It's such a different time now, and witnessing a woman your age live life on her terms, by herself, breaking all the old-fashioned rules that we grew up adhering to. It's beautiful to watch."

CHAPTER 16

DAY 51 - BALI, INDONESIA

Thanks to life on the Lido Deck, I was tanner than I had been in years. I looked at myself in the mirror, enjoying how vibrant colors no longer washed me out. Not to mention how my elliptical therapy sessions had my butt and legs looking mighty fine in any outfit I put on. I had never looked or felt so good. So healthy.

We pulled into port late in the day and half the ship, it seemed, had the same plans for our first night in Bali—to watch a cultural performance called the Kecak, a "must-see" recommendation from the Indonesian crew.

As the sun set and the tiki torches were lit, fifty shirtless men in black-and-white checkered sarongs rapidly repeated one word—"kecak," which sounded like "keh-jeh"—while moving their hands up and down like they were bench-pressing the air in front of them. My favorite was the lone bass keeper, who shouted, "Bohm, bohm, bohm," keeping a steady beat for the entire forty-five minute show.

The chanting was unbelievably fast, and performed with great enthusiasm. I became so entranced that I lost the storyline. I knew a princess arrived, followed by a dragon, and then there was a battle. I could only stare, mesmerized by their moving arms, their high energy, and total commitment to chanting "kecak" over and over again until it was time to take a bow.

Half the crew on board was Indonesian, and this was their dance, their chant. I wanted to connect with them by learning how to do it. I practiced in my cabin, but would mess up within seconds. It became stuck in my head for weeks, and I found myself doing the hand movements in public, especially when my favorite crew members were watching, which always made them laugh.

DAY 52 - BALI, INDONESIA

The next morning, I ate breakfast on an empty Lido Deck. Anne Marie walked up surprised to see me, explaining that most passengers booked resort stays for our three days in Bali, since it was very cheap for Americans.

I could have booked a last-minute stay somewhere, but wasn't in the mood. For the first time ever, I felt the pangs of not having a partner and had zero interest being in a romantic setting alone like I normally enjoyed doing. I found this feeling of loneliness very odd, quite annoying, and perhaps a little unpredictable. Maybe I didn't feel as lonely as I did left out. I wasn't sure, but I did know I didn't want to think about it anymore.

I reminded myself that it didn't matter what anyone else was doing; I had already planned to spend this day alone, conquering a fear and stretching my limits by doing something that felt far scarier than parasailing or swimming with sharks: surfing. This was an extraordinary pledge, considering that when I was three years old, I almost drowned.

At my grandparents' pool, I'd had a full-blown tantrum over using floaties. I just wanted an inner tube. My mom gave in, then inevitably turned away for a second, which was just enough time for me to slip through the tube. I remember sitting at the bottom of the pool watching bubbles come out of my mouth, not afraid, just curious. I didn't know I was in danger. Mom pulled me up by my swimsuit and into the air as I choked. Soon after, my Pop taught me to swim.

I felt comfortable swimming only in the enclosed walls of his pool. In my twenties, after a few strong waves dragged me under and rolled me back to shore, I shied away from swimming at the beach. Today, I would not only face the waves, but learn to ride them.

Arriving at Kuta Beach, I suited up and signed my life away. I wanted to quit as soon as I saw the waves, but I refused to let myself.

As I got closer to shore, I saw trash everywhere, as well as plastic containers bobbing up and down in the ocean. I asked the instructor about this.

"It is a problem on this particular beach. The current seems to gather it from far away and bring it all here."

I wanted to abandon surfing and spend the day cleaning up, but my instructor told me that today, my only job was to stand up on a surfboard. I tried to follow his lead, but had a hard time focusing while milk cartons and yogurt containers floated around me. I knew I was a contributor to this; I loved single-use plastic and didn't always recycle. Silently I promised God that if I didn't drown, I would do better.

Surfing was extremely difficult. After hearing one hundred times that I need to breathe and relax, I caved and divulged my fears to my instructor. I felt silly and vulnerable, considering the waves were not huge, but because I did so, he changed his way of teaching and swam out with me, giving me a huge pep talk before each attempt. The first time I stood up, riding the longboard to shore, his cheers traveled down the beach, making me look up to see people clapping.

I won't claim that I wound up loving surfing. I also didn't conquer my fear. I did, however, lessen it a bit, which to me, was a victory.

Afterward, my hired driver Made (Mah-deh) took me to the most pristine places on that part of the island. I tried to make conversation and get to know him more, but he always walked ten feet behind me as if he were my security guard. I knew he was being respectful, but his distance exacerbated how I'd felt at breakfast—alone.

One of the prettiest beaches he showed me wasn't even exactly a beach, but a waterway accessed only by going down a crazy set of stairs. I looked over the railing, loving the view—until I saw Hendrik with his surfboard and one of the shop girls next to him. She was rubbing his arm as they walked up the stairs. Turning around quickly I stared at the ground so they wouldn't see me.

As we drove away, we passed Hendrik and the shop girl walking down the street. I gazed out the back window of the car, realizing that he was just some player, but also realizing I was insanely jealous. I couldn't turn around. I kept staring until I heard Made's voice, "Ma'am, is there something important back there? I can stop if you wish."

"No sir, nothing important, but thank you for asking."

DAY 53 - BALI, INDONESIA

I woke up excited to leave the busy streets and exotic beaches behind to head into the mountains of Ubud, a more artistic part of the island. Outside the port a line of tiny, antique-looking cars lined up, barely fitting two people each.

"Hang back. We'll ride together in the last car," I heard my favorite Greek accent whisper, and turned to see Kiki had returned early from her time at a resort.

"Come on, it will be a romantic date for just us two," she laughed. I shook my head at the irony of her words and felt my loneliness dissipate like fog clearing from the warmth of the sun. I got into the tiny back seat and wondered if Kiki was real, or some mystical being who seemed to appear out of nowhere when I needed it most.

We drove past endless rice fields, and I leaned out the window, staring at the water floating above the rice, awed by how it looked like glass mirrors reflecting the sky. Kiki asked the driver to pull over and stop at a fruit stand on the side of the narrow road. She got out of the car and looked back at me through the window.

"Have you ever tried durian?" she asked.

"No. Is that the fruit they say smells really bad?"

"Yes," she said, "but it apparently tastes way better than it smells. Want to try some?"

At first sniff, it smelled terrible. At first bite, I thought it was going to be okay. But no. While exhaling as I chewed, a horrible taste took over my mouth. I started gagging. Kiki cracked up, but the guys at the fruit stand did not.

"Oh, come on, it can't be that bad," she said.

"Your turn," I said, handing her the fruit. She refused until I insisted.

Within a minute, she too was gagging. Feeling bad, we tipped the men well before leaving them with the rest of the durian.

We spent the day touring villages where life had barely changed in over a hundred years, before walking around the Pura Kehen temple, built in the eleventh century. After we covered our shorts in customary sarongs, Kiki wandered off, leaving me to feel the silent, eerie air while observing a montage of carved dragons and monsters. When I was ready to leave, I slowly made my way down the main steps and spotted her to the left, swinging upside down on a hanging vine.

"Come join me," she shouted.

"I can't. What if it's offensive?"

"To who? Come live a little," she insisted, so I made my way toward her.

As fun as our day was, lunch stole the show. I walked inside the restaurant and saw zero glass, just open air connecting us to the lush green blanket of trees and Mount Batur off in the distance. We were high enough up that the cloudy air left a dewy shimmer on my skin. Feeling like a plant in need of water, I chose a table on the terrace, taking in the view while the mist enveloped me, fueling my soul and revitalizing me in a way I didn't expect—a connection to nature I never felt while mountain biking or lying on the beach.

Midbite, I heard a few familiar voices, and turned to see Ken, Detta, and Pete walking toward us. They had heard me speak of both Mark and Kiki often, making her introduction more of a chance to put a face to the name.

"Kiki, we would like to host you and Mark for dinner tomorrow night," Pete said while I looked on in shock.

"I can't believe it. They passed the dinner invitation test," I said, poking Pete's arm with my finger. "But you forgot to tell her they can only stay one night."

DAY 54 - AT SEA

I ran to the dining room early, purchasing two bottles of red and two of white to be displayed on the table while also asking the manager to set two extra settings. I stood as our guests came down the stairs with Pete and Detta behind them. I formally introduced Kiki and Mark to everyone they hadn't yet met before sitting down to a very full table.

We had invited guests only twice before. Both times, the officers came decked in uniform and our dinner felt very formal. Sally would spend the evening complimenting the ship. Detta would ask about their families, and Pete and I would tell stories, silently on a mission to make the table laugh. Ken and Don would wait and fill in where needed. Like a well-oiled machine, we worked together to make sure the conversation flowed, and our guests felt welcomed.

Despite Kiki and Mark's casual attire, the night started off very formally. I felt honored that my tablemates tried, giving respect to two people I had grown to cherish. I didn't know if it was the wine or the relaxed energy, but halfway through our first course, the entire table let loose, abandoning the pleasantries for banter. I didn't want our time together to end.

Mark's understated humor meshed well with Ken and Sally's, and his soft-spoken demeanor was quite compatible with Don's. Kiki's loud, vibrant, fun personality enthralled Detta and Pete. It was the perfect storm. While the table sat gasping for air following a joke at my expense, I felt Sally clench my thigh. I looked over to see Pete helping Detta. She was white as a ghost, holding her chest with one hand and her abdomen with the other. Ken shot up and called for help as people started scurrying around. A minute later, medics rushed in. My heart was in a panic. It was all happening so fast, and I prayed it wasn't serious. As they rushed her off in a gurney, instructing us not to follow, I looked over at Pete to see every ounce of color drained from his face.

We tried to continue eating, but it was no use. We canceled dessert. Seeing as how my cabin was next to Detta's, I promised to send word the minute I heard her return.

I walked with a deflated Pete, knowing he didn't want to be alone. He cared about Detta to an extent I sometimes suspected was beyond friendship.

"You aren't going to trust me to call, are you?" I asked Pete.

"No ma'am, I am not. I'm going to find Detta."

"I'm coming with you," I said as we broke our direct orders and headed to the clinic.

It was after hours, but the door had been left unlocked. I pushed it open slightly to see a dimly lit reception area and a small desk.

"Pete, we shouldn't be in here."

"Oh, never you mind," he said, barreling in.

Before I could stop him, he had hit the bell on top of the desk a bit too hard, making a loud, echoing ring. Heavy footsteps advanced. A very tall, robust, blond woman dressed in officer's clothing came out looking alarmed and annoyed.

"We're closed."

"We are here for Detta," Pete said.

"Are you her family?"

I watched Pete fumble his words.

"We eat together," I said quickly.

"Sit down!" she practically shouted before walking off.

Pete and I sat in two of the three blue plastic chairs against the wall with our heads down and hands folded like scolded children.

"We eat together? Really?" Pete whispered.

"Shhhh. We wouldn't be in this mess if you didn't slam the bell so damn hard."

An hour later, the doctor came out with a warm smile.

"You must be Detta's friends."

"Yes sir, is she going to be okay?" Pete asked.

"I can't share specifics, but I can assure you, she'll be just fine." Pete's face lit up. My breathing quivered as I tried not to shed tears.

"We will monitor her for a while and then send her to her cabin to rest all day tomorrow."

"I live next door. I'll help in any way I can," I said as the nurse came out, walked right past us and opened the door to see us out. Pete gave her a dirty look. Thankfully he waited until the door shut behind us to unleash his thoughts.

DAY 55 - AT SEA

I softly closed Detta's cabin door behind me and headed to dinner. Despite hearing from Sally how well she was doing, I'd needed to see for myself. To my relief, Detta looked as if she'd never felt ill, but she did want to rest up one extra night just to be sure.

As I descended the main spiral stairs, I hated the vision of Detta's place setting and empty chair. It wasn't like she was off in port and that was the reason for her absence. Knowing it was due to her illness left a void in my heart.

Pete had a shrimp cocktail in one hand while the other hand was waving around as he told his dramatic tale. Now that he knew Detta was okay, he had the green light to run with his enticing account of our quest to find her, "breaking into" the clinic, and the villain of the story whom he now called Nurse Ratched.

"You are quite the rebel, Pete," Sally interjected, enhancing the gleam in Pete's eye. Pete looked over at me like I was the Bonnie to his Clyde.

I couldn't help but partake. "Oh, you should have seen him storm into that clinic and slam that bell!"

"I know, I did, didn't I!" His face was red with pride.

Telling the full story over appetizers wasn't sufficient for Pete. He brought it up again during our main course, and again during dessert. Each rehash, he laughed harder and shouted Nurse Ratched's famous line, "Sit down!" even louder until Ken finally quieted him before, once again, changing the subject.

CHAPTER 17

DAY 56 - SEMARANG, INDONESIA

As Pete and Detta boarded the bus in Semarang, Ken stayed back, waiting for me to arrive.

"Stick with me on this one," he said casually, finding two open seats for us. His protective assertiveness paired with a cheeky grin made me feel like he had some insider info. The bus took off, lurching around the corner way too fast. I felt my stomach drop; letting out a small whimper of fear, I held on for dear life, making Ken laugh.

For an hour we endured winding, narrow roads with steep ledges at top speeds, and a driver who seemed to enjoy nearly crashing into other cars and almost running over motorcyclists. Our bus swayed back and forth as if it were trying to dodge police and I repeatedly slammed into the window, then into Ken. Between my screams, I could hear Pete laugh-shouting, "Oh, my God!"

We arrived at our destination, and I was too worn out to yell at the driver like planned. I sat on a nearby bench pale as a ghost, dumbfounded that Ken looked so cool, calm, and collected.

"I don't think I can get back on that bus."

"Then enjoy your new life here in Indonesia." He laughed.

"I'll be sure to write."

"I was warned about it. Apparently, it's common and not just our driver. Here, I brought you some gum. It will help your stomach."

"Thanks. Save me one for the way back," I said as I popped it into my mouth.

"Actually, we're taking a slow antique train back that goes through the rice fields."

"Thank God!"

Just like at the temple in Bali, we were given sarongs to wear over our outfits before walking up to Borobudur, the largest single monument in the Southern Hemisphere, dating to AD 840. It was deserted and buried under volcanic ash in the forest for over a thousand years until Sir Stamford Raffles discovered it in 1814. He then went off and topped this discovery by being one of the founders of Singapore a few years later.

The temple, with its perfectly square, symmetrical design, was so huge that I needed to stand back to take it all in. From afar, it looked as if lava had been poured into a giant temple-shaped sandcastle mold, then turned over and plopped right onto the land. Up close, it was a work of art.

On our way to the entrance, Ken, Pete, Detta, and I came up behind two unnaturally slow Buddhist monks wearing maroon robes.

"This place is amazing," I said to the monks as we passed them on the left like a car on the highway.

"Yes. We came a long way to visit," one of them said in a heavy accent.

"Well, then we must capture this moment." I pointed to my camera.

"Yes, but only if you join us in the photo."

Ken took my camera and I stood in the middle, feeling the air from the space between us as we posed.

"What's your email? I will send you the photo tonight."

"It's okay. We are happy to just have the photo taken."

Huh? I wonder if it's a Buddhist thing. Or maybe monks can't have photos. I have no idea, but I'm very intrigued.

The design of the top of the temple—with its huge, carved, bell-shaped structures—was fantastic. I walked around, taking in the magnificent views of the land in every direction I turned.

Damn, this place is cool.

Ken and I made our way down to find Pete and Detta, who had wandered off. Ken leaned in as if he were about to tell me a secret. "I heard the temple used to be surrounded by homeless people, but the government cleared them out. They felt it would enhance tourism if the surrounding areas were kept nice."

"So, the government cleared out the homeless to draw tourists to a Buddhist temple? I don't know anything about Buddhism, but that can't be in line with their beliefs," I said.

Ken used his hand to signal that I needed to lower my voice. A nearby guide, looking rather insulted, said, "Yes, but nobody wants to see homeless people loitering and trashing the grounds of this magnificent temple."

"No, no, they don't," I mumbled, keeping the peace despite my strong opposition to his words.

On the train, I stared out at the rice fields, enjoying the peaceful ride home. Borobudur had been incredible and worth seeing, but I left uncertain if I would return. One thing I was sure about—always take the train.

DAY 57 - JAKARTA, INDONESIA

I walked off the ship in Jakarta and noticed an area off to the side with decorations, tables, and chairs. Families of crew members were waiting anxiously to see their loved ones. Some even held signs, making it hard not to get emotional. *Look at how missed these kids, wives, husbands, mothers, and fathers are. I don't think there is an attraction in this city that could top watching this big reunion.*

The crew on board, who mainly served food and drinks and managed our staterooms, came from either the Philippines or Indonesia. Without the ability to have visitors like officers could, they did not see their families for the entire nine-month contract unless the ship pulled into their home port, making this day special for some, and I suspect painful for others. The crew were not permitted to drink or dine with passengers, but that didn't stop us from getting totally attached. Just that morning, Jahn, James, and Anne Marie crowded around me as I ate my breakfast, eager to know what I had planned to see in Jakarta, their home city.

Anne Marie had become a favorite early on. Her black hair, large eyes, and mocha skin were naturally gorgeous, and her voice never raised nor sped up from its natural cadence. She always made it a point to find me and say hello. Her slow-moving, soothing nature felt like a warm cup of tea, especially at the beginning of the trip when I'd needed it most.

James was the quieter one of the bunch, but very popular on the ship. I'm not sure who started it, but he was nicknamed "007." Now, any time I would see him, he would stop and give his best James Bond pose with hand-guns blazing.

Then there was my little Jahn, who was one of the happiest people I have ever met, and although he was an adult, he looked about ten. He giggled constantly. Jahn was hell-bent on collecting all fifty U.S. state-specific quarters. Anytime I found one for him, he would jump up and down repeatedly, giggling even louder.

Even though he wasn't at breakfast that morning, I must mention Eric, who I believed was from the Philippines. His handsome, wide smile and charismatic charm were like rays of sunshine anywhere he went. Eric noticed immediately that at trivia or happy hour, I would decline the peanuts they served and ask for Goldfish crackers. The ship would often run out, so anytime a shipment arrived, Eric would look for me so he could hand me a glassful and say, "pishy pishy." I lived to hear those words. I would be reading or talking, and suddenly I would hear "pishy pishy" in the distance before Eric was even in sight. This phrase quickly morphed into his way of saying hello whenever I walked by.

The trip was rendered more colorful because of these moments, making my time on board even more precious than I could have imagined during my days of researching at the Drunken Monkey.

Today, in Jakarta, I wanted nothing more than a full report and some good stories for the crew of my time in their home city.

After a tour of the downtown area, I found a store Anne Marie mentioned where I could buy a batik dress to wear to the Indonesian show they were putting on for us all next month. Then, I stopped into the Indonesian Jester Puppet Museum, as James had suggested I do. The angry faces on the puppets freaked me out, making me race through it—something I suspected both James and Eric would find rather funny. I ran out into pouring rain, which helped me decide to cut my day short and head back to the ship to see if the reunion was still taking place.

I came through the gangway to find a crew member giving a tour to his spouse, and walked past colorful signs and decorations into the Lido Deck to eat a late lunch. There, a father was bouncing his five-month-old child whom he'd just met for the first time. Parents sat eating lunch with their kids. Husbands and wives were taking every moment they could together. My heart melted.

"Ma-am Step-anie!"

Anne Marie was sitting at a table with two people who looked like her mother and maybe a sister. I ran over and hugged her.

"Meet my family." She turned around to them. "This is the American I write to you about."

Me. She wrote home about me. I didn't know what to say, so I hugged them and told them how happy I was to meet them.

"Please join us," Anne Marie's mom requested.

They haven't seen each other in months, and they get only a few hours together—and they want me to join them. I filled a plate with some food and sat down. They bombarded me with questions about my life, from living in America, to not being married, to being on this trip. What was my favorite this? What was my favorite that? I equally wanted to know about them, but let Anne Marie and her family ask the questions. Whatever they wanted to know, I wanted to tell them, sharing as many details as I could before leaving the women to spend their last hour together in peace.

I walked down to my cabin with a quiet sense of happiness. Seeing the crew so thrilled to be with their families made me miss my own. *I wonder what Charlie is doing. I wonder if he even notices that I am gone.*

DAY 58 - AT SEA

"Ladies and gentlemen, this is your captain speaking. I hope you are enjoying this beautiful morning at sea. While we have a splendid day planned on the Lido Deck as we cross the equator today, I do have news that is of some concern. Norovirus cases have been reported on this ship. If it spreads to enough passengers, we will be refused entry into port, paralyzing our travels. It is vital that you wash your hands, and do not touch food and put it back. Please use the hand sanitizer stations before entering the dining room. If you fall ill, please alert the clinic at once and quarantine in your room until cleared by our doctor. Together we can stop this dead in its tracks."

I discarded my oatmeal, not thinking much more about the announcement. Today was a huge day. While technically this would be the second time crossing the equator during our trip, it was our initiation ceremony which I'd been forewarned about. Fish would be kissed. Officers would be roasted. King Neptune, ruler of the sea, would come forth and grant us Polliwogs our new, official title: "Shellback."

I scurried down the stairs to my cabin, eager to prep and arrive early. I had zero desire to kiss a fish again, but hey, it was a small entry fee for the laughs and craziness that were going to take place on the Lido Deck.

As I stood in the shower, washing my hair, a wave of dizziness hit me. I grabbed the safety railing on the wall to support myself while slowly sitting down in the tub. A stabbing pain hit my abdomen, and I couldn't decide if I was going to lose my bowels, throw up, or faint. Within ten minutes, I managed to do all three in that exact order.

I regained consciousness within minutes when my body alerted me that I was not done being sick. *Damn it, I can't sit on the toilet and lean over it at the same time. Grab the garbage can!*

An hour later, I felt like nothing remained. *Someone's knocking.* "One minute!" I shouted. I stood up and splashed some water on my face, which reignited my nausea.

I opened the door six inches and saw Sally's face staring back at me. She was dressed in one of her handmade sundresses, solid aqua like the sea with shell-themed jewelry to match.

"Why aren't you upstairs?" she said in a voice that sounded as if I were missing my own wedding.

"I think I'm sick."

"Today is your day. You cannot miss this. Everyone is expecting you."

"Sally, I'm not kidding. I am sick. I actually think you need to back up because I may be contagious."

She looked at me quizzically, despite my pale, sweaty complexion.

"Just try to make it, will you? It's a rite of passage."

"Just give me a few and let me try to come up, okay?"

She was right. It *was* important. Today was day fifty-eight. We had fifty-seven days behind us and fifty-seven days still to go. Today was the exact middle, as if our trip had its own equator. Was this the brilliant planning of our captain? Or was it Poseidon himself? Either way, they managed to line up the dead center of our trip with the dead center of the world.

Maybe I just have food poisoning, and it's almost over.

I put on shorts and a tank top and rode the elevator to the Lido Deck. As it ascended, I heard the laughter and cheering I was missing, which pained me more than the nausea.

Staying next to the elevator, I peeked around the corner. The Lido Deck was covered in Atlantis-style décor. The staff were dressed in various outfits that corresponded to the King Neptune costume worn by our main director—long white beard, robe, and triton. The whole thing looked like something straight out of *SNL*, making me want to participate even more.

As much as I wanted to stay, it wasn't going to happen. Within two minutes, I could barely make out the inappropriate joke King Neptune was saying about one of the first officers. The wave of dizziness returned, and I felt my body shutting down. I pushed the elevator button repeatedly, begging the doors to close. *Eight decks. Just eight decks, and you are home.*

I held onto the railing for what felt like an eternity, praying for deck 2. By the time the elevator doors opened, I was drenched with sweat and barely able to hold my head up. A couple who was waiting for the elevator took one look at me and offered to help.

"No, don't touch me! I'm sick and don't want to spread it," I insisted. Leaning against the wall, I made it five steps before crawling the last several feet.

I phoned the clinic and the doctor came to my cabin immediately.

• •

Over the next month, half the ship contracted the norovirus, making the matter quite serious. For all of March, my beloved gym was closed. Pools drained. The buffet shut down, and sanitizer became mandated across the ship. Thankfully, the captain's strict measures helped contain the illness before we were denied port entry. I was lucky to be one of the first handful to contract it and get it over with. But the timing of it bothered me greatly. *Why couldn't it have waited just one day?*

It was supposed to be my rite of passage, and I missed it.

CHAPTER 18

DAY 61 - KUALA LUMPUR, MALAYSIA

I found a little café tucked back from the main street, with a brown awning and gold letters spelling out words I didn't understand. No customers were inside, but I was hungry and decided to check it out.

A young man with large brown eyes and a pronounced nose stood behind the counter.

"Are you open?" I asked, hoping he spoke English.

"Yes. Of course, sit down," he said.

The norovirus was only a few days behind me, and not wanting to tempt fate, I stuck with something safe, ordering coffee and french fries. When the man brought me my coffee, I asked him his name and where he was from.

"My name is Kio, and my family and I immigrated here from Northern India."

"Wow, what made you choose Kuala Lumpur?" I asked.

He looked at me with his strong, warm gaze and a smile as if he were about to describe the love of his life. "Out of all the countries we could afford to move to, we chose Malaysia because the flowers bloom all year here like I imagine they do in heaven."

After a day of walking in ninety-five-degree heat, I have a hard time seeing it that way. I smiled back at him.

"I have only been to here and my home in India. I can't imagine what the United States is like in person," he said as he lingered for a moment.

Come on…you didn't come all this way to sit here and read your Kindle. Live a little. "Kio, would you like to join me? I can tell you all about it."

I took my time talking to him. In fact, I spent the entire afternoon telling him as much as I could, using any adjective I could think of to properly paint a picture. Enjoying the unexpected connection and not wanting to leave, I pushed the limit on time.

"I have to be back on board in thirty minutes. I wish I could stay longer," I said as I handed him my credit card.

"We only take cash," he said.

I looked in my wallet, mortified to realize I didn't have nearly enough.

"If you would let me go to an ATM, I promise you, I will return. I am good for it. I just need to go get some money."

He reached into his wallet and took out enough cash, then put it in the register. After having learned that he worked to help his father take care of his siblings, I knew his generosity was out of the question.

"Kio, I can't let you do that. Please, I will be right back," I said as I grabbed my things off the counter.

"No, please don't. I am honored to spend time with an American. Let me show my gratitude. Please don't insult me."

He values my time so much, he'd cover my tab with money I know he needed.

The look in his eyes told me not to push, that this was important to him. I fought hard to stop the discomfort in my chest.

"Kio, thank you. You are so kind."

"Of course. But may I ask a small favor, Stephanie?"

I smiled, knowing that the answer was yes, no matter what he asked.

"Can we take a photo together?"

••

I walked back to port wondering if that had really just happened, or if I'd somehow managed to dive headfirst onto the page of a poem.

DAY 65 - YANGON, MYANMAR

Myanmar, formally known as Burma, recently reopened after being closed to tourists for fifty years, making me overly eager to experience this rare opportunity. Today, we were heading to the legendary Shwedagon Pagoda, also known as "The Buddhist's Mecca."

I stared out the bus window as we made our way down a dirt road, passing groups of shacks with plastic communal tables in the middle. A young boy, who looked to be about six, stood in front of the table wearing no shoes. Our eyes met, and he smiled and waved. I matched his greeting, then used my hands to make a funny face. *Look at him laugh. I love it.*

"Monks from all over the world make a pilgrimage to this pagoda," our guide said as we made our way toward the city of Yangon. "It is legend that eight hairs of the Buddha reside there." I wondered if the monks I met at Borobudur had ever been here.

It was midday, sunny and hot. I could see the pagoda in the distance, covered in gold. The sun's light reflected off the main stupa, blinding me.

We stood in an area just outside the gate. Even though the pagoda was outdoors, we had to take off our shoes. As I did so, I felt a clump of goop land on my head. Bird poop slid down the side of my face and onto my shirt. I didn't find it as funny as Ken, Detta, and Pete, because I didn't see anywhere to go wash up. Thankfully, Detta had a wet towelette which I used to clean myself off.

We walked in to find shrines of gold everywhere and more Buddhas than I could count. One particular section had a Buddha representing each day of the week.

"Pour the water on the Buddha statue that represents the day you were born," our guide instructed.

I found Monday and picked up the ladle of water.

"Gently, from the head first. Just like how you were born."

But I was born feet first. Does that matter? Never mind.

I gave my Buddha a quick bath, realizing that the other people waiting to go next were real Buddhists. I watched as a couple bathed the Buddha slowly and with great care. I looked around; it seemed like people from our ship were the only tourists there. I felt like an impostor. Out of respect, I pulled away from our guide and faded into the background, curiously observing while trying not to intrude.

Our guide had arranged a set-menu lunch at a beautiful restaurant, and we headed there next, prior to visiting some smaller pagodas. The appetizer arrived right as we sat down. *Jellyfish.* After some encouragement from Detta, I tried it, instantly regretting my decision.

I listened to Ken go on about how the pagoda was made up of ninety tons of gold and how he couldn't wait to go back at night to see it all lit up.

"I would rather do something else," I protested.

"Why?" Ken asked.

"Because it's not like Thailand with tons of tourists crowding the pagodas. Here, we're intruding."

"Then pray with them!" Pete said.

"I'd like to learn more about Buddhism, especially since meeting those monks at Borobudur. But, that's not the point, Pete."

"I could see you becoming a Buddhist," Pete continued, but I stopped him with my hand.

"Pete, whatever joke you were about to say, don't." Pete gave me a look, before we both caught a bad case of the giggles, making Ken and Detta wonder what was wrong with us.

As night fell, we returned to the pagoda. Standing outside waiting to go back in, I felt a big clump of goop hit me right on the shoulder and down my arm. *Again? Are you freaking kidding me?* I looked up. There was no ledge of birds. No tree branch. Nothing.

"Looks like you've got your sign. Time to start studying," Ken said while Detta rushed to help. Pete kept his head down, and his shoulders shook as he tried to hide his laughter, declaring,

"She just got baptized by the Buddhists!"

DAY 67 - THANLYIN VILLAGE, MYANMAR

The bird poop made for a good story, but my third day in Myanmar is the one that will forever stay with me. While Yangon was a traditional city, underdeveloped villages—similar to those I first rode past while on the way to the pagoda—began just outside its perimeter.

We arrived at Thanlyin Village, where I was greeted by a man on a bicycle with a side seat, waiting for me. As we rode through the neighborhoods, children ran outside from their homes to wave as if I were royalty being escorted through the town. Everyone seemed so happy—and I'm not talking about normal "happy"; I am talking about "what-is-in-your-water" happy. I noticed it at the pagoda on our first day, and all through the previous day while touring Yangon. It was baffling.

We stopped at the village market where there were no souvenirs to purchase but plenty of dried fish, spices, food, cloth, and more. This market was the center of village commerce, where I watched ordinary daily life unfold. A woman was selling boxes of pencils and paper at her stand, and I remembered someone saying that Dolly brought school supplies to an orphanage every time the ship pulled into India. I bought as many as I could, hoping this would help break the ice between us.

"Pay her in American if you can," my guide suggested.

"Why?" I had sufficient local money.

"The American dollars are from fifty years ago. New money is very exciting," he said as I pulled out a crisp ten-dollar bill.

Some kids ran up saying hello, proud that they knew an English word. They started rubbing my arm, amazed at how white my skin was, despite my tan. *I wonder how shocked they would be if they saw me in my natural pale state.* The children had painted their own faces a light tan; my guide explained they'd used a paste from a tree root that both protected them from the sun and also made their skin lighter.

Before heading back, I felt compelled to ask him one last thing weighing on my mind.

"Is everyone secretly injected with happy serum while they sleep?"

He laughed. "Ahh, you noticed. It is not medicine. It is our way of thinking, derived from our Buddhist beliefs."

"Can you explain it to me?"

"Yes, of course. We believe that true joy comes from detachment to material possessions. The less one has, the happier they are. Poverty is the biggest blessing life could give us."

"Financial freedom is a blessing in the United States."

"I know the ways of your country. Being free to do what you want isn't necessarily freedom. Because as much as you think you will reach a point where you feel like you have enough, I assure you that day will never arrive. One who wants more will always want more."

"I sold most of everything I owned and spent almost all my money to take this trip," I said.

"You are very wise, Miss," he replied.

Wow. Not the response I'm used to getting...

"But remember, if you cannot find happiness with what is in front of you, you will never appreciate it in the places that you seek to get to. Now, in this moment, you are here with me in this village.

Enjoy it. Find its beauty and take it in. Be here fully, as if it is the only place on earth to be. Every place you go, do the same."

I had so many thoughts in my head, and I wanted to say something equally profound back to him. Instead, I simply replied, "Yes, sir."

DAY 70 - SRI LANKA

I didn't know what to expect in Sri Lanka, since it had been hit by the tsunami in 2004. I had no concept of how long a place took to rebuild following such a catastrophic event. To my surprise, it looked as if nothing had ever happened.

I walked up and down the camel-colored sand of my hotel's beach. Signs were everywhere, warning of turtle eggs buried beneath, waiting to hatch. I sat down in a safe area and tried to turn my mind off but couldn't.

This beach felt different. It was gorgeous and tropical, but I couldn't imagine myself basking there, sipping a piña colada while covered in suntan oil. *It feels like this place has something more to it. Something deeper. Is it possible that the beaches in Sri Lanka have seen too much tragedy? I'm probably just crazy and imagining things.*

I thought about Myanmar and how yesterday, I'd found out how much those ninety tons of gold were worth. Billions! *Yet their people have nothing. That money could fix it.*

Shaking my head to clear the thoughts, I remembered the words of my guide, and the Buddhist book I'd borrowed from the ship's library, and how both stressed the importance of staying present in each moment. But I couldn't help it. Thoughts raced around in my mind, igniting my anxiety.

I returned to the ship needing to talk, but I'd already ruined one formal night with my absence; I didn't want to ruin this one by dampening the mood. We all donned white, according to the theme's instructions, and eagerly waited for our escargot. I smiled, watching my table behave like always, finding their banter soothing. I inserted myself when necessary but contributed much less than usual.

On autopilot, after dinner I headed toward my cabin, falling back into an old habit from my first month at sea of self-loathing alone. Halfway there, I caught myself. *You promised you wouldn't do that anymore. Remember?*

I turned around and rode the elevator to The Crow's Nest, finding it empty. Our back-to-back port days were starting to wear on people, and tomorrow we would arrive in India. I too should have been resting, as I had plans to fly and see the Taj Mahal. While deep in thought, I heard a voice I had grown to love.

"Surrrree," Kel said, approaching me.

"Nice outfit!" I pointed to his white T-shirt with a silkscreen tuxedo printed on it. "Did you really get away with that?"

"They said 'tuxedo,' but never specified in what fashion," he said proudly.

I looked him in the eye, tempted to make a further joke about his bright red sunburn, but simply shook my head.

"What on earth were you thinking about? You looked like you were solving the world's problems."

I need a better poker face.

"Eric, champagne, please," Kel said, waving over one of our favorite bartenders. "Actually, make it two. And get Stephanie a glass as well." He laughed at his own joke, and I giggled.

"If you insist," I replied, pushing aside my coffee.

"Cheers!" he toasted. He barely let me swallow my first sip before he took aim. "Okay. So, what were you thinking about?"

"The Taj Mahal."

"Nope. Not buying it."

"I don't know," I insisted.

"Yes, you do."

He's not going to let me out of this conversation. No point in fighting it.

"I sat on the beach today and couldn't stop thinking about my life after we return. Don't get me wrong, I am loving every single minute of this trip and this experience has been all I ever could have imagined. The novelty has not worn off. Not an ounce of it."

"Nor should it. It is a once-in-a-lifetime trip for someone your age." His words perfectly mirrored how my heart had felt since I'd drawn that black line on the map back in Orlando.

"Life on board has become so familiar. It's become my home. Currently it is all I have, and I don't want to leave. I'd rather live my life here on this ship just like Dolly does," I said, trying to stop the burn in my nose.

"You would get so fat." We laughed.

Eric came over with a glass of Goldfish. "Pishy pishy?"

"Not tonight, Eric." He looked at me, shocked.

"Keep going, Stephanie," Kel nudged.

"I tried not to expect something big to come of this trip. I have learned and grown so much, and believe me, that is more than enough. But, I did expect the path forward to be illuminated with runway lights. So far, that hasn't happened, and I worry that it won't. Kel, every aspect of my life is up in the air, and every single decision I make when I walk off this ship will matter greatly," I said, choking down my fear.

"Yeah, it's hard to go with the flow when you have no solid ground under your feet, literally. Or a stool that you actually fit on." He chuckled, recalling our first meeting on the Lido Deck.

"Kel, I'm about to cut you off."

Ignoring my comment he got very serious and looked me dead in the eyes.

"Listen, the fact that you did what you did and came on this ship tells me you are different. From night one, when we met you, we knew you were special. You need to stay on course and keep going. Just keep going. No matter what happens. Try for big things. Huge things. No one does that anymore. It will seem like madness, but it will get you to a level where I know you're meant to be. It won't be easy, and you will probably be tested a time or two, but remember two things. Keep going, and don't be afraid to go broke."

I laughed. There was no way I was going to let that happen. The look on my face told him so.

"No, seriously," he said. "It happens to people who aim for greatness. And what you will gain from climbing back out will be life-changing. I am not saying you will. I just see it all the damn time—people holding back. The fear of going broke makes them play it safe. You can't play it safe and get where I believe you're meant to go. I can't say this enough to you. Go big...and if you fall down, get your ass up and keep moving forward. Cheers!" he said, clinking our glasses.

"I don't want my old life back," I said, "but I'm afraid I only know how to make decisions that will inevitably recreate it."

"You doubt yourself. Stop."

"I am just so happy you are here. You and Julie have been incredible to have around."

"We feel that way about you, too, my dear. Unfortunately, kiddo, we are getting off the boat in two days."

"Wait, what?"

"We were never supposed to be on this trip. We were on the previous cruise."

"I didn't know that."

"We planned on a month-long cruise and then decided to stay on a bit longer. Actually, we were going to stay the whole time, but we have some things to tend to back home," he said with a solemn look.

He gave me a long hug before signing his tab.

"Kel...you and Julie have to stay a part of my life," I insisted. "I mean it."

"Don't you worry. We will hound you until we see 'Stephanie in Lights,' so get off this ship in Fort Lauderdale and just do it. Whatever 'it' is, just go do it."

CHAPTER 19

DAY 72 & 73 - NEW DELHI, INDIA

The plane was covered in thick dirt from the previous night's sandstorm, and no one was doing anything about it. This couldn't be good.

News headlines popped into my mind's eye. *"Woman sells everything to go on trip around the world. Was dying to see the Taj Mahal so much that she actually died trying"...* *"Woman who travels world on ship, should have stayed on ship as plane she boarded crashes, leaving no survivors."*

I shook my head to dissolve the dramatic headlines. A panic attack was on the verge of erupting. *Stephanie, don't you dare make a scene. God, I would kill to have Pete, Ken, and Detta here with me.* Swallowing my fear I boarded the plane, where I found a familiar face in the seat next to mine: a woman I'd wanted to meet ever since night one, watching her limp across the Lido Deck in a sailor's costume. She introduced herself as Jeri. As we made small talk, I quietly left indentations in the armrests from clenching for dear life as both the plane and five tons of dirt became airborne.

We landed safely in the capital, New Delhi. Architecture was the focus of the day's tour, and our guide spewed off nonstop facts.

"On our left is the Gate of India where over 180,000 names of soldiers who died in the war are engraved, and just past that…"

I felt disengaged. *You came all the way here, pay attention.*

But every time I tried, I failed. Staring out the window, I watched the streets change from picturesque to slums, back to picturesque, with each turn we made. I couldn't focus. Something in the guide's voice had a weird sound to it.

"This estate up ahead is where the president resides. Behind the main mansion is a three-hundred-forty-acre garden. They have fifty employees whose sole job is to chase the birds from the gardens."

Maybe that could be my new career path. Bird chaser.

• •

The next morning I jumped out of bed, eager to make the trek to the city of Agra. I sang in the shower, danced around the room, giggling while running in place. I couldn't contain myself. After a fantastic breakfast of mysterious Indian food, I was so excited about seeing the Taj Mahal that when I bolted out of the hotel, the six-foot-seven guard standing outside the door was a blur. I stopped dead in my tracks, then turned around and looked at his stone-cold face, so official in his uniform. When I asked to take a picture with him, he moved his head slightly.

I'm not quite sure that was a yes.

"Smile," I said. Despite his unwavering expression, I think he liked me.

The minute I sat down in the van my uneasiness returned, but I stuffed it down, refusing to have it get in the way of my day. Jeri boarded with a foldable cane. I asked if she'd hurt herself, to which she responded, in a way that made it sound almost enchanting, that she had MS.

I felt unsure how to respond. "I'm so sorry. I love that it hasn't stopped you from traveling, though."

"It sure hasn't. It did cause me to retire early from teaching, but that's quite all right."

"Well, it seems like retirement is treating you nicely."

"My father taught me how to invest. I have been preparing for my retirement and my love of travel since my twenties."

"How fortunate," I replied.

She smiled at me warmly before turning the conversation back on me. "You are fortunate too, that your financial planning allowed you to take these kinds of trips so young."

Jeri's words reminded me that despite now knowing half the ship and feeling like I was one of them, I most certainly was not. Nothing will change the fact that I was an outlier flying by the seat of my pants. Nevertheless, I smiled, agreeing that I was indeed fortunate. Because I was. Just in a different way.

The van came to a screeching halt, jerking us forward.

I stood up but couldn't see any signs of an accident.

Police sirens filled the air. One of the men in our group asked our guide what the issue was. Just armed rebels blocking the highway, refusing to let any cars pass, we were told.

I started to pray that no one was going to get shot.

"Plane lands just fine, but world traveler dies in ambush on highway."

Our guide exited the vehicle, returning soon afterward. The driver put the van in gear and slowly we made our way through. *That's it? So anticlimactic.*

We pulled into a gas station for twenty minutes to take a bio break and grab a snack. I walked back outside with potato chips and a bottle of water and found a stray dog lying in the shadow of the van. *Poor thing. He needs a break from the sun. He's probably dying of thirst.*

I went back inside the store, got an empty coffee cup, and poured water in it. I approached the dog slowly, hoping it wouldn't bite me. It was golden, the size of a Labrador, but more of a mixed breed. I set the water down, and the dog stared at it before drinking the entire cup. I kept refilling it until the dog was satiated.

"You know, that was probably one of your deceased relatives. Good job," our guide said.

Huh?

Then I remembered the Hindu reincarnation beliefs I'd learned about in Bali.

"You're probably right." I smiled, going along with it. *Hey, you never know!*

"Who do you think it was?" he asked.

"Well, it's definitely not my Pop."

"What made you think it wasn't him?" he said, smiling at my answer.

"Because if it were him, I would have felt inclined to pour him a Heineken."

DAY 73 & 74 - AGRA, INDIA

Cows roamed, weaving in and out of the dirt-floor, open-air stores lining the streets of Agra. *People are buying fruit, completely ignoring a cow staring at them two feet away.*

"Cows are sacred. They are the highest form of incarnation possible and are more important than people," our guide shared after noticing our reactions.

We pulled up to a set of twin barnyard-like brown doors, which opened to reveal a high-end hotel, impossible to see from the street.

The hotel was quaint, but impeccably kept, and waiting for me in my room was a glass of white wine. I moved onto the balcony to take in the midday sun. *Ahh, this is perfect. I have a balcony and a view. Wait a second. Is that…?* It was. Off in the distance stood the Taj Mahal herself. *Wow, she is gorgeous, even from this far away.*

As the sun slowly set, we finally made our way to her. Despite the stark whiteness of this famous landmark, her color changed as the sun moved. On that night, she was a combination of tangerine and rose. As I walked toward Jeri, our guide approached us, flooding us with facts.

"The Taj Mahal is the first large mausoleum constructed for a woman, after the emperor, Shah Jahan, mourned the death of his wife. The entire place is perfectly symmetrical except for where he had his own casket placed, off-center and next to hers."

"So, he followed all the rules of symmetry down to every last detail and then broke them all when it came to his own tomb. I love this guy," I said as I excused myself to go walk inside.

Every glance revealed intricate, detailed perfection, from the white marble to the carved floral work engraved with gemstones. The grounds were crowded, but it didn't matter. No amount of people could take away from the brilliance of this landmark.

That evening I got to experience eating curry in India. My taste buds did backflips. I stuffed my face until I became a curry puff myself. Then I looked around the table, noticing the energy had fallen flat. I raised my glass for a toast.

"Being Italian, I must start by apologizing to my people, but curry in India is way better than pizza in Italy. Cheers!"

It was the perfect combination of cheesiness and fatigue, making everyone laugh. Except my guide, who blatantly stared at me from across the table. Chills ran down my spine, and I realized that he was the reason I had felt so uncomfortable these past two days.

At three thirty the next morning, I was out of bed and getting ready. I chose simple clothes: flip-flops, jeans, and a T-shirt. I had packed a necklace that my sister Amie had given me last Christmas. It was a chain with seven different key-shaped charms to choose from, each with a different word inscribed on the front. I looked at the seven keys: Peace, Happiness, Love, Hope, Faith, Trust, and Freedom. The right choice felt obvious. After my talk with Kel, I would bring Amie with me to the Taj, as I now call her, with the perfect key attached: Freedom.

The trip back to the Taj Mahal that morning was clouded in night's final moments. As we walked the pathway up to the mausoleum, the darkness broke, and the soft, dewy grass reflected the pale gray of the world onto the stark white front of the building. The closer we got, the more everything awoke. What started as pale grays slowly turned to soft shades of blue and purple. I stared at this work of art in the reflection pond, watching the colors dance as the water moved. *This is absolutely surreal.*

I walked to the side of the building, which was identical to the front. A man approached and asked if I wanted my picture taken. An idea came over me. I gave him the camera with instructions: "When I say go, just press and hold the button."

I climbed up on a small ledge and looked over to see no one else in sight. Just me and a building that represented love, self-expression, ego, beauty, and loss.

"One, two, three, press!" I shouted, jumping as high as I could. I felt the Freedom key hit my face and as I landed, hoped he'd pressed the button on time.

After we finished our tour, I climbed back into the van and sank into my seat, watching my dear Taj fade in the distance. I pulled out my camera and peered at the photo. *There's no way it actually came out this perfect.* Her white stone, appearing pink in front of a purple sky, was the ideal backdrop. The photo was backlit, making my silhouette a total shadow leaping across the Taj. I couldn't see my face, but I could feel the energy of strength, confidence, and joy radiating outward.

I put my camera away, smiling. This was me; this was who I felt lay buried underneath the shell I had created around myself.

This jump was a celebration of freedom.

DAY 74 - MUMBAI, INDIA

The Taj Mahal was an experience I would never forget, but the ship had become my home, and I was homesick. I missed my routine, the gym, the Lido Deck, and trivia. But most of all, I missed my table.

We arrived back at the airport in New Delhi. As I waited for my plane, I wandered into a sunglass shop. I was eyeing a particularly purple pair of Ralph Lauren shades when our guide approached me.

Wait, I thought he was back at the gate with the rest of the group.

"Having fun on the trip?" he asked.

"Yep. Thank you again for teaching us all that you did," I said, trying to keep the conversation businesslike.

"No problem. So, the ship leaves tomorrow?"

"Tomorrow night," I responded, starting to feel uneasy. Chills raced down my spine. The guide began to follow me as I walked around the shop, pretending to decide which sunglasses I wanted.

"I would like to show you Mumbai at night after the tour ends. We can get some drinks, and I will take you to some places you wouldn't normally see."

I looked at him, not knowing what to say. *Something's wrong. Don't create any resistance.*

"I will wait for you outside the port," he continued. "When you get out of the van, board the ship. Then come out twenty minutes later and walk outside the main gate. My friend and I will be waiting with a car."

Go along with it. Just agree and go back to the others at the gate.

"Sure! Sounds fun. I'll go change my clothes, and then come meet you."

He smiled and walked away. Before I could process his words, he turned back around. "Don't disappoint us. We are excited to show you the city."

"I won't," I assured him.

"Oh, and don't tell anyone." His tone made me want to vomit.

I purchased the purple sunglasses and put them on to hide the fear in my eyes.

I have met plenty of strangers in my life and had zero red flags about spending time with them. This time, I am in trouble. Tell someone. No, don't. He had mentioned this was his first tour and he isn't from here. Who knows who he is and what he is capable of. Breathe. Stay calm. The safest thing to do is to act like nothing is wrong and get your ass back to the ship.

Every step I made, his eyes were on me. He kept taking calls on his cell phone, something he hadn't done at all during our three days together. When we boarded the plane I switched my seat to sit next to Jeri.

"You okay?" she asked.

"Yeah, yeah. I'm just afraid to fly," I said. *This plane feels so safe compared to how scared I am.*

"I figured. I noticed you clenching the armrests on our way here." She rubbed my hand, and I desperately wanted to tell her how terrified I was. *I want to hold her hand so bad. I feel like a child right now who wants her mom.*

Our plane landed and we boarded a fifteen-passenger van to take us to the ship.

"Does anyone want a mini-tour as we head back?" our guide said. Everyone cheered while he stared at me.

Cheer, goddammit. I clapped along with Jeri, smiling widely. *He is staring at me. Seeing if I look suspicious. Now he is making a call. This extra tour isn't about us. I think he is buying time.*

The van pulled up to the port after what felt like a year-long tour around Mumbai. Before entering through the security gate, our van pulled off to the side and the guide exited, telling the driver he would be right back. I saw him run to a car, but I couldn't see anything else. As he returned, the van pulled into the port and I exhaled, knowing I was almost to the ship. *He isn't going to physically grab me, is he? Come on. Just keep looking happy.*

He stood at the door of the vehicle, collecting tips as people disembarked. When my turn came, I focused my attention away from him, helping Jeri out of the van. As I turned, he leaned in and whispered, "Stephanie, I have arranged a great night for you. I expect you out here in twenty minutes."

I dipped into an acting technique, channeling a genuine feeling of excitement to mask my fear. I smiled, nodded, then walked onto the gangway ramp and went straight to my room, where I sat, safe but stoned with shock. I tried hard not to blame myself, but it was impossible. *Maybe if I stood taller, looked meaner and smiled less, I wouldn't look like someone to prey upon.*

I shook off the thought, knowing deep down I'd done nothing wrong, and shifted my focus to what would be the best part of my day—dinner. My table had equally missed me and spent the entire meal asking about my adventures. I divulged it all except for one detail, which I decided to save for Pete up at The Crow's Nest later on.

"You played it smart. You did what you had to do to get out of there safely," he said, trying to hide his concern.

"I keep asking myself if I made it all up in my head."

"No, you did not. His behavior was alarming."

"Sometimes, I feel like I have a bullseye on my back."

"People who shine bright often do."

"And you know what the worst part of the whole day was?" I asked. "I passed Dolly in the hall before dinner, and she didn't even say hi, or thanks for all the notebooks and pencils I had delivered to her stateroom for the orphanage."

"Knock it off with the Dolly obsession. And don't change the subject on me," Pete said.

"I know. I do that when I'm complimented," I admitted.

"Well, knock that off too."

"I just keep replaying my actions and wonder if I should have done something differently."

"You handled it perfectly, Stephanie. Trust me, and trust yourself."

"I decided not to report it to the captain. I don't want to draw more attention to myself."

"If that's how you feel, then I respect that."

"And I only told you and not the entire table because I don't want them to worry. I just want to forget it and move on."

"There is only one way to forget a trafficking attempt," he said.

I looked at him, curious as to what he could possibly say.

He grabbed my hand, leading me to the wide open, empty dance floor. "We cha-cha. That's what we do."

CHAPTER 20

DAY 78 - DUBAI, UNITED ARAB EMIRATES

Dubai greeted me with a phone call from the head of hotel, Henk. "Miss Stephanie, good morning. Port officials have reviewed our manifest, and they would like to look in your cabin before you disembark."

Here we go again.

"May I ask why?"

"Here, they don't have to tell us why."

We both know damn well it's because I'm a younger woman traveling alone.

"No problem, Henk. What do you want me to do?"

"Just come to my office in an hour, and then we will let them enter your room, and you can wait here."

I hung up and sat on my bed, waiting to spiral like I had in Sydney, pushing the time, knowing I needed to prepare for my time off the ship.

But nothing came. No trigger. No flashbacks. Nothing. I got up to shower and dress, almost as if I were walking on eggshells, expecting my PTSD to rear its head at any moment. But it didn't.

"Stephanie. Thank you for your cooperation. I am so sorry about this," Henk said as I entered his office.

"They're just doing their job," I said, taking a seat.

He excused himself to join the officers.

• •

After I was cleared, I walked off the ship smiling wide, feeling different. Feeling good. The excursion I booked fit my mood perfectly. Some speed, thrills, and a small dose of danger were on the agenda.

As two other passengers and I were driven into the desert in an all-wheel drive SUV, our driver asked where we were from.

"California," the couple answered, assuming he knew the names of our states.

"I'm from Florida in the United States," I said. "Are you from here?"

"Yes, I am. I wanted so much to travel after my schooling, but I was set to marry. Now, my new responsibilities as a husband prevent that."

Having no idea how to respond, I smiled at him warmly, and through the rearview mirror, he smiled back. I stared out the window feeling immensely grateful for my own freedom.

Our silence was interrupted by a jerk as the driver turned off the road and down the steep desert dunes. How we didn't roll over is still beyond me. This was the exact dose of adventure I was looking for. But the joke was not lost on me: for a trip around the world on a ship, I'd had my fair share of crazy driving. My thoughts were drowned out by my screams as our driver slid us sideways down a forty-foot sand dune.

"How do you not flip the vehicle?" I shouted in between screams. "Very carefully," he said, which didn't help.

After a half hour of thrills, our vehicle came to a standstill atop a large dune, where we sat, taking in the vast desert.

"You have one hour before we head to a tent with camels, henna, food, and a swirling dervish just for you this evening," our driver announced.

I trekked to an adjacent dune to sit alone. I thought about the earlier events, then tried to scare myself by wondering what else I would be subjected to as we sailed through the Middle East. It didn't work. I didn't care. *Whatever happens, so be it.*

The peaceful feeling within my heart soothed me. I grabbed some sand in my hands. *It's so tan and soft but not powdery like the beach.* I lay back, letting it mold perfectly to my body. *I could lie on this forever.*

DAY 79 - DUBAI

The next morning, Ken, Detta, Pete, and I stood at the top of the world's tallest building, the Burj Khalifa. Below us was a city plopped in the middle of the desert, actively under construction in every direction. *From eighteen hundred feet up, it looks as if someone brought a Lego set to the beach and built Dubai on top of the sand.*

The goal of every building project in Dubai was to make it the largest, biggest, tallest, or the first. And then, to top it off, an entire housing development out in the ocean had been constructed in the shape of a palm tree. Because, why not.

"Do you really think people work or live this high up?" I asked Ken.

"No, almost a third of this building is vanity height. Uninhabitable." He had obviously done more research than I.

Vanity height. Just for looks. Interesting.

Dubai was undoubtedly "extra" in every way, but what I found most unique was the harmonious cohabitation of the traditional Emirates culture and those who came to visit from all over the world. It was suggested we cover our shoulders and knees without resorting to yoga pants or tight clothing. But even in full dress-code compliance, I still felt almost naked standing next to a native woman who had every ounce of her body covered except a thin slit for her eyes.

My first close encounter occurred in an elevator, on our way to the biggest mall with the biggest indoor ski slope in the world. I was minding my own business but still felt the woman's eyes on me. I wish I could have spoken to her because I couldn't tell if she was staring at me in disgust, envy, or curiosity. I kept my gaze toward the floor and couldn't help but notice her vibrant, expensive Valentino shoes and matching handbag. *If the only visible part of me were my shoes and handbag, I'd do the same thing.*

That evening, Kiki, Mark, and I went to a low-key dive bar with a live band.

"The vibe in Dubai is weird," I said, trying to make sense of how I felt.

"I get it," Mark said. "It's a bit overwhelming with all the world records. I mean, the largest indoor ski resort. It's a desert. Why do you need that?" The way he said it didn't sound like an insult.

"Forced greatness," I said. The words rolled off my tongue unexpectedly. I now understood why this city felt off to me.

"What do you mean, exactly?"

"Some things are great because they are what they are. This place is making itself great on purpose. Now that I think about it...sounds like how I used to live my life." I winked before grabbing us another round of beers.

DAY 81 - MUSCAT, OMAN

Muscat, Oman was very bright. When the sun hit the white buildings, it was blinding. Unlike in Dubai, tourism here appeared to be minimal.

Our guide approached the ten of us with his shoulders back, head high, and a strut, as if he were a prince about to greet the people of his kingdom. His regal behavior was clearly an act, because he could keep it up for only a few minutes before his quirkiness began showing through. He had to be in his midforties and was missing a few teeth, which really messed up his pronunciation of English words more than his foreign accent did. He smiled with his entire being. I genuinely wanted to know more about him.

To my satisfaction, he freely told us about his family: his mom, wife, and two kids. He was absolutely hilarious, not because he said anything funny, but because he owned who he was with zero apologies and a small dose of childlike excitement. I couldn't take my eyes off him—that is, until he announced that he was in the market for a nice second wife.

"Here in Oman, second wives have the same honor as the first. They are equal," he announced with pride.

Pete elbowed my ribs. I curbed the corners of my mouth to hide an inescapable need to laugh. *Dear God, he is looking right at me.*

"Stop, Pete!" I whispered out of the corner of my mouth. "You don't believe in marriage. Why are you trying to have me become someone's second wife?" Just then our van stopped in the middle of the road. Camels. They were everywhere, forcing us to inch our way through.

As we arrived at the main mosque of the city, I finished tucking my hair into my head scarf and left the van. When I stepped down in my black, long-sleeved, floor-length dress, our guide looked at my arm and noticed that my sleeve was an inch too short, revealing my wrist bone.

"You be careful as men will fall in love with you if they see you showing off such a beautiful wrist!" he said, causing a second elbow in the ribs from Pete.

Since no services were taking place, we were allowed to see where the men gathered to pray. The women had their own section, we learned, because otherwise the men would get distracted and not focus. The women's section was rather small and not as decorated. Odd, considering that with multiple wives, the women would technically need more space.

I walked through the area, taking in the garden that was sculpted to look like a two-foot-tall maze. The guide caught up to me and asked where I was from.

"Florida. The United States," I said.

"Do you like it there?"

"To be honest, I am not quite sure anymore," I replied, suddenly realizing what I had just said. Before I could do damage control, he ran with it.

"Would you ever want to live here?" he asked. *It's not the time to be polite, Stephanie…*"Probably not," I said as nicely as possible.

His face told me everything. *Holy shit, this guy isn't joking around.*

As we boarded our van, he stayed toward the front, talking to one of the guys in our group. We all settled in and silenced ourselves, just in time to overhear him telling the guy he wanted me to be his second wife.

The van erupted in laughter, making him realize he'd said it way too loudly. He then decided to compliment me in front of everyone.

"A woman like you is worth three racing camels," he declared.

The look on my face told him I had no idea what that meant. So, he did a little math on my behalf. "That would be about three hundred thousand U.S. dollars. Tell your father I will pay it."

I heard a few gasps. By this time Pete was hunched over, laughing. He looked up at me and said, "I don't think this is an act. I think this guy is serious. Tell him your age. That will end it."

"Pete! I mean it. Knock it off. I don't want the attention. It's making it worse!"

"He will think you are way past childbearing age, and his heart will break, but eventually he will find someone else."

"Pete, thank God you aren't related to me because you would totally have just sold me."

"I would have!" he said, catching his breath.

When it came time to bid farewell, I approached the guide.

"Thank you for everything. I hope you find a second wife worth *four* racing camels." I smiled and proceeded to walk away. He waved goodbye. I knew I didn't have to worry about a parting creepy handshake, hug, or hand on my back. He would never think of such behavior. I felt safe and appreciative of this culture's limitations in that respect.

Soon after, I dipped my toes into the Arabian sea, then returned to the ship. I messaged my mom about how a man in Oman offered her three racing camels to buy my hand as his second wife. Casually I mentioned how much they were worth before telling her I missed everyone and that I would see them soon.

A day later I received a one-sentence response: "Can he just send the cash instead? Love, Mom."

While her response was brief, the only thing her email lacked was the sound of her laughing at her own joke. A sound I dearly missed.

DAY 84 - THE RED SEA

After two days in Oman—one fighting off marriage proposals and the other studying frankincense—we were now sailing the Red Sea, heading toward the Suez Canal. The ship had planned an Arabian-themed sail-away party before dinner. Tents with pillows were set up with hookahs, specialty drinks, and crew walking around with hors d'oeuvre trays.

We were encouraged to dress in full Arabian-themed costume. I'd somehow missed that memo when packing, so I wore the same garb as in Oman. Then there was Pete, who came dressed in full costume, claiming he was our sultan.

I sat with my entire table in a decorative tent up on the Lido Deck, where bottles of wine flowed like water. The whole time was filled with, "I'm your sultan, bow to your sultan. I am royalty, do what I say." I was about to remind Pete that it wasn't Halloween, then I realized that for the first time on board, he was drunk.

Taking a break from the craziness, I looked out to sea, viewing the faint shoreline of Yemen. I could see tiny smoke billows rising from the ground. Passengers who were keeping track of international headlines told us how close we were to the turmoil of a civil war, both now and while on shore in Salalah the previous day.

"It breaks my heart to see Yemen up in smoke," I said.

"It's not safe for us right now," replied Sally.

"I'm not scared. I'm sad for the country," I clarified.

"Oh, no, you should be scared."

"We'll probably get a notice tonight in our cabins," Ken said, "but with four days at sea, we are at risk of pirates. So, tomorrow there will be pirate drills."

Pirate drills? Don't laugh. They all look so serious.

"We'll sit in the hallways outside of our cabins for the drill."

"Why there?"

"If pirates came after us," Detta explained, "the ship would need to make swift maneuvers to outrun them. It's the safest place for us to be."

"Wow. I did not know this." I took a sip of my wine in an attempt to hide my amusement.

"There is barbed wire wrapped around the Promenade Deck so pirates can't climb on," Sally added.

"Stop it!" I was struggling not to laugh.

"Go check for yourself," she said, as if I should have known this.

"Did you see the naval escort?" Ken asked.

"The what?"

"Yeah, the military is escorting us through the Red Sea until we go into the Suez Canal," Pete said. My mood shifted.

"Okay, now I get why maybe I should be concerned," I said softly.

Just then Hendrik walked up holding a sign that said, "3 Camels For Your Wife." *Ahh, he heard about what happened. He got the sign wrong, though. It should have said, "Be my 2nd wife for three racing camels," but I'll give credit for his effort.*

Pete insisted on taking a picture of Hendrik and me together, making me blush.

"Hendrik. Why don't you, Kiki, and Mark join us for our Suez Canal party in my suite. I upgraded to the luxury deck, so I'm allowed to invite you," he said proudly but with a bit of a slur.

"Thanks, Pete." Hendrik smiled before walking away.

"Time to eat!" Pete shouted. "Your Sultan is hungry."

CHAPTER 21

DAY 87 - THE RED SEA

'I've canceled the Suez Canal Party," Pete said as he answered his door.

"Then why did you ask me to come help you plan?" I said, annoyed.

"April Fools'!" he shouted.

It's April already? Damn it.

It was time to look at the calendar. To count the days I had left. In the faint distance, my return home started to appear on the horizon, whispering softly in my ear that soon, I would need to make some major decisions. Anxiety set in. *I'm not ready.*

I switched my focus back to the present and my utter excitement over our arrival into Egypt the next day. This ship could cross the equator ten times and make me kiss a million fish, but seeing the pyramids was *my* rite of passage, and I couldn't wait!

Pete's Suez Canal party was as important to him as the pyramids were to me. As I spent the afternoon in his cabin, helping order bottles of wine and plan the appetizer trays, a letter was slid under the door. I got through the first paragraph before stopping. *This can't be happening.*

"What does it say?" Pete asked.

"We aren't going to Egypt. Both stops have been canceled due to the threat of violence. How can we sail the world and not stop at the pyramids?" I looked at Pete. "Could this be an April Fools' joke?"

"No. Too many on board would have a heart attack, literally."

Without finishing the letter, I picked up Pete's phone.

"Shore Excursions, Mark speaking. How can I help you, Mr. Thompson?"

"Mark. It's Stephanie. I'm in Pete's cabin. What's going on? Why can't we stop in Egypt?"

"There have been some threats," he said.

"What kind of threats?" I asked.

"I can't say."

"Oh, come on. It's me," I pleaded.

"There were threats to bomb tourist buses," he whispered. "That's all I can say. I have to go. Please don't repeat that." He hung up.

Shrugging my shoulders, I told Pete the ship didn't want to put us in danger and that was that. He asked me to continue reading the letter, from which we learned we would now be stopping in Sicily, then Israel during Passover and Easter. I was stunned that we would have the option of booking a pilgrimage to go around and learn about Jesus—all during their holy days.

"I just want to go float in the Dead Sea," Pete said, sounding like a kid.

"Of course, you do, Pete." I shook my head. *I wonder if I will ever get to see the pyramids. But the universe has other plans for me, and I am just as ecstatic as I am sad.*

"Too bad it wasn't an April Fools' joke. That would have been hilarious." Pete laughed.

With his words, an insane idea came into mind. Something I couldn't believe I hadn't thought of sooner.

"Actually, I think I have the best idea for an April Fools' prank," I said.

"Just make sure I'm around to see it."

"Then just make sure you are at the happy hour spots before dinner."

• •

An hour later, after gaining Henk's permission and borrowing some supplies from Anne Marie, I stared in the mirror at my April Fools' masterpiece. My hair was slicked back in a bun. An orange top with a pearl sheen was paired with a long, shiny, maroon skirt. I found a photo of myself and put it in an official name tag holder with my new name: "Nada Crew." *Wow, I look exactly like them.* I entered the common areas dressed like a lounge server in full uniform with a serving tray in hand. People did a double take. First, they'd say, "Miss, may we ord..." Then they would realize it was me and start laughing.

Word spread fast, and people crowded the lounge to see the spectacle. Even the captain came to find me, impressed with my prank as I delivered Anne Marie's drink orders.

I'd taken a misunderstanding that made me feel vulnerable at the start of the trip and turned it into something to laugh about. From my vantage point, the sense of community between me, the crew, and the other passengers had grown even stronger.

• •

Later at dinner, I learned that the pranks did not end with my cocktail service shenanigans. I was the second to arrive at the table, finding Ken already seated with a glass of wine. I greeted him but focused more on the extra place setting. Unless I was left out, we were having an "unapproved" guest joining us, and the look on Ken's face told me he had everything to do with it.

The table settled into their seats as the extra place setting sat vacant. Of course, Pete had no will to wait, demanding to know who was arriving.

"Renee," Ken said simply.

"Who's Renee?" Detta asked.

"An officer who works in the clinic," Ken replied just as Nurse Ratched walked up to our table.

I tried to hide my shock but couldn't.

We all greeted her politely, except Pete who couldn't form a thought.

Pete's obsession with both Nurse Ratched and his desire to tell the story of our night in the clinic never wore off. Just like Eric's "Pishy pishy," shouting "Sit down!" had become Pete's new greeting anytime he'd see me around the ship. I could tell by looking around the table that everyone found this entire situation hilarious. Well, except for Pete.

I wasn't sure if she was going to acknowledge our encounter with her in the clinic. She didn't. Actually, by the level of comfort she displayed, I wasn't quite sure she even remembered.

Renee's proper etiquette charmed Sally out of the gate, while Don took to her brief, concise responses. Slowly, very slowly, the conversation took off, like a plane that had trouble getting into the air. There was no making her laugh, but as our hero of the night, Detta, got her to speak about her family and life back home, under her rigid essence a humanness shone through. I learned that her life had been a series of circumstances that left her in charge of taking care of things or leading the way, which explained her no-nonsense nature.

As much as Pete and I liked to joke, he impressed me greatly over dinner, listening intently and engaging in conversation. Being a man who lived to laugh and tell funny stories, he was also a gentleman, and that showed through.

Later, up in The Crow's Nest, a shocked Pete went on and on over that night's dinner.

"I am so mad," he declared. "Stephanie, I am mad that she is so nice. I can't call her Nurse Ratched anymore." He sounded like a disappointed child and I tried not to giggle.

"I agree. I think she is now officially Renee. But you can still yell at me to SIT DOWN!"

DAY 88 - PETRA, JORDAN

Centuries ago, a sandstone mountain stood, minding its own business, doing the only thing it knew how to do: be a mountain. Until the earth shook beneath it, that is. The stubborn strength of the hard sandstone was not nimble enough to move with the shaking, giving the mountain no choice but to split into two, leaving a mile-long narrow crevasse running through it.

After its split, water flooded through the crevasse and slowly smoothed out the rough edges of the gorge, creating a beautiful passageway connecting the East and West. With trade now possible, the mountain was further "broken" as Petra, one of the Seven Wonders of the modern world, was carved into its side.

Just outside the entrance, I stood sipping Jordanian coffee that was so thick, I almost needed to chew it. My heart raced. *This stuff makes espresso look like water.*

I stared up at the six-hundred-foot-tall sides, amazed at and overwhelmed by this magnificent natural passageway we were entering. Something felt eerie to me, like I had been here before. A hand rubbed my back before giving me two pats; Detta was letting me know it was time to begin.

The chatter between Pete, Ken, Don, and Detta echoed back and forth between the sides of the gorge we were walking through.

I stayed silent, unable to find either words, or the attention required for talking. *Did the mountain feel defeated when it was split into two? Or was it wise enough to know its destruction had a purpose?*

I let the group go ahead of me and placed my hand on the wall to feel the soft sandstone designs. Instead, I felt something in my body ignite like electricity and run up through my heart and down my arm. *Okay, maybe that coffee is a bit strong. Even still, something isn't normal with this place.*

Twenty minutes later, the crevasse became dark, backlit by the light of an open area ahead. The darkness became a picture frame, giving us a partial portrait of the ancient treasury building. I entered the open area to take in the entire carved building, which looked like someone had stamped it onto the red rock. I had to catch my breath.

A hand rubbed my back. *Oh, Detta found me.* I turned around to see my huge-haired Greek friend instead. "Kiki, you came!"

"Of course. I was just on a different bus. I can't miss Petra. I have seen it a few times, and it never gets boring."

"Honestly, I wasn't prepared for the intensity. Do you know what I mean? Don't you feel it?"

"Feel what? Here, take a picture of me doing a handstand with the treasury in the background." A minute later, she walked off with her group.

Is it me? Am I going crazy? It's just a split mountain. I get it. It's cool. But why do I feel so drawn to it? I don't want to leave, but the supernatural feeling in my body is freaking me out a little.

A hand touched my back again. This time I knew for certain it was Detta.

"Does this place feel odd to you?" I asked.

"Yes, it feels a bit claustrophobic. Here, have some water." She handed me a bottle from her purse. "You know, that coffee was very strong."

I drank it down in three long gulps as we headed back out and to a restaurant just next to the park. No sooner did we exit the gorge than the feeling subsided, leaving me convinced it wasn't in my head.

It was real. Inexplicable, but real.

DAY 90 - THE SUEZ CANAL

And just like that, we were already at the Suez Canal. Our Panama Canal crossing on day seven had felt like a gateway into this trip. Now, with just under a month remaining, this canal felt like the gateway to home.

We were anchored in the Red Sea among various types of ships waiting to be called to enter the canal. Ken, Detta, and Sally had just sat down, while Pete, who was convinced we didn't have enough wine and appetizers, was on the phone with his deck's concierge ordering even more.

Someone knocked on the door, and I opened it to find that Pete had invited this week's onboard celebrity chef, James, and his partner, Billy. Hendrik, Kiki, and Mark were the last to arrive, completing our afternoon party. Seeing Pete's exhaustion, I launched into full server mode and took everyone's drink orders.

As the party got underway, the captain's voice came over the intercom. "Ladies and gentlemen, there is quite a long line, and I just got word that we will not be called to enter the Canal until after dusk. Unfortunately, the Canal isn't well lit, making viewing quite difficult in the dark. I apologize as I know we all looked forward to the event."

The cabin fell quiet with disappointment.

"Why isn't it well lit?" I asked.

"Because it isn't a lock system like the Panama Canal. It's a narrow river we coast through," Mark said.

Attempting to lighten the mood, I grabbed my wine glass. "I would like to make a toast. To hopes of cutting in line! Cheers!" The room erupted in laughter.

"I would like to add to that," Pete said as he raised his glass again. "I've been talking about the Suez Canal since we were at the Panama Canal, and I am happy you all are here. James and Billy, thank you for coming. Kiki, Hendrik, and Mark, thank you for making our trip so fun and for befriending us all. You are welcome here any time. And Stephanie, thank you for helping me today as this old man is tired. You are a dear friend. Cheers!"

James, the celebrity chef, lowered his head into his hand. "I am so sorry, Stephanie. This whole time, I thought you were Pete's kept woman."

Everyone paused.

"It's just because of the way you were serving us," he added.

"No, not here, but she almost was in Oman," Pete joked, making light of the embarrassment that crossed every face in the room.

"What is a kept woman?" I asked James.

He started to fumble his words. "It's just that I have watched you serving us all day, and worrying about our drinks being refilled, and taking care of Pete, that I thought you were with him, and he paid for you to come."

"I'm not." I paused, needing to gather my thoughts.

"I am so sorry. I didn't mean to offend you. You just look so young."

"Boy, did you dig your grave, sir," Pete said, laughing. "But telling her how young she looks should help matters."

His partner, who was sitting next to James, looked at me with eyes begging me to help diffuse the moment.

"James, to be honest I would have thought the same. I am so grateful that Pete invited my friends and treated us all to this amazing day. I wanted to thank him by making sure every guest was taken care of so he could relax. But I paid my own way on this cruise."

"I am most impressed by that," he said. "Go, you."

We both smiled as the captain's voice interrupted.

"Ladies and gentlemen, this is Captain Mercer. I am happy to inform you we will be going through the Canal in roughly thirty minutes. They decided to put our ship in front of the line for safety reasons."

The cabin erupted in cheers.

"To cutting the line," I shouted as loudly as I could off the balcony before turning to James. "Sir, may I get you another glass of wine?" I said flirtatiously.

He hugged me tightly. "Actually, I will take over now and act like a kept man."

The incident didn't offend me, but rather brought me back to my lunch with Detta in Australia. I could hear her words:

It's such a different time now, and witnessing a woman your age live life on her terms, by herself, breaking all the old-fashioned rules that we grew up adhering to. It's beautiful to watch.

That day helped me fully understand the power of my presence on board.

DAY 91 & 92 - ISRAEL

"Happy Easter!" Jeri said as she appeared beside me, pulling me out of a trance. I kept my eyes locked on the large square tomb that was built to resemble a castle.

"I thought Jesus's tomb was a cave with a round rock in front of it," I said, disappointed.

"That's how it was in my schoolbooks growing up," she replied as she tugged my arm, signaling it was time to head to our next location, the Sermon on the Mount.

Our? small group eagerly entered the tiny church to touch the oval-shaped rock where Jesus had stood while giving his famous sermon. I sat on a similar oval rock fifty feet away that overlooked the tan-colored town of Old Jerusalem.

"Are you not wanting to take a picture of the rock, Stephanie?" our guide, Sarah, asked as she sat down on an adjacent rock.

"It's just that you use the words 'as tradition states' when you explain things. So, are you saying that the rock inside that church isn't the one Jesus actually preached from?"

"It represents it. It's symbolic," she replied.

"Then why take a picture of it?"

"I understand how you feel. But the Sermon was here in this location, if that helps," she said with a smile.

"It does, actually, because that is truthful."

"Having something be symbolic isn't lying, necessarily. It's choosing to have something represent something bigger."

I felt lost. *What does she mean? She has a PhD in this stuff. I do not.*

A while later, I sat in our van, staring at the armed officers in front of a gate to Palestine. We had special permission to enter and see the location of Jesus's birth in the town of Bethlehem.

"This is The Church of the Nativity. Tradition states that Jesus was born below the church, which was ground-level during his time. How wonderful you get to see it on Easter. Please stay in the background and be quiet and respectful of the church service taking place," Sarah said as we were ushered inside.

• •

A bit later, Sarah found me sitting in the church courtyard. "Done already?" she asked.

"Yes. It was a bit crowded, but I did go down below and touch the spot of Jesus's birth—even if it wasn't the exact spot."

"Good for you. But you know what the best part is about this church?"

"What's that?"

"We just witnessed some of the Roman Catholic service. Those people over there I saw you watching? They are with the Armenian Apostolic Church. Next week, the Greek Orthodox will come and celebrate their Easter as they are a week behind the others."

"I've never heard of the Armenian Apostolic Church before."

"What I want to point out to you is that they are all different religions that don't always agree with each other. And yet they gracefully share this church together. That's the power Christ has here in this location, whether he was born in that exact spot or not," she said. "It is also Passover. You have come at such a great time to witness so much ceremony. We will now head to the Wailing Wall, which is the actual remains of the old temple of Jerusalem."

"Not as tradition states?"

Sarah laughed. "Correct. We will get there at dark, and you will see the crowds of people offering up their requests to God."

• •

"Wow, they really are wailing," I whispered to Jeri as I stood behind a massive crowd of people pushing toward the wall of the old temple of Jerusalem. They had come with written prayer requests to stuff into the cracks between the stones in the wall.

There is so much pain here. So much need. I can't just stand still.

I took a piece of paper out of my purse and thought of the people in my life who outwardly longed for things like partners, children, or health, then wrote their wishes down and made my way into the sea of crying people.

An hour later, I reached the wall and softly put my hand on it as I'd seen others do. I bowed my head and began to pray. "God, I can't ask anything more of you after all that you did to help me take this trip. But I come with prayers for people who aren't here. Please accept them. Amen." I placed the folded paper into a crack and headed back.

I never told anyone I'd prayed for them. Within a year, every single request I had left in the wall came true.

• •

The next day, I sat with my feet dangling in the Jordan River.

"Your feet are quite baptized by now," Sarah said as she sat down next to me. "Did you enjoy the day today?"

"I did! Seeing Mary's home in Nazareth was cool, even if it may not be real. I might have been a bit hard on Israel and 'tradition,' " I said, making air quotes with my fingers.

"What made you realize that?"

"The Sea of Galilee put some things into perspective. I must have seen at least five hundred tents camped around the lake—the same lake where Jesus walked on the water centuries ago. People were hanging out, relaxing and barbecuing, as if it were no big deal. Made me relax a bit about it all."

"Well, I suspect many of the campers are Jewish, but that isn't the point. What we do know is that the people from ancient years undoubtedly shaped the life we live now. And we all connect to that in a different way."

"What do you mean?"

"What I noticed is that you are moved by people. I saw you write wishes at the wall. Were they your wishes?"

"No, they were for other people."

"I suspected as much. Then, I noticed you were moved when I told you about the three religions sharing a church." She joined me by putting her feet in the river. "But my point is, Stephanie, you found the connection for yourself. That is what it is about. For some, it is kissing a rock that may or may not be the exact rock. They need the visual. You needed to see the pain of those crying, the unity of those sharing a church, and the joy of those celebrating a holiday together on a lakeside. Does that make sense?"

"Kind of. Thank you."

I paused for a second, wondering if I should elaborate.

"It's just, I've been questioning truth, my truth, a lot on this trip. What to think, what to believe, and how to live my life more authentically. I'm sorry if I was cynical. I feel like I was a bad student these past few days."

"Nonsense. Students who question things and seek their own truth are my favorite kind." Sarah gathered her shoes and mentioned it was time to head to the van.

I wanted more of a response from her. More answers. More information. I lifted my baptized feet out of the Jordan River and dried them with my sock.

DAY 94 - EPHESUS, TURKEY

Men in tuxedos carried beverages or hors d'oeuvres. Tables lined the ancient streets with soft blue tablecloths. The ship had spared no expense for our evening under the stars in Ephesus, their way of saying thank you to us passengers for coming on the trip. Even the CEO of Holland America flew in for the event.

I selected some food from the buffet and wandered around, staring at the intact front façade of the ancient Ephesians' two-story library. I continued my walk up the aged streets, admiring the rocks that glimmered with sparkles, shiny bits I could easily see now but could not detect earlier in the day.

Soon after dinner, we were called over to the amphitheater, a part of Ephesus I hadn't seen before. After panning the crowd for Pete, Detta, Ken, Don, and Sally, I carefully climbed the amphitheater steps and sat down on a portion of its remains next to a couple I hadn't previously met.

"Ah, it's the girl who likes to cha-cha," the man said in an off-putting tone.

"I can never say no to a dance invitation," I said, trying to suppress my annoyance.

"I'm Kate. That's Doug. You came alone, right?" his wife said.

"Yep"

"Oh, we noticed," Doug said as Kate tapped his arm and gave him a look.

I was well aware that not everyone on the ship welcomed my presence, but this was the first time someone like that actually struck up a conversation with me.

"Did you visit here during the day or stay in Kusadasi?" Kate asked.

"I did both. First, I went to the bazaars in Kusadasi. Bought friends some of the Turkish candle holders. Then I came here."

"Isn't the library fantastic?" Kate gushed.

"It is. I just didn't know they had so many books that they needed a two-story library back then."

"Well, they didn't have books in tenth century BC. They had scrolls," Doug explained like a condescending teacher. "And the library housed over twelve thousand of them, with the bottom floor as a place to gather, read, and have official meetings."

Books. Of course they didn't have books. There is nothing I can say to recover. I stayed silent while mentally building a brick wall of protection between us.

"Cleopatra and Marc Anthony roamed these streets if that interests you," Doug said.

"That I do know. I love the notion that I've walked down the same street as they did."

"Many historically important people did. This was The Big Apple of ancient times. Ya know, New York City?" he asked.

"Yeah, I know."

"Where are you from?"

"Florida." I wanted the conversation to end.

"You should move to New York City. You would fit in," he suggested.

He must be referring to my leather jacket.

"Nah, it's too angry and fast. Not to mention dirty."

"So, did your dad buy you your ticket?"

"Doug!" Kate said.

Before I could say anything that could get me in trouble, I was saved by the most beautiful sound coming from the Aegean orchestra on stage. The music echoed off the ruins, making it feel like I was in a surround sound theater. My body relaxed and the brick wall I put up between me and Doug began to fall. Mixed with the cold breeze, both the music and his words flew right into me and out the other side, leaving me completely and utterly at peace.

CHAPTER 22

DAY 98 - INLAND, GREECE

Greece is perfection. The stillness I felt up in Meteora, visiting monasteries set atop of one-thousand-foot-tall rocks, was surreal. It was so quiet; everything below was so small. It felt like a more spiritual, calmer, and much safer version of parasailing in New Zealand.

I celebrated Good Friday for a second time, walking through a small village behind an entire church congregation for the Orthodox Good Friday. Mark, who came along to monitor the overnight tour, joined me. We walked slowly holding lit candles. Villagers who didn't attend leaned out their windows with candles to join in the silent celebration.

The entire experience was beautiful, but nothing compared to my first Greek Orthodox Easter Sunday. And, I mean NOTHING. Yes, the roasted lamb was the best I ever tasted, and the yellow potatoes—well, I couldn't stop eating them. Of course, I had to join in on the ouzo shots with complete strangers in the courtyard who shouted toasts in Greek as we laughed and hugged. That's when I turned and realized Ken was there, too.

Our exchange was warm but brief, then he returned to the friends he was dining with. As the party began and the entire restaurant circled up, I didn't think much more of it. Music blared and people danced with their hands on each other's shoulders, kicking their legs out before switching directions. Ouzo shots were being slammed everywhere I looked. Real plates smashed against the wall and on the ground.

I thought I would be the highlight of the party when the server pulled me up on top of a table to dance with him, but I wasn't. Well, not in my eyes, at least. It was Ken, the covert partier. Out of nowhere, and to my utter shock, he walked into the center of the circle and began to dance his very own solo interpretation of the traditional Greek dance—the sirtaki.

I loved this side of Ken. *Where the hell is this version of him on the ship?* I wanted to slap him for every time he held back over the three months we'd been together.

Dessert soon hit the tables and the festivities died down temporarily. I made sure I crossed paths with him as he walked to his seat.

"You know I'm going to make you do that on board, right?"

"Not a chance," he said without stopping.

I stood there, watching him walk away, unsatisfied with his answer. He must have felt my eyes on him.

Ken turned around, looked me straight in the eye, put his left hand on his hip, his right hand in the air, and shouted, "Opa!"

DAY 99 - CATANIA, SICILY

With Sally staying on board, the rest of the table ventured off the main square in Catania onto a side street too narrow for a car. It curved toward the left, leading to a set of stairs. We made our way up the coffee-colored stone steps to find a row of restaurants. After Pete randomly chose one, we were led to a courtyard with one large table dressed in a white cloth with fresh purple flowers. The floor was covered with the same terra-cotta tiles that my Grandma and Pop had had in their home. Plants and flowers growing up the sides like vines surrounded the square dining space and mysteriously smelled just like their backyard.

"Do you have a local menu?" Ken asked "We will eat anything you make. We want authentic."

The manager's face lit up. "Absolutely! I maka-you something special." He scurried off.

"So much for a light snack before dinner," Don whispered into my ear. He'd never think of making a comment like that aloud for fear of offending someone.

"That's the sauciest thing I've ever heard you say, Don," I whispered back, making him blush. Hoping enough time had passed on our trip and he'd be comfortable enough opening up, I said to him softly, "Don. I feel like I know nothing about you still."

"There's nothing to know," he said. "I've just enjoyed getting to know you. You're the interesting one." He smiled warmly and I patted his shoulder.

"Stephanie, what are your plans in Italy?" Detta asked. "You are welcome to join us."

"Thank you, but I have family to visit in both Naples and Rome."

"I didn't know you had family in Italy," Pete said.

"Yeah. My grandmother immigrated to the U.S. during World War II and left behind her parents and nine brothers and sisters. I have a ton of extended family here."

"Have you been to see them?" Ken asked.

"Yes," I said, "after trying to study abroad in France my last semester of college. When I got there, it turned out the program didn't even exist. Huge disaster. They let me stay in the dorms, but I felt a bit of culture shock. So, my grandmother flew me to Italy for three weeks to stay with her brother, Zio Ernesto and his wife, Zia Maria Luigia, before I returned to France."

"That was nice of her," Detta replied.

"Oh, yeah. She was so mad I wanted to learn French and not Italian. I can still hear her yelling into the phone, 'They you-a family. You-a heritage. No-a France.' My only protest was I had no way of communicating with my relatives. They didn't speak English."

"What did grandma have to say about that?" Ken asked.

"She shouted, 'Use-a your hands.' " Everyone laughed, which sparked anecdote after anecdote across the table about how each of us had spent time in Italy...until the swinging doors abruptly opened.

Both the manager and a server barreled onto the terrace, holding large oblong dishes in each hand. They set them down in the center of the table with serving spoons so we could help ourselves. As the manager left, he flipped a switch and the large bulbs that hung in the shape of an X above our heads lit up. It wasn't dark, but the shady courtyard was now suffused with a soft glow, making the glasses and plates glisten.

Don passed a dish to Pete, and Detta served some of the pasta onto Ken's dish before telling Pete what she thought it was. Pete passed out rolls without anyone asking. It was the most beautiful three-ring circus.

I couldn't help but drift back to when I first arrived on my Zio and Zia's front steps. How they greeted me with open arms. How cold their marble floors were on my bare feet. How every morning, Zia made me warm milk with a breakfast pastry as if I were her young child.

The whole time I had been there, we couldn't converse. I could only watch Zio's and Zia's routine—a dance they had perfected over many decades. Moving around the kitchen, interacting, and never getting in each other's way, but each needing the other. Then, every night, we sat together on their couch in the den and watched TV with a small space heater in front of us. I had no idea what was happening on the shows but would laugh when they did and gasp when they did. I wanted them to feel as though I was comfortable in their home. Happy. Because I was. Their simplistic way of existing grounded me in a way I couldn't describe.

The table came to a halt the minute they noticed I hadn't moved.

"You okay?" Detta asked.

"Yeah. I just was having a moment."

"Nervous about seeing your family?" Don asked.

"Yeah, kind of."

"Out with it," Pete said with one of his downward stares.

I took a deep breath. "My Zio has advanced dementia, and I don't think he is going to recognize me." Something in my chest tightened. I grabbed the dish of carpaccio and offered some to Don.

DAY 100 - NAPLES, ITALY

I sat in my cabin, drenched in regret, wishing I had better kept in touch. To have learned Italian so I could have called them. To have taken vacations to Italy instead of traveling with friends. To see Zia Maria Luigia again before she passed away. I couldn't undo it. Even if I could go back in time, I wouldn't have had the maturity then to know what mattered most. Instead, I now had to walk off the ship and head back to the three-story villa in Caserta once more, praying that my Zio would recognize me so that I can tell him "thank you."

• •

"Wow, you look like you belong here in Italy," the security officer said as I walked off the ship in jeans, a white T-shirt, black leather jacket, and a bottle of red wine swinging in my right hand. *Yeah, I know, pal.*

My heart was racing. Elvira, the granddaughter of my Zio Ernesto, was coming to get me. She couldn't have been ten years old the last time I saw her. Now she was driving me to see him.

We arrived at the villa, and it felt as if I had gone back in time. Every aspect of it looked exactly the same, even inside. Zio Ernesto, now in his late eighties, sat in the kitchen. I entered the room— and the look of confusion on his face confirmed my worst fear. He mumbled as he slowly shuffled up to me. Elvira shouted, "Estephanie. Estephanie," explaining who I was.

It didn't help. He didn't recognize me. My heart sank.

We all sat at the kitchen table while Ernesto, Zio's namesake grandchild opened a bottle of Prosecco to toast the reunion. Zio Ernesto's grandchildren hovered around me, hugging me, holding my arm or my hand, or playing with my hair.

Zio Ernesto sat quietly with his head lightly shaking back and forth, almost like someone with Parkinson's. I listened to everyone chatting and took all the photos they wanted. But as I did so, a vision of Zio and Zia engaged in the dance of their old kitchen routine shimmered before my eyes.

Needing a moment alone, I excused myself to go to the bathroom but went and peeked into the room I'd once stayed in. All was exactly as I had left it. I walked into the den to see the same small couch where the three of us sat to watch TV. Now, Zio Ernesto sat there alone.

The villa smelled exactly the same, making me want to breathe it in. All these years later, my appreciation—not only for their way of life, but also the way they took me in—now had a deeper meaning than it did when I was a wide-eyed twenty-one-year-old with zero appreciation for my heritage. Now, I could feel the thread tying me to this culture, reminding me that part of my path forward included tying myself back to my roots.

Elvira found me, telling me that Zio Ernesto had had enough. "Stanco, stanco," she repeated, which I knew meant "tired."

"You, us cousins, go restaurant. Dinner," she said.

"Va bene," I agreed, using some of the few words I knew in Italian to show respect for her attempt to speak English.

I walked back into the kitchen, not ready to say goodbye. Little Ernesto was showing my uncle a photo of me, Zio, and Zia, taken thirteen years ago. Zio Ernesto looked up from the photo as little Ernesto pointed at me.

"Estephanina!" Zio cried as he tried to stand. I went to him and hugged him for what felt like an eternity, and yet was nowhere near long enough. *Thank you, God. Thank you so much.* I ached to tell him how much he meant to me, how grateful I was for both him and Zia, and how sorry I was. All I knew how to say to him in Italian was, "Ti amo tanto. Grazie, Zio, Grazie."

CHAPTER 23

DAY 102 - AT SEA, APPROACHING SPAIN

We had one day of rest before arriving in Cartagena, Spain. I craved this sea day, especially after six straight days of back-to-back ports. Like riding a bike, my normal routine returned without thought.

Except, unlike on any other sea day, every familiar face I met on the ship mentioned "the jive."

"Good luck dancing today, Stephanie!"

"Have fun with the jive later!"

"Go get 'em! We can't wait to see you dance!"

This happened everywhere I went: the stairs, the gym, the sauna; even at the breakfast buffet as I attempted to have my first cup of coffee, Bill and Larry approached me with the same question.

"Ya know, you are the sixth person to mention it. But no, I'm not," I said.

"We figured since you missed the waltz and cha-cha while you were off the ship in Greece that you would definitely dance the jive," Larry replied.

"I honestly have no idea what you all are talking about. Other than trivia, I don't pay attention to the activity schedule."

"Oh. It's a dance competition today at three p.m. They teach you the steps of the jive and then you get to do it with one of the professional dancers," Bill explained.

"I don't want to upset anyone by having an age advantage."

"Believe me, the people competing can dance," Bill said.

"Live a little, Stephanie," Larry poked.

"What do you mean, 'live a little'! I'm doing this trip, for crying out loud!" I winked at them and walked away with my coffee and a bowl of oatmeal.

I wandered across the Lido Deck, waving hi to everyone but staying far enough away to ward off any additional comments about the jive. I basked in the warm breeze while eating—a feeling I had dearly missed as we'd traveled through colder climates.

Too full to finish, I pushed aside my oatmeal and kicked up my feet. Anne Marie came over and took my plate.

"Anne Marie, you don't have to do that. I can take them."

"You are funny, Ma'am Step-anie," she said with a soft smile before ignoring my suggestion.

Closing my eyes I thought of all the moments from the past week which I had yet to absorb, quizzing my memory to make sure it was all captured. Before I could finish mentally replaying the dinner in Sicily, I was sound asleep.

I woke to a poke in my arm that felt all too familiar. "Pete," I said with my eyes still closed, "can't you see I'm trying to sleep?"

"Wake up. It's almost three. You've been sleeping all afternoon! You are starting to act like the old people on the ship," he said as if he were excluded from that group. I smiled, remembering my first night on board and seeing people asleep during the 10:00 p.m. show. *I have become one of them.*

"Let me grab a water, and we can walk down to trivia," I said.

"No, ma'am," he said with his typical stare. "You are dancing the jive."

"Oh, come on, you too?"

"I'm serious. It's only one hour, but it starts at three, so you have to go now."

"What about trivia?"

"We'll live without you. Besides, you never have any answers," he added as he walked away.

Minutes later, I stood in a group of about forty people watching professional dancers teach us the steps to "Shake Your Tailfeather." *This is harder than I thought.* I lost focus when a familiar silhouette caught my eye from a distance. Pete was lurking by the back door, watching. I shooed him away as he gave me a huge grin and two thumbs-up, and then pointed at the teacher as if scolding me from afar for not paying attention. I tried to scold him back, mouthing for him to go to trivia.

After a handful of run-throughs, one of the dance pros pulled me onstage for my turn to dance the jive. As much as I didn't want to do it, and without fully understanding the steps, my inner performer couldn't resist and I put on one hell of a show. My body might have failed, but my face looked like that of a Rockette at Radio City. I couldn't tell if Pete was still watching, but it was all for him.

• •

Later at dinner, I walked up to my table and sat down nonchalantly. Pete was the last to arrive with a huge smile and a newly poured Bloody Mary.

"Having two this evening, Pete?"

"I have reason to celebrate," he said.

"Celebrate what?" Detta asked.

"She won the jive!" he shouted.

"I thought it was just an isolated event. Nobody told me that I would have to dance again in the finals."

"It's the Dancing with the Stars at Sea show, and it's a big deal," Sally said.

"That's fantastic!" Detta said. Ken motioned for our server to order a bottle of wine to celebrate.

"Actually, I think I will let the runner-up compete with the other finalists. I don't think I have the guts to get onstage in that big-ass theater and dance the jive in front of the entire ship," I said.

"Absolutely not. Don't you dare let us down," Pete said. "Otherwise, you will be voted out of the table, and you can go eat at the buffet alone."

DAY 103 - CARTAGENA, SPAIN

I had originally booked a tour of the city, but decided to cancel it and invite Kiki and Mark to play hooky instead.

"We can have a big picnic in the town square," I told them. "What do you say? We'll get some sandwiches and wine, and chill out?" Kiki loved the idea, insisting she was rubbing off on me, which was true.

We spent the entire day sitting on a blanket in a small grassy area in the center of town, watching locals walk by and kids laughing and playing after school with their soccer ball. We laughed like old friends who had known each other much longer than the four months we had sporadically spent together.

I disengaged from the conversation and observed the scene, enveloped by sadness. I knew this was the last time we could all gather together in port for one of our adventures. To me, it was my first goodbye in a way. I needed to do something to add to this memory, to make the day about more than just "the last time we…" Planning the picnic wasn't enough. I needed to bat away the sadness by creating a memory we would laugh about for years to come.

"We need a video," I said, grabbing my camera.

We all bopped our heads to the music playing and waved. I stopped recording.

"Not good enough, guys." My mind raced, frustrated at my lack of creativity while grasping at straws for something to savor. Then it hit me.

"Let's do that Kecak, ya know, from Bali!"

It took zero effort to convince them. Kiki and I began to do the chant and move our arms.

"Keh-jeh, Keh-jeh, Keh-jeh…"

Mark became the token bass, shouting, "Bahm, bahm, bahm," just as we'd seen in Bali. As much as we tried to do it correctly, our laughter got in the way. A gorgeous, cultural chant done for centuries was being absolutely murdered by a handful of idiots in Cartagena. It was exactly what I needed to begin my goodbyes.

DAY 105 - CÁDIZ, SPAIN

After my picnic in Cartagena's town square, I spent the next day in Málaga with my table touring historical sites and learning about Alhambra tiles. On our third and final stop, I needed to round off my perfect trifecta in Spain with alone time.

With aggressive waves and white caps as a backdrop, I wandered the winding, brown, rectangular-stoned streets, weaving in and out of shops. I sat down at a local café and ordered empanadas. I couldn't have said what was inside of them if my life had depended on it, but each one I tried was to die for. As I finished, I sipped an espresso, watching the day turning into late afternoon. This was our last day on the mainland in Europe before we headed to the Azores and then back to Fort Lauderdale.

Kiki suddenly appeared. "Lost in thought again?"

"You always catch me when I'm thinking." I smiled.

Instead of having her sit and join me, I solicited her help to find something special for Pete's celebration that coming Saturday. His birthday had been a few days prior while we were in port, but he wanted to celebrate while we were at sea during the weekend. It was important to me to find something to make the experience memorable.

We scoured the small shops, finding a wall of funny sunglasses: flamingos, beer mugs, even ones with Elvis's sideburns. No outrageous theme was left out. We decided to buy a bunch for a night of fun with crazy shades.

After we paid for our purchases, I told Kiki I was going to take one last walk before heading back to the ship. My tone clearly communicated that I wanted to go alone.

"Of course. But all aboard is at five. That's only ninety minutes away. Set an alarm on your phone."

"Yes, mom," I said obediently.

I walked around for a while before finding the right park bench where I could take in the scenery. An hour later, when my alarm sounded, I stood up and walked back into the center of town—or so I thought. *Wait, where am I?*

Turning around I saw water, which made me scurry back toward the shore to see which way the ship was docked. *No ship in sight. Where's the port?*

I started walking back into the narrow streets of the town. Worry set in. I arrived at the center, which had tall buildings and narrow streets, offering five different directions to choose from. *I'm lost. I don't have time to be wrong. I don't have my passport on me to fly to the Azores. I'll have to fly home and miss the rest of the trip. Shit!*

I jogged until I found a restaurant where a younger guy was standing out front.

"Do you speak English?" I said.

"No speak English."

What is the word for ship in Spanish? I have no idea. How do you even mime it? This is bad.

I ran full speed through the streets. I reached another shoreline. No ship.

I am in trouble.

"English? English? English?" I called out desperately to everyone I passed. No one responded.

I couldn't believe this was happening. My mind went straight back to wanting so badly to take this trip, to believing so hard it would work out—and it had! Now, I was about to miss the ship again, but this time, it was all my fault. And I couldn't fix it because I couldn't find the ship. No last-minute miracle could help me now. *I will never forgive myself for this.*

Come on. Get smart, Stephanie. The ship leaves in TWELVE minutes.

The craziest thought came to mind. *I know the French word for boat. Maybe someone here speaks French!*

"English? French? English? French?" I shouted over and over to anyone who could hear me as I ran. Some kids who were gathered at a park bench heard me and pointed to their left. A French patisserie. I ran inside.

"Parlez-vous français?" I shouted as a guy came out from behind the swinging door.

"Oui, oui, qu'est-ce qui se passe?" he said. *Yes, yes, what's going on?*

"Grand bateau. Grand bateau. Je cherche le grand bateau." *Large Boat. Large boat. I'm looking for the large boat!*

"Là bas, là bas. Tout droit, puis le troisième à droite" *That way, go straight, and make the third right.*

"Merci!" I shouted as I sprinted out the door and down the street.

I ran so fast my legs no longer felt attached to my body. The port slowly came into view. I tried to run faster, but it wasn't possible. The ship was still there; however, if the gangway had already closed, it would be too late.

"Miss Wilson, walk, it's okay. You have one minute," an officer shouted.

My body wasn't going to stop running until it was on board.

"You almost didn't make it," he said, scanning my badge.

Upon hearing his words, I began to bawl my eyes out while trying to catch my breath.

"God, I'm so stupid," I said between sobs as I leaned against the metal detector.

"Miss, it's okay. You made it. No need to cry."

"You don't understand. This makes twice now."

"But I am here every port, and I don't remember this happening another time," he said, confused. I gathered myself and tried to explain.

"Back in Fort Lauderdale. It's a long story," was all I could say before I headed straight to change and right up to the elliptical to process the stress I'd just carelessly created.

DAY 106 - AT SEA, APPROACHING THE AZORES

I clung to Sergei as the ship took on a swell. "I already can't dance well, and this isn't helping," I said.

"You will be fine. Relax. Just have fun," he said as we practiced our jive routine.

"Let's run it ten more times, and then we can call it a day."

"You know it. Don't over-prepare." He thought for a second. "Actually, you know what I think you need?"

"Some dance skills?"

"No, a big move."

"A big move?" I was petrified of what that could possibly mean.

"Yes. At the end. A big finish. It will make our dance. Here like this." He held me by the waist. "Now, just lightly hold onto my shoulders, and trust that I won't drop you. The minute I say 'pose,' you put your hands over your head, bend one leg at the knee, and smile."

Before I knew it, I was hanging upside down, hearing him shout, "Pose!"

"Can I interrupt you two for a second?" the ship's director asked. He was the one hosting the show.

"Yes, of course," Sergei said as he swung me upright to put me back on my feet.

"Stephanie, I would like to interview you on camera. Ask you a few questions. We just filmed you practicing, which we'll include in the video we play before you perform."

"Sure," I said to him. "Sergei, no 'big move,' " I said, walking away.

"Yes, big move!" he shouted back.

I sat down in front of a video camera as the host asked about my lack of dance experience, my favorite part of the trip thus far, and a few other questions that were cute, but boring. So very boring.

"One last question for you, Stephanie, before we all watch you jive. What's it like dancing with Sergei?"

"Well, he is an amazing teacher, but he does something that scares me," I said, building suspense.

"Scares you? What could that be?"

"Well, there's a part in our routine where I come up behind him, grab the sides of his butt, and we run backwards together. He has buns of steel, and it's so distracting, I forget my steps."

The director began to laugh.

"I was just messing around. Don't put that in there," I said.

"No worries. I won't," he assured me.

DAY 107 - AT SEA, APPROACHING THE AZORES

This can't be normal. Why isn't anyone else fazed by this severe rocking?

I sat in The Crow's Nest with Pete and some other regulars, trying to act normal while my stomach turned in circles. I knew I should head to bed, but I wanted to be with everyone.

"Did you not hear the news?" Kiki asked. "Letters are being delivered to all cabins. There is a storm system developing in the Atlantic, and our second port in the Azores is too far north. We will sail right into it. So, we will remain at our first port an extra day, and then duck under the storm and head home. Oh, and tours are pushed back to day two."

"So, tomorrow is our last stop?" I said, praying I misunderstood.

"We get an extra day there, though," she said, as if that made it all okay. It wasn't okay. I wasn't okay.

The ship took on a huge swell, and I grabbed the bar while watching our drinks slide two feet. "Holy shit! This is a bit much."

"The navigation screen says there are sixty-mile-per-hour winds out there and sixteen-foot swells," Pete said.

"Why isn't the ship in high alert? Isn't this dangerous?"

"Nah," Kiki said.

The room is spinning. I need to put my head down. "I think I am getting seasick, guys," I groaned. "I thought this only happened once, and then you are over it for good."

"Yeah, but this weather is a lot for a rookie," Kiki said, rubbing my back.

I couldn't decide if I should try to walk, or just hold on as tightly as I could to the bar's metal railing and sleep there for the night.

"Oh, no, Pishy Pishy is sick!" Eric said, returning to the bar with a rack of clean glasses.

"Yeah, guys, I think I need to try to walk back to my room."

I slammed into the walls as I made my way down to deck 2, partly because of the intense rocking, and partly as a result of the dizziness that pushed in the minute I felt seasick. I climbed into bed, waiting for the anti-nausea pill to kick in, clinging to the letter from the captain that canceled our final port, making tomorrow our last stop. The true beginning of the end. Whatever lay ahead, I had to trust that my time on the ship had prepared me for it. But it still didn't diminish the feeling that I wanted more time. I needed more time.

DAY 109 - HORTA, THE AZORES

The weather gave us a day of misty reprieve. Stepping on the solid ground, I realized that the next time I stepped off the ship, I would be walking away from it forever. *I need today to be special. To savor every moment. Every detail.*

Everyone except, Sally, piled into a small van that drove us up the mountainous island. Horta looked like so many places we had already visited merged into one. The lush tropics, volcanoes, picturesque scenery, ocean, historical villages, and culture combined felt like the world had set off all the fireworks at once for a grand finale.

We stopped to see two attached volcanic craters that had since become large lakes. I stood, staring at how one lake glowed neon green and the other neon blue. The two lakes had merged, joined at one small area.

"How on earth do they not mix together into one color?" I asked Ken. By this time in our trip, I knew he was the one to ask.

"It's not the water that's a different color. It's what's growing inside of each lake that is creating the different colors."

"So, even if the water flows back and forth, it won't change the lake?"

"Exactly," he said. "Remember that in life."

"Wait, Ken…were those your parting words of wisdom for me?" I asked with a cheeky grin.

Ken blushed, patted my shoulder and kept walking.

The next stop was a small town in the middle of a valley, where we spent the day exploring. The detached little buildings looked like they came from Germany. Everything was quaint, spread out, and peaceful. It was so tucked away that it felt protected, despite the volcanoes surrounding it. We found a local pub with white walls and dark wood beams and trim. It barely fit us all inside. I ordered some cold ones, and topped them off with special pastries that were made locally by the baker "just down the way."

"These are like butter cookies, but better," I said to Detta as she took her first bite.

Pete motioned us to stand in a circle. "I want to take a moment and thank you all for such a wonderful trip. Each one of you made it special. I'll never forget it. Here's to our last time off the ship together!"

"Cheers!" We loudly clinked our thick, old-fashioned pint glasses.

Detta, Ken, and Don took turns thanking everyone for the memories, confirming their interest in doing this again in 2017. Their speeches were sentimental yet brief, as if everyone wanted to finish so that it could be my turn. I gathered myself and forced a smile but that damn burn in my nose started, glassing my eyes over. My voice trembled before I even tried to speak.

I wanted nothing more than to laugh and do something funny like the Kecak, but it felt wrong this time. I knew I needed to stand in the discomfort of my sadness. As hard as it was to do, I looked every single one of the people who meant so much to me in the eye.

"I came on this trip excited to see the world. You weren't part of the plan I had in my mind when I thought of the reason to leave my life behind and board this ship. Then you showed up, all so welcoming, despite giving me a hard time with all your crazy rules," I said with a teary laugh.

"We were giving you a hard time," Detta said as everyone inserted similar comments.

"I know, I know," I chuckled. "I now believe you all were the reason I was meant to come on this trip." I felt Pete's hand rest on my back while Detta wiped her eyes.

"When I find the strength to walk off our ship, I will do it so very grateful that I got to see the world with *you*. I don't think I can express in words what you all have done for me. How you have changed me..."

I couldn't continue. I had no choice but to make a joke.

"So with that said, I have an announcement to make. I've decided to stay here and hide out a while. So, you all be safe heading back to the ship."

"Oh, stop," Pete said. "You still have great things to do. I believe in you and cannot wait to hear about all that you accomplish."

"You are so loved," Detta said. "This trip wouldn't have been the same without you." Everyone took turns giving me a hug.

"You are one-of-a-kind," Pete added, "and I know your life will be unique."

"Thanks, Pete. After all the jokes you have thrown my way, you sure know how to make a girl feel special."

CHAPTER 24

DAY 110 - THE ATLANTIC OCEAN

Ladies and gentlemen, this is your captain speaking. As you all know, we have canceled our last port to navigate around a large storm system. Unfortunately, it has strengthened into a tropical depression, and our passage around it is going to require your help. Please secure any loose items above knee height onto the floor of your stateroom. The ship will be securing itself during the day and closing down immediately after dinner. All passengers are to be in their cabins by nine p.m. This matter is serious, and I urge you to comply for your safety and the safety of others."

So, sixty-mile-per-hour winds and the sixteen-foot swells we had coming into Horta didn't require bracing the ship. But now we need to? How bad is this going to be?   ••

Never before had I seen us eat fewer than three courses and gulp our food as if we were in the military. The water swayed back and forth in my glass as if it were drunk. Waiters held on to our chairs to balance themselves when standing at our table.

"It's getting bad. Time to get to our cabins," Detta said as we noticed other tables following suit.

"Even if you aren't tired, lay in bed. Trust me," Ken said.

"Is this going to be like our bus ride to Borobudur, Ken?" I asked.

He chuckled. "This will be much worse," he said, heading toward the stairs.

Forty-five minutes later, the ship engaged in full battle against the storm. After one tumble across my cabin and a hard hit to my right shoulder, I realized I needed to follow Ken's advice. I got down on my hands and knees, turned my desk chair over onto its side, and tried to better secure the belongings I had put on the floor. Even on all fours, I still struggled. I crawled to the bathroom, took some Advil for my shoulder, and crawled into bed, vowing not to move until the storm was over.

With each huge wave, my feet rose up over my head, only to be rocked back down to almost a standing position. Over and over, the ship rocked, nose up, nose down, and then side-to-side like an intense carnival ride. Yet never once did I feel weightless or airborne. The ship stayed grounded, no matter how much slashing it received, never losing its sense of gravity—the sole reason I never fell off the bed.

To add to the intensity, each crash of the waves sounded like an avalanche of cement rocks hitting the ship, followed by a shaking as if we were a maraca being played by the ocean. A shake so loud and so violent it felt like the ship was breaking apart.

I found the dramatic way we were beginning our crossing of the Atlantic rather poetic. I wondered what the captain and officers were doing up in the bridge. *Are they concerned? Do they have everything under control?* Oddly, I wasn't afraid; I trusted this vessel I called my home. But that didn't take away from the fact that it was going to be a long, long night.

DAY 111 - THE ATLANTIC OCEAN

I held onto the wall as I made my way up to breakfast. The rocking was still strong, but last night had desensitized me. *I am going to need five cups of coffee, especially because today is Pete's big day.*

I found the birthday boy eating on the Lido Deck with Detta.

"We lived!" Pete shouted, holding up both hands like a ref calling a field goal. "I didn't think I was going to make it to my eighty-second birthday dinner."

"What was it like sleeping in your bed?" I laughed, knowing that he preferred to sleep on his balcony in a lounge chair.

"Very funny," he said as Detta pulled out a chair for me.

"So, I was thinking," I said. "We need to do something more than just cake at dinner for your birthday, Pete." I was pretending I had zero plans up my sleeve.

"Maybe we will hit up The Crow's Nest after dinner," he suggested.

"That works! Maybe we can convince the entire table to join us for once," I said as I took a sip of my coffee...and sneaked in a wink to Detta.

My countdown to Pete's birthday had consumed my thoughts the past two days, forcing my countdown to Florida to retreat to the back burner. I'd found every close friend of Pete's, handed them a pair of sunglasses, and instructed them to be in The Crow's Nest at 10:00 p.m.

Kiki had grown to love Pete as much as I did. Still, he was surprised to see her at dinner, as well as the bottles of wine on our table waiting to be consumed. Our frequent joking around had already earned us a reputation for having a little too much fun at dinner, so that night, people at tables around us weren't shocked when I pulled out the sunglasses and told Pete we were wearing them for the rest of the evening.

While wearing huge sunglasses with big plastic birthday cakes on top of each lens, Pete opened a gift from a passenger who had stopped by: a plastic pig wearing lipstick and a red dress, which, in the midst of dancing, suddenly lifted up and flashed him. Pete couldn't stop showing his new toy to every person who walked by.

With only four days left of the entire trip, we gathered and laughed as we took our last dinner table group photo. For the first time since karaoke night, every one of us went to The Crow's Nest afterward.

Pete, walking around in his shades on our way to the bar, thought he was the star of the ship.

"Happy birthday, Pete!" his friends shouted as we entered The Crow's Nest, standing gathered together with their crazy sunglasses. Pete grabbed onto the railing attached to the bar to collect himself. I grabbed his other arm to make sure he didn't lose balance.

"I can't believe you! Look at what you did!" he said before giving me the biggest hug.

The band was playing and I rotated partners, dancing with everyone. I wasn't sure if our unsteadiness was from the rocking or the wine, but as soon as I took a dance break and stood by the bar, I could tell I was rather tipsy.

I watched Pete laughing as he showed someone his flashing pig.

"Hey, Stephanie." A head of loose blond curls entered my peripheral vision. Hendrik. "Did you do all of this?"

"Yes, I did."

"Pete's a lucky guy!"

"Go wish him a happy birthday," I said, wanting him to leave. I watched his gorgeous tall figure stroll through the crowd to hug Pete, and stared at the shape of his ass in his blue uniform until he slowly made his way back to the bar.

"Wow. You made his night. It's a shame you didn't do this for my birthday."

"I would have done it for you, but I didn't know when your birthday was."

"You would have?" His wide smile lingered, making his desires quite clear.

I looked at my watch. *It's midnight.*

"It's getting late," he said.

"Yeah, it's usually dead by now."

"Want to go hang in my cabin? We can watch some old TV shows I have on my computer."

I knew no TV would be watched.

Have I been misreading everything? Is this him, or is it me? You know what—screw it.

"Okay," I said.

"In fifteen minutes?" he suggested, finishing his wine. "I'll grab us another bottle. The door will be cracked. Be careful. Same as last time."

As I walked past the matching stateroom doors on Hendrik's deck, I felt empowered. The closer I got to his door, the more I realized what this was. *I am throwing caution to the wind here and I am fine with it.*

Opening his cracked door, I caught a glimpse of him lying in bed. I quickly entered and closed the door behind me—and made a beeline to join him.

DAY 114 - IN THE MIDDLE OF THE ATLANTIC OCEAN

Wow, I think everyone on the ship has come to watch. It's packed out there! I stood in the back, nervous after watching the other dancers during dress rehearsal earlier that day.

"Breathe and just have fun," one of the pro dancers, Rebecca, said after noticing my fright. She looked down at my skirt. "Turn around."

I had done my best to look the part: a green fit-and-flare skirt, black ruffled top, and a pair of horrible low heels with an ankle strap I'd found in Spain.

"Oh, Stephanie, your butt is hanging out of your bloomers. We can't have you going out there like that," Rebecca whispered in my ear.

"I don't have bloomers. These are my bikini bottoms."

"Here, let me run to my cabin. I have a pair of clean ones you can borrow," she said, darting off.

"Relax, it is going to be fine," Sergei said in his heavy Russian accent.

We listened to Ben dance the waltz and Dina kill it with the cha-cha.

I'm next and no bloomers.

The host of the show came onstage to announce our dance, but he still had to play the video he'd made, buying Rebecca another minute.

The video started, showing Sergei and me practicing, and me answering various questions, including my impromptu confession about Sergei's butt. I looked at my dance partner, embarrassed for what he was about to hear. I had not told him what I'd said, because I trusted it wouldn't be aired. Sergei leaned in to hear better. A look of concern crossed his face when he heard me say on the video that I was scared.

"Well, there's a part in our routine where I come up behind him, grab the sides of his butt, and we run backwards together. He has buns of steel, and it's so distracting, I forget my steps," I said on the screen. The theater erupted with laughter, and the video came to an end.

Sergei blushed and shook his head as Rebecca came running up with bloomers, which I quickly put on over my bikini bottoms.

"Go-go-go," she urged.

I scurried out onto the dark stage and stood there alone, my heart beating in my chest as the music started. The song "Shake Your Tailfeather" began and Sergei slowly entered the stage. Seeing his smile I relaxed. He moved me into our dance hold, and I felt so led, so guided by his strength and abilities that I let go and just moved. I didn't want it to end. Then it was time for the move where I grab the sides of his butt. An idea popped into my head. As he shuffled forward, I held onto his butt, refusing to let go while making a face that looked like I was hanging on for dear life. *I have become Lucille Ball.*

The crowd roared with laughter, and even Sergei played into it as we separated in time for our solo moves. The performer within me nailed it. Before I knew it, I was hanging upside down in our final pose, and the audience was on their feet. *I did it! I started this trip by almost falling off a barstool, and I'm ending it dancing the jive on the main stage.*

Sergei hugged me, and we stood onstage waiting for the judges' remarks. After amazing feedback from the first two judges, the mic was handed to Hendrik, the third judge. I looked at him for the first time since our night together.

"Stephanie...I must say. There was one small misstep, but your passion, precision, and overall performance were spot-on."

"Wow, Stephanie! Those were some comments from the judges," the host said. "And I must say, it's not often Hendrik gives out words that begin with a *p*."

Words that begin with a 'p'? You mean, like penis? I get your joke, you asshole. So, he told you...and now you want to secretly mock me onstage. Ugh, this sucks. Just smile and act like you don't care. Don't let them take your power or rain on your parade.

As the host turned to the audience for their vote, I was overwhelmed by how loudly they cheered when my name was called. After the crowd went silent, an envelope was handed to the host.

"Ladies and gentlemen, the winner of Dancing with the Stars at Sea is… Stephanie Wilson!"

The entire theater rose to its feet. I stared into the audience for a second in disbelief, then hugged the other two contestants before taking a final bow and running off to change my clothes and find my friends.

As we walked through the ship, Pete held my arm as if he were my agent, parading me through every lounge. We finally settled at the piano bar with the rest of our table. A little old woman walked up and tapped me on the shoulder.

"I must tell you," she started to say in a thick Brooklyn accent. Whatever it was, she wasn't going to begin with pleasantries. "You were not the best out there."

I braced myself for what was to come next, while Pete's face turned red hot.

"She was too," he snarled.

"No, she was not. Not by a mile." She spoke to Pete with such anger that I thought she might slap him. I patted Pete's leg to tell him it was okay.

She turned to me and stuck her head way too close to my face. "But you had the most fun up there. That's why you won. Congratulations." She turned her hunched-over frame and slowly walked away.

DAY 115 - AT SEA, APPROACHING FORT LAUDERDALE

I got to the gym and stopped dead in my tracks. *Why am I working out? I should spend as much time with everyone as possible.* I headed straight for the Lido Deck, eager to participate in our normal sea-day chats. Walking through the automatic glass doors, I expected to see people in their usual seats, engaged in their usual activities.

Instead, I stood, frozen and heartbroken. It was empty. *It's already over.* People were probably in their cabins doing exactly what I was hoping to put off until the very last minute—packing.

I returned to my cabin and began undoing all that I had done over the past 114 days, returning my room back to the way I had found it. I gathered the gifts I had bought and put them in the duffel bag provided by the ship. Next, I turned to one of my suitcases. It, too, quickly filled up with memories. In order to bring it all, I was going to have to shed some of the things I had brought on board with me. I looked at my clothes spread across the bed. *You served me well. Thank you.*

I grabbed my key card and went to find Anne Marie.

"I'll be quick," I said once we were back in my cabin. "I don't want to get you in trouble for being here." I pointed to the pile of clothes folded on my bed. "These are for you if you would like them."

"No, ma'am, I can't."

"You would do me a great favor because I can't fit them in my bag."

"They are so nice and beautiful," she said softly. She grabbed one of the dresses and held it up.

"I'm glad you think so. I would hate to throw them out, and I know you're my size from wearing your uniform on April Fools'," I reminded her.

"Ah, yes." She gathered them together. "Thank you. I will miss you so much, Step-anie." She teared up and hugged me. It was the first hug I gave knowing almost for certain I would never see her again.

• •

My last night at dinner felt exactly like my first. Fun, but a bit formal. We laughed, we joked, and we reminisced, but with a distance that told me everyone was protecting themselves. I could tell we all had so much to say, but instead said very little, only polite statements of how wonderful everything had been. Maybe that was easier than all of us losing it and jumping off the deck into the ocean. Because that was what I felt like I might do if I let the flood of emotions take over. Toward the end of dessert, Sally asked about my plans. Naturally, I was the only one to be asked; all the others were heading back to the same life they had left.

"I don't know yet," was all I could say.

"That's okay." Sally put her hand on my thigh and gave it a squeeze.

We lingered a bit past ten at the table. No one wanted to get up. When we finally had to, we all hugged and vowed to do what we had already talked about at least ten times throughout this journey: to come back in 2017, together. I told them I would. As we walked away, I prayed to every god in the universe to make our promise a reality.

Pete and I made our way up to The Crow's Nest, where Kiki and Mark were already having a drink with Hendrik. They had a crew party to attend below deck but wanted to spend at least a little time with those of us they had grown close to. After a hug and a promise to keep in touch from Kiki, a hug and farewell from Mark, and a high-five from Hendrik, I sat with Pete at the bar, nursing one last drink. We laughed with the other Crow's Nest regulars until one by one, they too said goodbye and left. Finally, it was time for Pete to head for bed. He gathered his thoughts and then looked me in the eyes. He was welling up.

"Before I go, I want you to know how special you are, Stephanie. Don't give up your pursuit of a life on your terms. You made this cruise ship come to life just by being you. It's quite the superpower. And no matter what life brings, try to have fun. Keep in touch, come visit me sometime, and know that I am always here for you."

"Thank you, Pete. I honestly don't know how I am ever going to get used to not having you around. Life won't be the same. And thanks for stirring up some gossip on the ship with me." This time, it was me making light of a heavy moment.

"You were the perfect partner in crime." He laughed.

"Agreed, Pete. I couldn't have chosen a better person to bum around with."

"Any regrets?" he asked as he got up.

"No. It was a trip of a lifetime. It was everything I could have hoped for. But maybe I do have one. I never got to know Dolly," I said. Pete rolled his eyes.

"Yes, you did. She's a fighter and she lives life on her terms. You are Dolly, just younger." He hugged me goodbye.

"I'll see you in 2017," I said, fighting back tears.

"2017!" he echoed, walking away without turning around. I watched his lengthy frame head slowly toward the exit, and stared at him until he turned the corner and was gone.

PORT EVERGLADES - FORT LAUDERDALE, FL

"Ladies and gentlemen, the blue group can now make their way to the gangway to disembark. Once again, the blue group can now disembark."

The hall intercom blared in full force. It was 6:00 a.m. No sleeping in today. Not that I could anyway. I'd been up all night tossing and turning.

We were grouped by colors, depending on flight times, so that the U.S. Customs line wouldn't get backed up making people miss their planes. Those of us, like me, who didn't have a flight were last to disembark. *I am totally okay with that. Hell, I would prefer to be the last person off the ship.*

I went up to the Lido Deck for some breakfast, where I sat facing the wall. I didn't want to look out and see the port. I pushed around my oatmeal for thirty minutes before discarding it.

My color group disembarked around ten, so I decided to spend my remaining time on board wisely. I began at the top deck of the ship, in the gym, staring at the elliptical machine with overwhelming gratitude. I gazed at the pedals, thinking of all I had released while moving them in circles. So much healing had occurred in this room.

I made my way around the Lido Deck, trying to picture it full of people on a sea day with all the familiar faces sitting at various tables. Kel and Julie doing their crossword. Dolly sitting on her throne. Pete and Detta off in a corner, giggling and eating their post-breakfast snack. Soundbites from all the conversations I'd had there with so many passengers blended and blared like an intercom in my mind. I tried to savor those conversations, the visuals, but grew frustrated at the thought that there may have been some I'd already forgotten.

At the piano bar, I envisioned Debbie playing Carole King while we sat behind her, trying not to fill up on Goldfish and peanuts before dinner. I looked over toward the corner where we had played trivia, and thought of my team laughing at my lack of knowledge of pop culture. Those moments felt so simplistic compared to the heaviness I now felt.

I wandered into the theater and sat on one of the seats, pretending to watch myself dance the jive, or see the Alleycats singing again. I laughed, thinking of the first night and how I hadn't been a fan of the shows. *How ironic that I wound up performing in one.*

My heart swelled with love as I took a lap on the Promenade Deck and remembered Valentine's Day, or any time I'd felt the need to watch the waves. Or the time a large group of us walked a 5k around the deck to raise money for cancer. I headed back in and saw the knitting group's area, where I once desperately tried to knit after the captain's wife invited me. *Thank goodness she understood when I dropped out.* Before leaving deck 3, I glanced down the hallway that led to Hendrik's cabin, deciding that that unsatisfying part of my trip wasn't worth revisiting.

I took the elevator up to The Crow's Nest and sat one last time at the bar, remembering so many conversations with Pete and the other regulars. Hearing Eric say "Pishy pishy" and Anne Marie calling me "Ma'am Step-anie." I stared out at the dance floor—how I'd graced it with horrible karaoke and subpar cha-cha moves. I looked at the small, empty stage, jealous that it would again be filled with a band I wouldn't be here for

As I headed to one last stop on deck 5, I promised myself I wouldn't cry.

I made my way down the huge red staircase to the dining room like I had that first night, but instead of entering candlelit warmth, I walked into a cold, barren shell. The tablecloths were packed away. Not a soul was in sight. I approached our table but couldn't sit. *Not without them.*

I wished I could go back in time for just one dinner and focus hard on every second. To make sure I had everyone's laugh perfectly memorized. To feel the starch in the napkins. To listen to the sound of silverware hitting dishes. All of it. Every single bit of it.

I kissed my fingers and touched the table.

"I'll miss you guys," I whispered.

As I turned down the passageway toward my cabin for the final time, my color was called over the loudspeaker. Our bags had been taken the night before, leaving me with only my purse and backpack.

I sat on my bed in the exact spot as when I'd entered my room for the first time. I remembered looking around with excitement and wonder, having no idea what any of it would be like. Now I was leaving it all behind with a heart full of memories that would stay with me for the rest of my life. I just wished there would be breadcrumbs leading me forward. Instead, tomorrow was a blank canvas—and I had no idea what to paint on it.

Stuffing down the fear I lifted my chin. *It's fine. The plan is coming. I didn't come this far to only come this far! I had the guts to wager my entire life for an adventure that I will never regret. The world is a blank slate, and I am going to expect the unexpected. I am going to "go big" like Kel said. I might not see the next steps, but they will show themselves.*

My inner Tony Robbins was right. *There is no need to worry. I dared the universe, and I won. There is only one way to go, and that is up!* With a hopeful heart I stood up, grabbed my bag, and sauntered steadily down the hall with my head held high.

When I got to the gangway, Captain Mercer and Henk hugged me tightly. Then I turned around and took my first step on the solid ground I had left behind 115 days ago.

Was it sea legs or nerves? I didn't know, but my legs were shaking.

PART 2:

WOODEN BENCHES

CHAPTER 25

FORT LAUDERDALE, FL

The Customs officer reviewed my passport and disembarkation paperwork, then hovered over his computer longer than my patience would allow me to smile for.

"Miss, please step aside," he said in a deadpan voice.

"Is there a problem, officer?"

"I am going to need you to come with me," another officer said coldly as he approached. He escorted me into a gray room with no windows and left me to wait.

I was at the point of losing my cool when the officer returned, escorting another man dressed in a suit rather than the typical dark green shirt and pants. He introduced himself as Agent Moseley. His cold, stiff demeanor told me he was someone important. I smiled at him, but he didn't reciprocate. He sat down and stared at me while the other officer stood in the back corner.

"Ms. Wilson, I am going to ask you some questions," he said. "First, I need to know why you were on this trip."

"I wanted to see the world," I said calmly. I calculated my next words. "Like everyone else on board."

He looked at me as if I was supposed to say something further.

"Ms. Wilson, you can make this easy on yourself and talk now, or you will stay here all day in this room until you do," he said.

A female officer wearing rubber gloves rolled my three orange and silver hardshell bags into an adjacent room.

"Go ahead, go through my bags. You won't find anything, but you're welcome to take a Turkish candle holder home to your wife."

"Ma'am, I need you to cooperate with us."

"I can't cooperate if I don't know what you want from me."

Agent Moseley paused, then exhaled sharply. "You are wanted in the state of California."

"For what?" I asked.

"I can't give you that information, but I do need to look at these surveillance stills and compare them to you." He glanced back and forth between my face, my body, and his computer screen as I sat on the plastic office chair, my hands gripping its sides.

"Sir, I don't know if this is part of the issue, but I was burglarized almost two years ago. They broke into my safe and stole all my documents. My passport, my birth certificate and social security card…even my extra credit cards. Someone is posing as me. Please give me a chance to prove it to you."

He looked at me with raised eyebrows.

"May I access my email to show you the police report?" I asked.

He excused himself from the room. The other officer in the corner stayed behind, staring at me while I frantically searched my inbox. Agent Moseley returned with yet another man in a suit. They reviewed my police report carefully and then returned to the photos.

"We understand, Ms. Wilson, that this may not be you, but it is uncanny how similar you two look. I can't tell you apart."

"Can you show me the photos?" I asked, both curious and disturbed.

"No, we cannot, but can you show us your ankles?" I nodded, then lifted up my light gray jeans and lowered my socks. Agent Moseley came around the desk and examined my skin closely.

"Nope, no tattoo and no signs of a tattoo removal," he said to the other agent, signaling him to follow him out of the room.

The past I'd left behind had been waiting for my return, threatening the hopeful, positive energy I walked off the ship with. I stared at my feet in disbelief for over an hour before the door swung open again.

"Ms. Wilson, we are releasing you. Just give us a few minutes to clear your new passport in the system so that you aren't detained any further while traveling. But I have to warn you that this matter could resurface if this woman isn't apprehended."

It took a second to digest his words. *It's never gonna end, is it?*

Staring at my spilled-over suitcases on the floor of the adjacent room, I sighed, grabbed the first one, and began to slowly repack.

• •

Sitting curbside on top of my largest suitcase, I took comfort in staring up at my ship's bow towering over the port. My phone pinged a text message, the first in four months: "I'm pulling up." As Angela's red SUV curved around the cul-de-sac, I felt a rush of gratitude.

We drove onto the highway and I watched the MS *Amsterdam* getting smaller and smaller until it was gone, forcing me to turn my head away from the direction of the port. I listened to new, unfamiliar songs on the radio while entertaining Angela with the most upbeat and outrageous stories from the trip. After an hour, she placed her right hand on my arm. "Hon, I know you must be feeling so much right now. If you need to let it out, it's okay."

"I just need to keep moving."

"Okay, boo. Let's get you to Orlando." She turned on a Taylor Swift playlist and began singing at the top of her lungs—an old inside joke between us. I smiled at her and joined right in.

Hours later, after saying goodbye at a car rental in Orlando and promising to get Charlie in a week or so, I got in the car, realizing I hadn't driven since my brief attempt in New Zealand. I looked over the dashboard to make sure I knew where all the buttons were before heading to Yanira's for a brief stay. As odd as driving felt, the realization that I was alone for the first time since walking off the ship was even stranger. A buildup of pressure inside seemed like it was going to explode.

At the first red light, the dam cracked. I punched the steering wheel until the pain in my hand forced me to stop. I screamed.

"God, I can't do this. I can't. I don't want to be here. It all feels so wrong." I sobbed, trying to catch my breath.

A loud, long honk snapped me out of my dark despair. I lifted my right hand, gave the car behind a middle finger, and shifted back into drive.

• •

Yanira ran out of her home, arms open wide, screaming, "My Fef's back!" Her loud, emphatic craziness drowned out the "WTF am I doing" playing on repeat in my mind. Despite my weariness from the fit I'd just had, I smiled and ran out of the car to jump into her embrace.

"Mamacita!" I shouted. "I've missed you!"

"Come inside. Let me feed you," she ordered.

"I'm not hungry."

"Well, you better be thirsty. I opened up a nice bottle."

We sat on her back porch, wine in hand, and I regaled her with the stories I'd told Angela.

Later, after a quick shower, I opened my suitcase and sifted through the few items of clothing I'd kept from the cruise. I selected the blue floral top I'd worn to my first dinner on the ship, holding it tightly to my chest and inhaling. It smelled like the ship's detergent. Fighting back tears, I slipped it on with a pair of jeans.

Yanira's gang was waiting for us at the Wine Room down in Winter Park, a place I frequented before my trip, mostly with Caroline, who was, unfortunately, too busy to join us. The Wine Room overflowed with its usual Friday night crowd. Everyone in our group was laughing and enjoying the breezy May evening, and since my birthday was around the corner, discussing what I should do. I observed the scene in silence, watching as if they were all swimming around in a fishbowl. As happy as I was to see them, I couldn't help but feel like I'd returned to life as I once knew it—but now only as an outsider.

• •

The next morning I woke up late to the smell of Yanira cooking brunch. I sat on her couch next to two grocery bags full of my forwarded mail. Just the thought of going through it exhausted me. We spent the afternoon lounging in our pajamas, and "Party Yanira" was quickly replaced by "Truth-slapping Yanira."

"Fef, you had this amazing, once-in-a-lifetime trip. Now it is time to get a job and continue your life."

"Yanira, everything looks the same, but feels foreign. It's messing with my head. I have to keep moving forward. I just don't know how…and I don't know if it's meant to be done here in Orlando."

"Fef, Orlando is your home, and we want you here. Don't get me wrong, I will always support you and your dreams. But are you really ready to leave again?"

"You're right. I'm not. I'm in limbo, Yanira."

• •

Later, I met up with Yvonne at Hillstone, our favorite restaurant where we'd often lounged on their lakeside back patio. I craved both the artistic connection and the smoked salmon that she always ordered for us—and the only salmon I somehow enjoyed.

"I have something for you," I said out of the gate, excited for the gift I'd bought her. "It's a silk scarf handmade in Georgetown, Malaysia. They take the silk and draw on it with wax before they dye it. Then, they boil the wax off leaving a cool design. It was brilliant to watch and something I thought you would like."

Yvonne put the scarf on proudly before gliding across the patio in her bohemian, yet regal manner. She stopped over at the firepit, lit her cigarette, and looked at me with her brown doe-eyes, seeing through me just as she always did. Instead of addressing practicalities such as housing and work, she went straight to the heart.

"What are you feeling?" she asked.

"I'm happy, sad, in shock, unsure, and super emotional."

"Wow, that's it?" She laughed.

"It changes by the minute. But being here in our spot feels nice. Yesterday was horrible. Thank God Yanira and her friends were so understanding. I was a zombie, Yvonne."

"Dive right back into Art Sake. Come to the advanced class tomorrow. It isn't the same without you. And before you know it, Play de Luna will be around the corner, and you can both direct and act in it. It will help."

Yvonne excused herself to go to the restroom, which allowed me time to process my thoughts.

Everyone seems to think this trip was a hole to fill before settling down. It wasn't. But, I do need to mobilize, and I think I should do that here in Orlando. Get a place to live, get my dog, and get work. If I can stabilize, without falling back into my old life, I will be able to follow the current forward. Okay, I think I have a plan.

Yvonne returned. "I'm surprised David isn't here. Did you invite him?"

"I wanted to see you first, but I'm dying to see him." I texted David to come join us. As if he'd been secretly waiting around the corner for my call, in only ten minutes he came running up behind us. I jumped up. He twirled me around, shouting, "What's up, bitches! I ordered you both another round when I walked past the bar."

CHAPTER 26

I woke up the next morning on a mission. Like a madwoman, I secured an apartment, bought a car, and ordered all the furniture and décor I would need to complete my new base camp—all within ten days.

To my surprise, I discovered that my tastes had changed. Instead of the Tuscan style and darker feel of my last home, I opted for a brightly lit apartment, with an office area for the new career that I knew would soon present itself. And the best part: it was right around the corner from Art Sake. I purchased distressed wood furniture and accented it with bright blues, yellows, and magenta. My new home would look like the perfect combination of a cottage near the sea and an artist's haven.

As soon as the movers set down the last box and closed my apartment door, I stood frozen, realizing how much I'd depended on Yanira's constant presence while staying with her, as well as on all the dinners out reconnecting with friends. I hadn't been left alone with myself until now. I turned on the radio to break the silence and began to frantically unpack and set up. Charlie was arriving tomorrow. *Having him here will make everything better.*

By eight o'clock my stomach began to growl, so I ordered takeout from the restaurant downstairs. I carefully arranged a place setting on a TV tray: glasses for water and wine in perfect position; flatware, including a fork for each course; and a folded napkin over the cream-colored china plate my Italian grandmother had given me as a housewarming gift. I served myself the appetizer before sitting down and placing the napkin over my lap, then stared down at my plate until the crisp definition of my food grew blurry. I couldn't bear to look up and not see their faces.

• •

Charlie's return was heaven, and I decided to give us both a month to reconnect and decompress in the new space, as well as to allow the high of my trip to wear off. To watch the movies I missed. To visit the friends I hadn't yet seen. Most of all, to slow down enough so I could see the way forward.

By month's end, my place was impeccably decorated, but somehow, it still didn't feel like home. In the corner of my bedroom, a bag full of gifts I'd bought now sat collecting dust. A part of me didn't want to reach out to my old college friends. My time away from them, as well as the hours on the elliptical, had clarified their mean treatment and toxic behavior. I expected that would help curb the pain when my group text suggesting we get together went unanswered by all. It didn't. The rejection stung. Even worse, I started to see their social media posts about the upcoming Dave Matthews girls' trip. For the first time in nine years, I wasn't invited.

I decided to further decorate my apartment with the gifts meant for them. Candleholders from Turkey, glasses from India, and tchotchkes from Thailand graced my shelves. I displayed everything I bought except the gifts for Caroline, Brad, and their kids, which I wrapped and kept safe in a closet.

Life had gone on without me while I was away, and although I felt the love from Yvonne, David, Yanira, Angela, and my acting friends, inserting myself fully back into my community felt harder and made me more vulnerable than I had imagined it would. I latched onto Caroline, trying desperately to see her. Unfortunately, she was traveling and wasn't available. I was happy for her but needed my best friend. I missed our conversations. I missed her.

A single text to David on a Friday afternoon with two words—*I'm stressed*—was my SOS. He immediately planned a pool party at my apartment for the next day.

I sat dangling my feet in the water, judging the pool for having chlorine in it instead of saltwater like the ship's pool had. My friends were all joking around in the shallow end. Then, Yanira and David made their way over to me.

"You two look like alligators slowly approaching their prey," I said.

"What are you doing over here all by yourself?" David asked.

"Out with it," Yanira demanded.

"It's just I've been home forty days and still haven't seen Caroline," I admitted softly.

"You haven't seen Caroline?" Yanira was shocked.

"No. She texts me to make plans, and then cancels at the last minute. She has this exciting new job that requires her to travel all over the country. I'm happy for her, but it's been hard to get together. Yesterday, I mailed her the gifts I bought. I couldn't stare at them any longer."

"That makes no sense. She loves being a stay-at-home mom," Yanira said.

David looked confused. He hadn't had the chance to really get to know Caroline. She'd always preferred to have dinner with just the two of us before getting home to her kids.

"You haven't seen her Facebook posts with all the fancy restaurant food pics from her work trips?" I asked Yanira.

"No." She climbed out of the pool and grabbed her phone. Seconds later she showed me Caroline's Facebook page. No travel posts at all. Yanira then opened Caroline's page from my account and saw tons of posts detailing her trips. She pressed a few buttons and looked at me, pissed. "Fef. She made these posts private, so only you can see them. And the pictures were copied from the restaurant's website. She didn't take those."

"Oh my God, she is faking it. What a bitch," David said as Yanira showed him my screen.

"No. No way. She would never. Maybe she doesn't want anyone to know she got a job."

"Stephanie. No. She's fucking with you." David gave me a look that said he wanted to find her and kill her.

"Caroline wouldn't do that to me. She's my best friend," I insisted.

"Fef. She is being passive-aggressive. She has zero intentions of seeing you."

"You guys. I don't think I can hang anymore. I gotta go."

"Nope, you aren't leaving. You are staying right here with us," David insisted.

"We've been best friends since I was twenty. Her mom is like my second mom. I go to their family functions. There is no way. Not her." I started to cry.

Yanira handed me my phone. "Text her and confront her."

Consumed with shock and sadness, I began typing out a text.

• •

Three days passed without a single response from Caroline after sending several messages. On day four, she blocked me on all platforms. Our friendship was over.

I ran a bath, got in, and cried my eyes out. For the next two weeks, I cried in that tub once, sometimes twice, a day. It was the only place where I felt safe to fall apart.

Maybe she was jealous. But why? She has the life she always wanted, with a husband and two gorgeous kids. And I supported that choice for her. I always stood by her. Maybe I upset her while I was gone. I barely emailed anyone. Maybe I was too self-absorbed in my trip. I should show up at her door and demand we talk and fight for our friendship. She's worth it. But I can't. I'm just too hurt.

I clung to the belief that she would come around. But as the weeks passed, I had to face that she was gone for good. She broke me. I couldn't take anymore. I never conceived of coming home to such heartache and confusion.

I had trusted Caroline like I had trusted Pop—with my heart and soul. My spirit was crushed. The inner guidance which had led me this far fell silent, and I no longer trusted myself with any decisions about my life. I desperately needed reassurance and direction. I needed someone to tell me what to do.

My prayers for help were answered within two days. An acquaintance I ran into while food shopping boasted about how amazing her life was, all because of a woman who was giving her guidance using unconventional methods. After asking her a few questions, she suggested I should give it a try. She was completely unaware of my struggles, which made her words feel like divine intervention. Even though normally I never would have agreed to something like that, I eagerly said yes without questioning it.

CHAPTER 27

This time, the sign on the office door did not say "Psychologist and Life Coach"; it said "Healer."

"What does a Reiki healer even do?" I'd asked the woman who referred me.

"She channels information and clears out old programs by working on your energy."

Her words were as incomprehensible as Greek to me, but I understood her next sentence perfectly.

"She can get answers from the other side."

I stared at her in the middle of the produce section with wide eyes. She seemed like someone who wouldn't suggest something that wasn't legit. *This is exactly what I need. Answers.*

It seemed as if I were somehow cheating, but I didn't care. I wanted the shortest route through the woods. To be told what to do next.

Ten minutes late, the healer came floating in like a fairy. She was around my age, had long, straight blond hair, a pointy nose, and a flowy robe that overwhelmed her tiny five-foot frame. She began by burning dried leaves that smelled like marijuana while chanting something under her breath. To finish her ritual, she sat down slowly and grabbed two crystals to hold in her hand.

"Stephanie, I am honored you are here today," she said in a high-pitched whisper. "Please lie down on the table. I am going to ask that you close your eyes, relax, and focus on your breath."

I peeked a few times to see her hands moving six inches above my body. Consulting with someone invisible to me, she worked the air above my torso as if she were molding Play-Doh, and asked the invisible entities to clear out "muck" and replace it with "gold light." Thirty minutes later, she asked me sit up.

"Let's chat," she said. "There are parts of your energy in your heart and in your core that are stuck. I worked to remove them, but aligning you will take some time."

"Okay," I said, not fully grasping what she meant.

"It is a vital time for you. You are at a crossroads, and every decision you make moving forward will be life-altering."

Come on. You could say that to anyone, and it would be true. But… it *was* true. Her words lured me in.

"Stephanie. You have an energy of both a creative and a go-getter. But you also have a knowing. I can tell by the magenta glow around you. You are very powerful if you just learn to ground yourself. You have a team of spiritual guides in the other realm who want to connect with you and help you."

I sat up straighter. "So, I am being watched?"

Ignoring my question, she continued. "Tell me more about your trip."

It all came spilling out. I told her about my travels, the month and a half since I returned home, the loss of my friends, and my love for Charlie.

"That trip must have been expensive."

"It was. I sold my home to finance it," I replied, then redirected her focus. "I just feel so confused. I want to find a way forward that financially supports me while allowing me to feel creative, free, and happy, and most importantly, lets me spend time with Charlie during the day. I promised him I would after leaving him. Those are my conditions. I just can't figure out how to do it. Do I go back to school? Do I build an online platform? I have so many facets about me between acting, real estate, traveling, et cetera. Which path do I take? I need answers," I said all in one breath causing me to gasp.

She listened intently, then motioned me to be silent as she looked up toward the ceiling to listen for messages coming from the other side. She conversed back and forth in a mumble while I waited, in disbelief over what I was witnessing yet desperate for a message.

"If you go back to your old career, you will revert to your old habits and undo all that the cruise did for your growth and well-being."

See, that's what I've been saying!

"You don't throw out a perfectly good blue sweater to just go out and buy another blue sweater. You throw out the blue sweater because you want to change up your wardrobe," she said.

She gets it. She really gets it.

The healer began burning more dried leaves and then grabbed a bowl and struck it, which made a high-pitched sound that hurt my ears.

"What on earth is that?" I asked, gritting my teeth.

"I am raising your vibration." She sat down again and resumed her conversation with the ceiling.

"They want me to tell you that the ship wasn't your real adventure, but a protective nucleus to nourish you and prepare you for what's next. Your trip's end was just the beginning."

"Whatever I need to do, I'll do. Can you tell them that?" I asked her.

"How long can you support yourself without working?"

"Six months," I replied, which meant through January 2016.

"If you take this time to rest from this transformation you went through, you will be beyond abundant come February," she assured.

My logical brain objected. "But what if that doesn't happen? I have student loans I could pay off, and I should work. I could do a few real estate deals on the side, but that won't fully support me." I could feel fear creeping in. "This is a huge risk."

"I assure you: you will have an abundance of money come February. And your path forward will be paved out in front of you. Trust me when I say, you will need this rest and recuperation for what is to come," she declared. Her words ignited a sense of excitement and hope within me, reinforcing the belief I clung to: this trip was meant to connect me to my next steps.

"But most importantly, you need to feel joy and expect good things during this time. Worry and fear will ruin the outcome. I want to have a session with you weekly. It will help greatly."

Dang, at two hundred dollars a session, this is going to add up fast. This is obviously my first test in trusting.

As I walked out, the healer hugged me and whispered softly into my ear, "Stay home, rest, and trust."

I was unsure if it was her words or the insanely close proximity of her mouth to my ear, but something gave me chills.

• •

Yvonne would have been the only one I suspected would understand, especially with her love for tarot cards, but I kept this decision to myself. I believed that no one could fully empathize with what I was going through, and I didn't want to risk any negative influence. With the assumption that I was doing real estate again, my close friends didn't ask for details. I think they were happy to see me happy—a look I tried to portray daily to further instill the positive emotions the healer said I needed for it all to work out.

Aside from my weekly sessions, I spent my time trying to rest and turn off my brain. Half of each day I spent with Charlie, sitting in the park next to my apartment building, feeling and allowing—just as instructed—as best as I could. Most days, I wouldn't make it till the afternoon before I'd cave and spend the remaining hours researching ideas and anticipating what would come my way in February.

After one of our sessions, I complained to the healer that I couldn't sit still all day; despite her disapproval for my need to take action, she gave me the task of creating a vision board. *The last time I did an activity like this, I drew four lines on a map—and changed my entire life.*

I filled a large poster board with pictures and words all related to storytelling, creativity, acting, people I admired, a photo of Charlie, words about love and happiness, and even a cruise ship. Lastly, for shits and giggles, I added a huge picture of the mirror ball trophy from Dancing with the Stars that happened to be in the gossip magazine I was clipping from. It reminded me of my jive, and I thought it was aesthetically the perfect centerpiece on my montage. I hung my creation on the ceiling above my bed so I could stare at it at night and as I woke up each morning.

After a month of trying to trust—and boring myself out of my mind—I was rescued by the fall production at Art Sake. I dove right in and decided to both direct and act.

Being back full swing in my craft was the best kind of healing medicine. That is, until I was met with challenges both as an actor and director. My abilities didn't disappoint me; time away hadn't faded my talents. However, difficulty after difficulty kept surfacing. I pulled a muscle in my back, making the very physically demanding role I played painful to perform. As a director, the risks I took with an already politically questionable script were criticized. Despite my pride in my directorial decisions, all of it created a disconnect and an underlying feeling of anger and frustration. Just like when I'd experienced the fishbowl sensation on my first night back, I felt like

an outsider, desperately trying to reclaim her place in the theater—
but no matter how hard I tried to blend back in, I couldn't. I hated
feeling like I didn't belong in the one place I called home. I figured
it was because of all the vulnerability brought on by the extreme
uncertainty in my life, and believed that by next year's production, it
would be different.

• •

Come November, as much as I tried to trust the healer, my suppressed
fears began to surface. Each night, at 3:00 a.m., I woke with a burning
pain in my chest and couldn't breathe. Rapid thoughts would flood
in before morphing into a visual appearing before me: a frog in a pot
of water, relaxing. Unaware of the slowly increasing heat, its muscles
became paralyzed. By the time the frog realized it needed to get out
of the boiling water, it was too late. Every night I watched the frog
struggle before succumbing to its fate.

I'd turn on the light, head to the kitchen, and shake off the
haunting vision with a glass of almond milk. Then, I'd stare at my
vision board, praying for an answer. Some nights, nostalgia set in,
making me regret putting the picture of a ship on there. I loved
keeping in touch with Julie and Kel, my table and Kiki, sharing
pictures and checking in on each other, but it wasn't enough. I
needed them back. I missed them terribly. Our conversations, our
banter, our dinners. Just having them near. I'd then pray for God to
send me back in time. Just to be on the ship again for a week. Just
one week, and then I would be able to leave it behind and never wish
for it again. Regardless of what I asked for, I always concluded my
prayers endlessly swearing that *I am trusting*, repeating the words over
and over in my mind until my eyes finally closed.

The night terrors continued until a week after Thanksgiving,
when I received two calls on the same day, each with astonishing
news. Either the universe was starting to mirror my vision board, or
my healer's promise was beginning to unfold.

CHAPTER 28

The two calls came as I drove up to Atlanta to attend an acting workshop.

"This is Andrew from Holland America. I am calling about the dance competition that you won on our world cruise."

I figured he wanted to use it for a promotion or advertisement.

"You have been selected out of one hundred fifty winners from all of our 2015 cruises to be a finalist on our official Dancing with the Stars at Sea cruise in mid-January. It's week-long, it's free, and you can bring a guest. Best of all, the cast and celebrity judges from the real Dancing with the Stars will be in attendance, and you will be competing for the *real* Mirror Ball Trophy. If you accept, we will send you all the paperwork via email."

"Yes, of course I accept!" I said, stunned. I had no idea my dancing on the trip could lead to a bigger competition. And for the real mirror ball trophy? The exact one on my vision board alongside a picture of a ship? *This is no coincidence.*

I felt as if my car and I were flying. I turned on old eighties music and sang along like I was on a karaoke stage. An hour later, my phone rang—the second call.

"This is Stephanie."

"So formal," a familiar voice with a heavy Greek accent replied.

"Kiki! How are you?"

"I am good. Our ship just pulled into Fort Lauderdale to do rounds in the Caribbean. I got permission to have a guest stay with me below deck on our New Year's cruise for free. Can you come?"

It's like going back in time for a week. My table won't be there, but it's close enough. Thank you so much, God. Thank you, thank you, thank you, for answering my prayers.

After telling her yes, I hung up needing to process. I pulled off the highway at the nearest rest stop.

Was this what my Reiki healer had been talking about? Was dancing part of my way forward somehow? My excitement was overwhelming; my faith restored. *It's all going to work out.*

Once again, I found myself preparing for adventures at sea. But instead of researching ports and selling off my life, this time I was consumed by getting in shape and buying fringed dresses and fishnet stockings.

•   •

I skipped my last two December sessions with the healer so I would have spending money on both cruises. I even called and verified that my passport was cleared for travel. Hearing that the matter was permanently resolved brought tears of joy. The woman who'd stolen my identity was still at large, but I would never again be detained by Customs and treated like a criminal. For now, this was enough.

I met Kiki at a brewery near port and hugged her so tightly. It felt like we'd never parted and these last months never happened.

As we sat catching up, we took photos to send to Ken, Detta, and Pete.

"It must be hard not seeing them every day," Kiki said.

"It has been insanely hard, but I try not to think about it."

A message from Pete chimed on my phone.

"Trouble!" he wrote.

"I can still hear his heavy accent when I read his messages," I said. We both laughed.

As soon as I walked across the gangway, I felt home again. On board, even though the décor and layout were slightly different, it was like I had traveled back in time just like I'd wished. While Kiki worked during the day, I relaxed on the Promenade Deck, watching the waves as we sailed the Caribbean. My old routine couldn't help but resurface. I kept catching myself thinking I would soon need to dress for dinner with Pete, Detta, Ken, Sally, and Don. Or even head down to trivia. As much as I missed everyone, those moments were a reminder of how they still lived within my heart.

On New Year's Eve, I sat in my same spot on the Promenade Deck reflecting on the year. I thought about my Pop, whose ashes I had laid to rest in the ocean, and longed to talk to him. To ask him if I was being adventurous and daring, or stupid and foolish. I kept hoping that maybe the healer would be able to speak to him. Each week, I had waited for her to mention my Pop, but it never happened.

"There you are!" Kiki said as she walked up. "I got off early so that we can spend time together before the big bash tonight." She sat down and got under my blanket with me. "You okay?"

I sighed. "I just had a ton happen since the cruise, and I'm banking on some things panning out. It's been really hard."

"Girl, you are the last person I worry about. Nothing gets you down. You'll be fine."

I hear this so often. I know it's a compliment to how strong and capable people think I am. But it makes me feel alone and reluctant to share my struggles.

"What about you? You are dying to get off ships. Why don't you do something else. Take a chance."

"Who, me? No. I like safe," she said.

"I think you could do anything," I pushed.

"You think anything is possible. I am not like you."

"Kiki, I doubt myself. I struggle. Sometimes, I even cry in the bathtub," I confessed, trying to convince her that I bleed just the same as everyone else.

"Yeah, but it's different. You're different. Come on, let's go get ready."

I knew better than to try to explain. Instead, I got up and followed her to the cabin.

• •

The Lido Deck was covered in décor welcoming 2016. I felt sad to leave behind 2015, which would forever be stamped by my trip around the world, but was excited for what lay ahead. While the band played, I stayed in the background with Kiki and the other officers, allowing the paying guests to be the center of the dance floor. The breeze and the night sky created the perfect backdrop. As the clock counted down the last seconds of the year, Kiki ran over to me and we hugged, wishing each other a Happy New Year, but she wouldn't let go. After a minute, the awkwardness subsided, and I melted into her embrace.

"I love you so much," she said in my ear.

"I love you, too. And I believe in you."

Kiki nodded before letting go of me enough to face me. "Ya know, hugging you for the ball drop was way better than kissing a cute boy," she laughed, grabbing my hand and leading me to the dance floor.

• •

Halfway through January, my money was running out, but I fiercely held onto hope. The dance competition *had* to be the event that would create my abundance, as foretold by my Reiki healer. Maybe I would meet someone on the ship who would take interest in me or my story. So many well-known people came on this cruise for the event. The opportunities had to be endless, which made me feel anxious and pressured.

I was permitted to bring one guest for free. I couldn't ask Yanira or David; they would see right through my masked despair. So I messaged my Art Sake tribe and was thrilled that both Kristy and Amber agreed. Unable to say no to either of them, and fearful whoever came would be bored while I practiced, I said yes to both, secretly putting one of their tickets on my credit card.

The MS *Nieuw Amsterdam* had the same layout as Kiki's ship the previous week, which helped me feel slightly more settled. I quickly gave Amber and Kristy a tour before dragging them up to the Lido Deck for a cocktail.

Live music and a cool breeze filled the air. I lifted my drink and toasted our friendship. As we clinked glasses, I saw the most beautiful, tall, dark, and handsome man come into focus.

"Dear God," I whispered to the girls as I ogled him. Amber quickly elbowed me as an equally beautiful woman popped out from behind him. She gave us a stare that warned us to stay back.

"Wow, if looks could kill," Kristy said.

"That's his wife. I saw their rings," said Amber.

As we laughed and carried on, I heard a familiar sound in the distance. "Pishy, pishy?"

I must be imagining things.

"Pishy, pishy?" I heard a bit louder.

I looked up to see Eric in full uniform, holding a tray and waving with a huge smile.

I jumped up and ran over, hugging him while screaming. "I can't believe you are here! This made my day, Eric. Is Anne Marie here? Or anyone else?"

"No. They are on different ships."

"Bummer, but I am so happy you are here. Come, I want you to meet my friends."

After a brief chat, Eric returned to work, and I swore to visit him at the bar he was assigned to after dinner.

"Wow," Kristy said. "I get it now."

"Oh, me too! Seeing you and Eric really gives us a glimpse of how meaningful it all was," Amber added.

The only response I was capable of giving them in that moment was a nod before changing the subject.

That evening, we had an informational meeting with all fifteen finalists. The host and co-host of the event, a husband-and-wife couple, walked onto the stage. My heart stopped. It was the guy I'd checked out on the Lido Deck along with his wife. She looked at me and realized the same. *I am going to have to dance really well to make it to the end of this competition.*

• •

Even though my dance partner spent a day and a half yelling at me to stop leading during practice, the first of our four potential performances went smoothly. Florence Henderson, the celebrity judge for that round, showered me with compliments about my waltz. I was enamored of her spunky, easy-going demeanor. *I want to be like her.*

Between dance practices and performances, I tried to look approachable to allow the universe to work its magic. However, all I felt was absolutely invisible. And as every day passed, I became a bit more anxious.

For our second dance, my partner and I were given the samba coupled with a rather fast song—"Fireball" by Pitbull. Now, I love salsa, swing, the cha-cha, and any other dance that has more of a side-to-side type of movement, but this one had booty-pumping, and my booty does not pump. At least I'd packed a bright pink, fringed dancer's dress which looked straight out of Miami, while my partner wore all white. We certainly looked the part.

After two long days of practicing, we decided to concentrate on having fun and exciting the crowd instead of worrying about technical merit. I held my mouth open in an attempt to look sexy. But on the replay, ironically, I looked more like a bird, hungry for its next meal. At the end of our dance, my partner threw me above his shoulders for a final pose and the judges went nuts—especially Carson Kressley, who spent more time flirting with him than he did critiquing our dance.

As we waited backstage for the results, my partner was called out of the room. When he returned fifteen minutes later, he said, "You must have pissed off the gods above."

Incredulous, I listened as he explained how even though technically, we'd gotten enough votes to advance, we couldn't. The host's wife had changed the rules at the last minute, making the scores cumulative; the first night's scores were added to that night's. Since the waltz never scored as high, our combined score put us just under the cutoff for advancing to the next round.

I sat in silence and disbelief.

"Honey, we placed sixth out of fifteen, and that is something to be proud of for a non-dancer like yourself," my partner tried to console me.

I ran back to the cabin before my friends could find me, where I fell to the floor, scared. Very scared. I wanted to call the healer and demand she wave her wand, rub her crystals, even talk to the ceiling if she had to. But she needed to fix this. Then, as if a haze of fog lifted, the reality of my foolishness and utter idiocy came flooding in.

Oh, God, what have I done?

CHAPTER 29

Following the cruise, I called the healer in a fury. "Nothing happened by February like you said it would. I depleted my savings, paid you an obscene amount of money, and you lied to me."

She tried to respond, but I wouldn't let her.

"I want my money back, NOW! Every cent!" I shouted.

Her reply was cold as ice. "Stephanie, you didn't trust enough. YOU are the reason things didn't work out, and I don't offer refunds."

"Are you kidding me? MY fault because I didn't trust enough? I met with you each week, and never once did you tell me I wasn't trusting enough."

"You skipped two weeks in December, and that's when you went off track."

"Do you hear yourself?" I screamed.

"Maybe you can call family and borrow money."

"That's your suggestion? To borrow money from my family? Screw you."

I ended the call and hung my head in shame.

By the lake outside my apartment, I sat in the grass with Charlie, retracing all the steps I had taken after walking off the ship last May right to where I now was, sitting there flat broke.

Before I had the chance to wallow further, or get even angrier at myself, Charlie moved into my lap and I cuddled him tight. I took out my notebook and once again, asked myself what I needed. This time, no directives came out; rather, I wrote: *I went broke.* I shook my head at those three simple words that brought me straight back to Kel's haunting advice from our chat in The Crow's Nest.

It happens to people who aim for greatness. And what you will gain from climbing back out will be life-changing...

I hoped to God he was right about the last part.

I wished I'd gone broke because I was aiming for greatness. Instead, I'd been foolish, trusting others when I was afraid to trust myself. I dug myself a massive hole and willingly dove into it headfirst. *Now, it's time to climb out.*

Not wanting to be driven by fear, I took my notebook, closed my eyes, and replayed that entire night with Kel while taking notes.

Go big...don't play it safe...will seem like madness...won't be easy... you'll be tested...if you fall, get your ass up...keep going...

Coming off of six months of listening to someone I shouldn't have listened to, I wondered why I was, yet again, listening to the words of someone else. As much as I tried to discredit Kel, I couldn't. He wasn't out for my money. He wanted nothing in return. I knew deep down that Kel shared those words because he had been there before, and he'd recognized his own kind the minute he met me.

Kel said out loud what my soul had been screaming into a pillow my entire adult life. This whole change of heart that began after my life crumbled wasn't just about finding something I loved doing. Yes, I had an artist's soul and passionately loved my craft. But my soul was also a seeker of experience, of adventure and story. My soul begged for me to go big. To dare greatly. And I never fully let it until I boarded that ship.

An inner surge came into my bones. *I might be riding on fumes with no money in the bank, but I am not going to let this stop me.*

I doodled a big heart under Kel's words, and then leaned back and stared at the sky. Within seconds, I shot back up and wrote underneath the heart: *Wait for it.*

I knew what it meant. Wait for the heart pull. That feeling I had at Art Sake. That feeling I had when I booked the cruise. To really listen to my inner guidance.

"I'm ready when you are," I whispered.

But first, let's stop the bleeding.

I needed a job, and I needed one fast.

Like a soldier on a special ops mission, I got in my car and drove to mine and Yvonne's favorite spot, Hillstone. With six years of serving experience from my teenage years, I had a job there waiting tables within three days.

• •

Hillstone felt like penance. I brought in just enough income to make ends meet, but not enough for the luxury of buying wine, or socializing and numbing out. I had to sit in my feelings of embarrassment and shame every night while icing my left shoulder, which throbbed from carrying heavy plates for seven hours straight.

Sometimes old coworkers would come in for lunch. I would see the look of shock on their faces quickly followed by a pity smile. Meanwhile I'd flash them a wide grin and wave before proceeding to move robotically around the restaurant, completing my tasks despite their stares. Even the healer dined one evening with her husband. When our eyes met she didn't react, but nicely introduced me before commenting on how it must be so fun working in such a beautiful restaurant with such a wonderful view of the lake. A part of me wanted to slap her, but instead, I owned my part in it. I smiled, nodded, and told them both to enjoy their meal before walking away to tend to my tables.

Of it all, the only part that truly stung was having my vantage point as an employee slowly ruin the backyard oasis where I'd always loved lounging with Yvonne.

On the other hand, the job did allow me to create stability, which was the first step in climbing out of the hole I had dug. I accepted my new life while waiting for the next adventure, and the free mental space helped me navigate self-forgiveness. At peace, I knew that soon enough the fire within me would return. I just didn't expect an extra shift I picked up one Friday to be the start of it.

That night, out of the corner of my eye, I saw a man in a light pink polo shirt and tan shorts enter with two kids. He glanced at me with a look of surprise, then sympathy for what he knew would happen next. As Caroline walked in behind him, I fled.

My tears made tracks down my cheeks in the frigid air of the walk-in freezer. I leaned my head back, trying to control my breathing as the door swung open. Danny, a fellow server, entered and handed me two napkins. "You okay?"

"My best...ex-best friend is here with her family. I can't go out there. If they sit in my station, please take the table. I beg you."

"I got you. I'll check on your tables. Take all the time you need, okay?" He squeezed my shoulder and left. Coldness took over not only my skin, but my heart.

I will not let her send me back to crying in the tub! It doesn't matter what she thinks of me. If I wronged her, she owed me a conversation. She isn't going to make me feel like I did last summer. Not today. Oh, no, no, no.

I wiped my tears, stood up straight, broadened my shoulders, and arranged my face into an emotionless mask. *I am going to look that bitch square in the eye every time I walk past her.*

After my shift, nothing could extinguish the fire in the pit of my stomach.

"And she refused to make eye contact?" David asked as he stood in my kitchen plating the Moe's he'd picked up on the way over.

"I walked past her three times, and she wouldn't."

I sat on the floor still in my work uniform, leaning up against my couch and petting Charlie.

"But *you* did, and that's what matters."

"Hell yeah, it matters. I'm done being beaten down. Seeing her ignited something within. I can't explain how or why, but I feel ready."

David sat down next to me. "I haven't asked why you are waiting tables. I don't need to know. I love you so much no matter what you do with your life."

"Oh, I know…" I tried to get up to go eat. He stopped me and looked me dead in the eye.

"Stephanie, listen to me. I have always known you as a risk-taker. The girl who challenges the norm. Who makes people think. Even when you direct plays, you make choices no one else would make. You aren't afraid to be bold, to be unconventional in your art and in life. Aside from Caroline's bullshit, I don't know what has happened, but I haven't seen *that* Stephanie since you returned."

"Yeah, I lost her there for a while, but David, I swear she's back."

"Good, get her back."

"I said she's back."

"And I have your back."

"I hate you." I lightly punched his arm.

"No you don't. Suck it up and find her."

"DAVID! Ugh. She's found!" I said as he laughed. He knew exactly how to diffuse a moment.

· ·

I ripped down the vision board above my bed and tore it to pieces, no longer wanting to be influenced or limited by the images I had cut from magazines. I wanted to reactivate my creative curiosity, so I began meditating and journaling, trying to quiet my mind. To allow myself the chance to hear my own inner compass. The simple answer was to get an agent and audition, but the State of Florida had lost tax incentives for commercials and films, which made auditions scarce. Yvonne's production wasn't happening until the fall. So, I searched for local plays and film screenings and watched the creative works of others for inspiration.

The next weekend, Lindsi from my Art Sake tribe and I went to see an afternoon screening at The Enzian, a venue that showed low budget independent films. After the film, the director got onstage to answer questions from the audience. I felt inspired, captivated. Watching him up there sparked my curiosity.

Following the show we sat at their outside restaurant. Lindsi was talking about politics; I began to stare off into the distance.

"You okay?" she asked, interrupting her rant about the candidates running for the 2016 presidency.

"Do I look like a cross between Amy Poehler and Tina Fey? People tell me that all the time."

"Um, yes, you do. It's actually kinda crazy. Why?"

"Maybe I can be their half-sister in the sequel to their movie, *Sisters*," I blurted out, not fully realizing what I was saying.

"Well, that came out of nowhere. You looked possessed!" Lindsi said.

She was right. It felt like that idea came through me, not from me. "I know. It just popped out."

"It was a little scary," she said laughing. "Do you even know the storyline?"

"No, but Lindsi, I've been asking for a creative outlet. For something to be excited about. Maybe it's filmmaking. Maybe I can make a fun, short film. Learn how to get into film festivals. Start super small. But a sequel to *Sisters* could be a fun start and a great learning opportunity. It would just be a fan film. The concept would be funny, wouldn't it?"

I looked at my phone to see where the movie might still be playing. "It's only at the dollar theater downtown. The next showing starts in an hour. Let's get the check."

Lindsi sat still, looking stunned.

"Want to come with me?" I asked.

"No, girl, this is all you."

I drove to the theater, thrilled that the feeling I'd had when I drew that black line on a map had returned. My brain kicked in, reminding me I would have so much to learn in filmmaking, but the first step was always to find a good storyline. This could be it. First, though, I needed a sign.

With my purchased ticket and soda in hand, I entered an empty theater. I would be the only one watching, which made the experience feel intimate.

Within fifteen minutes of the movie's beginning, my jaw dropped. The entire movie was set in Orlando…just down the street from where I was sitting. *My sign.*

I left the theater feeling a sliver of hope. Maybe this was a small breadcrumb toward a new career path hidden under the disguise of a fun creative outlet. Maybe it wasn't. What I did know was for the first time since I walked off the ship, I felt alive again.

CHAPTER 30

Yvonne sat relaxed out back at Hillstone while I couldn't help but notice plates that needed to be cleared. I had just told her about my new creative project, and she was pondering it in silence.

"Well, your idea is pretty funny," she finally said, then took a sip of wine before lighting a cigarette.

"I love theater, but I want to see how this feels."

"When are you going to film it?" she asked.

"I have to save up some money first. But I'm writing the synopsis now, and having a blast."

"If you need a backup idea, I'll lend you the theater if you want to put on a play. Would that fulfill you a bit while you adjust to being back?" she asked.

"Wow! Yvonne, thank you," I said as the server arrived, setting down our usual smoked salmon and some grilled artichokes. "Can I think about it?"

• •

Yvonne praised my abilities as an actress and director, but she was also one of my closest friends. I knew this offer was her way of giving me options, but her suggestion made me insecure, and I wondered if I was only good enough within the walls of Art Sake. If that was the case, I wanted to know now so I could redirect my time and energy.

I signed up for a weekly class under the direction of a well-respected acting coach, Rus Blackwell. He was the perfect mix of madness and logic, who always emphasized that anyone could be successful, but that their definition of success might change. His opinion was unapologetically honest, and exactly what I was looking for.

One night after class, he asked me to stay behind.

"I think you have a very strong instrument," he said.

"Thank you," I replied, releasing the breath I'd been holding.

"Have you ever heard of Stella Adler, the acting school in New York City? They have a full-time summer conservatory that I think would benefit you."

"You mean, go to New York and study?" I asked.

"I know it's a long shot, but it's worth looking into if you can make it work."

I agreed to check it out, not letting on that there was no way I could go.

After walking Charlie that night, I opened my laptop and looked over Stella Adler's program. My heart raced, begging me to go, while my brain reminded me I couldn't afford to. After some thought, I realized that Stella Adler's acceptance letter alone would offer me the validation I sought. I applied.

Days later, I received a call from a woman who had boarded the MS *Amsterdam* to visit an officer. During the one afternoon I'd spent with her on the Lido Deck, I managed to tell her some of my story; fascinated by it, she asked to keep in touch.

Through her awkward small talk, I could tell she wanted something, and after ten minutes, she finally came out with it.

"I am hosting my first women's conference at the end of this month. It's 'shero' themed, and everyone attending is an entrepreneur or soon to be. I know it's last minute, but could you come?"

"Linda, thanks, but attending a conference isn't a priority for me right now. I have a lot going on."

"I don't want you to attend. I was hoping you would speak at it. Just a short motivational speech. Something that would inspire all the risk-takers in the room. You have a great story and the perfect energy for it."

The idea sounded so fun and right up my alley, I was dying to say yes. I just didn't think I could swing it.

"Where is it taking place?" I hoped she would say the North Pole, which would justify my decline.

"New York City." She stayed silent to let me think, a sales tactic I knew all too well from selling homes.

"It might be too expensive to justify, especially so last minute," I said, trying to sound more like the powerhouse she'd met on board than a financially busted restaurant server.

"Aside from dinner that evening, your expenses will be covered."

Every extra penny was being saved for my film. Speaking at this event would delay my efforts a bit, but something about going felt so right. I couldn't bring myself to say no.

A few weeks later, I walked into Linda's conference in New York City just as it was about to start. People were busy chatting and getting seated. The maroon-and-navy plaid suit I had worn to the mingling event the night before apparently hadn't made enough of a statement because today, no one seemed to recognize me, except a woman about my age named Celeste. She was sitting toward the front, next to an empty chair, and motioned for me to sit next to her.

Celeste was also starting a series of conferences herself. I was intimidated by her hard New York energy and bright red hair. But her warm smile canceled out my trepidation.

"The speakers seem super nervous to get onstage," Celeste whispered.

"I noticed that myself. Their body language is so tense." The first speaker got up and nervously announced she wanted to take off her heels and talk barefoot.

"That's odd." Celeste's voice had a distinctly judgmental tone.

"She's just trying to ground herself and feel more approachable," I replied as I further watched the speaker struggle to connect with the audience.

"Are you speaking?"

"Yeah, a motivational speech," I whispered.

"On what topic?" Celeste asked.

"Don't know. Haven't written it yet."

The look of shock on her face made me laugh a bit too loudly, and I covered my mouth.

The barefoot speaker finished her section on marketing small businesses, giving us an hour break for lunch. I picked up my purse and looked at Celeste.

"Since it's 'shero' themed, I brought an old Halloween costume." I pulled out a shirt with a silk-screened Superwoman torso on it and a red cape hanging off the back of the shirt.

"Stop it! You aren't going to wear that, are you?"

"Not sure." I shrugged.

We finished lunch at one, which gave me one hour until taking the stage. I found an extra pen and immediately began scribbling out a list on my napkin. Seven in total. There, I had it. "The Seven Steps to Taking a Leap" was born. After a day of hearing constant foul language, I added a note at the bottom: "use the f-word." I popped into the bathroom and put on the Superwoman shirt under my sweater and tucked the end of the cape down the back of my pants, just in case I decided to use it.

My name was announced and I walked up onstage. I smiled at the speaker sitting in the audience who had taken off her shoes.

Dramatically, I took off my heels while cracking a funny joke and watched her shoulders relax as giggles filled the room.

I spoke freely, with my list on the napkin serving as guideposts. I knew I was walking around the stage. I knew I was using my entire body. I knew people were laughing and cheering, but the rest was a blur. At the end, I stood there in my Superwoman shirt and cape to a roaring applause.

Afterward, I was no longer a random person lost in the sea of women entrepreneurs. I was "that girl with the cape who gave a killer motivational speech." After the event, people approached me, telling me how ignited they felt by my words. Others expressed how they could never be that bold to get up onstage and say what I said, but that they loved every minute of it.

I enjoyed the feedback, but wasn't looking for acceptance, to fit in, or to impress. I wanted to get back into my power. To be that unstoppable version of myself that I'd been hell-bent on finding again. I found her on a stage sharing my story about the last-minute sale of my home. It wasn't just a speech. It was a catapult, flinging me back into the shoes of that girl who dared and won.

As I walked out the front door with a group for dinner, a woman I'd noticed earlier approached me. She had short blond hair, bright pink lipstick, and was standing in the back with a pissed-off look on her face.

"Ya know, I normally don't like people like you, but for some reason, I like you," she said in a heavy Staten Island accent.

Is that a compliment?

"Thanks?" I said.

"So you're workin' on a short film about Tina Fey's recent movie?"

Wait—I mentioned that? I told my idea to a roomful of how many people? Dammit, I should not have winged that speech.

"I sure am," I replied.

"I've done some work in the film industry. I know her people."

"Whose people?"

She rolled her eyes and sighed. "Tina Fey. Who else?"

"Dude, no way!"

"Dude? You sound so Florida. Listen. You write a pitch script. Okay? Film it. Can you make that happen?"

"Yes. That was my plan." I was trying to act more certain than I was.

"Good. My name is Lou. Here's my card. Get it to me ASAP, and I will send it to her rep."

I walked away in shock.

Midflight back to Florida, I sat laughing at how the entire weekend was so random, from my last-minute speech getting rave reviews, to the other speakers telling me I belong in New York, even down to the free drinks the hotel gave me. I'd been so mentally tired. I needed some fresh wind in my sails—and every aspect of this trip gave me exactly that.

I thought about Lou's offer. I tried to persuade myself that this was a coincidence but couldn't. Between that and Stella Adler, it all felt so exciting, But, at the same time, logic was right there, reminding me I was too broke to say yes, which made it all feel like one big taunt.

I looked up at the ceiling of the plane in surrender and silently spoke. *Universe: I need one more gigantic sign, and I will agree to consider moving to New York. But just consider it. Nothing more. And here's your deadline: tonight, before I lay my head down on my pillow. I am daring you to dare me.*

Arriving home, I unpacked my bag and cuddled with Charlie in front of the TV. It was early afternoon, but the heavy rain made it look like night. I put on *Pride and Prejudice* and drifted off to sleep. When I awoke from my nap I peeked at my phone and noticed I had a new email—from Stella Adler. I had been accepted into their summer conservatory from June through August.

The universe had doubled down and dared me back.

CHAPTER 31

I was cooking with gas but had no burgers. I would have to find a way to produce a short film, find the money to pay for Stella Adler, and move to New York City for three months. *Do I take the chance and just say yes? Nope, not this time.* I refused to commit to any of it before knowing in advance how I would pay for it.

The following week, Celeste reached out to catch up. She really liked my speech, she told me, and was hoping I could give her some advice on how to incorporate courage and creativity into her conferences.

Her request began a series of phone calls between us, sparking frequent brainstorming sessions that lasted hours. I felt seen, empowered. I was helping her create something amazing.

By the end of April, just as I had to tell Stella Adler that I would not be attending, Celeste dropped a bomb. "Come to New York City this summer and work alongside me. Speak at my events about creativity and taking leaps. The first one is the second week of June, so the timing is perfect."

She shared her plans for the summer—independent workshops and weekend conferences—and all the ways I could be involved. My lease was up at the end of May, making it all fit together so perfectly, even if it was a bit too far-fetched financially. I told Celeste I would think about it.

Over the next week, I avoided Celeste like the plague. Something in my heart whispered to wait to tell her no. That weekend, after I finished my lunch shift, I got into my car and turned on my phone to see a missed call from a friend I hadn't heard from in a while. She wanted to submit my name as her real estate agent on the purchase of a home. I wouldn't have to do anything but give half of the commission back to her. My cut would be thirty-two hundred dollars—the exact cost of tuition at Stella Adler. Or, the money could go into savings and I could breathe again. Either way, I agreed, thankful for the easy money.

The next day, I called Celeste to decline her offer.

"Celeste, I would love to do this, but to be honest, I can't afford it. I'm sorry, but I can teach whoever you do find to help you."

She stayed silent for a second.

"Ya know, I wondered about your situation since you mentioned you were waiting tables. Listen, I want you here. I have an apartment in Queens with an extra bedroom that has your name on it. For free, all summer while you study and work with me."

I paused. "I appreciate your offer. But your business is new and a bit of a gamble. I don't have extra money to float myself in case things go south and you aren't able to pay me. Again, it sounds great, but I'm looking for low-risk right now. I'm sorry, but I can't."

"I have invested everything I have into my workshops. I am all in, and I am not going to let them fail. Trust me."

The chance to give more talks and expand my acting abilities. It was everything my heart wanted. I had asked the universe for the means, and that's exactly what Celeste had just presented. I stayed quiet for a second, lost in my thoughts.

"Listen, money is your only hang-up here, right? Making money is the easy part."

In that instant, she took my biggest fear and reduced it to the ridiculous. I wanted to say yes so badly. But I held back for just a minute more, savoring my peaceful life, playing it safe as a poor server who just wanted to make a film.

"Have a little faith, and just get your ass up here," she said.

Without another thought, I shouted, "Okay, I'll do it!"

• •

In thirty days, I was moving to The Big Apple for the summer. Time to act quickly—not only because I had a short time to arrange everything, but because if I slowed down, I might have gotten too scared to keep going.

I broke the news first to my mom and stepdad. Surprisingly, they thought it a great opportunity and offered to watch Charlie.

Kristy, my Art Sake friend who had joined me on the cruise, lived in my apartment complex and gifted me her unused storage unit just down the hall. The only problem was that it wouldn't hold all my stuff. The idea of selling my belongings and packing up my life again, just one year after the first time, felt exhausting. But I loved how things were coming together so perfectly.

Now came the hard part. Yvonne and I met at Hillstone for our smoked salmon and wine.

"Stella Adler is a great school," she said in a serious tone.

"What are you not saying?"

"I feel like you are running away. Your home is here with your tribe."

"I'm not running away. I am running toward something. Following signs. Listening to my inner compass. I can't ignore that, Yvonne. If I did, what good would I be? Things wouldn't be the same.

I wouldn't be the same. Of all people, I'd expect you to know that," I said, almost wasting my breath. My dear, stubborn Yvonne would never admit I had a point.

"Just know you will be missed."

I had to stand firm on how I felt, but I also took a moment and assured her that Art Sake *was* my home. My refuge. I was a leader there. I had my picture on the wall of those who contributed immensely to the success and mission of Art Sake. While having a picture on a wall might not mean much from a literal standpoint, for me, it confirmed that I was as important to the theater as the theater was to me.

The next night, I sat with David, Yanira, Angela, and a few other close acting friends at dinner. Out of nowhere, my plans spilled out of my mouth like water.

"I'm moving to New York City for three months; can someone please pass the bread?"

Silence.

No one responded. They were watching David. I looked over; his face was an expressionless stone structure. But his eyes were glassy, and that told me everything. I should have pulled him aside to tell him first.

David left the table and walked outside, while I went straight to the bathroom to cry. I felt like my life had become a double-edged sword. I was tired of leaving the people who meant the most to me, but I knew that not moving forward on this crazy path would feel like a slow death. I would be gone for only three months, but I had lost friends after being gone for four. I didn't have the strength to lose anyone else. I'd made my peace with those who walked away, because those had been toxic relationships. These friendships were not. Jeopardizing my bond with Yanira, David, Yvonne, Angela, and my Art Sake tribe would kill me. Absolutely kill me.

I walked outside. David's eyes were as red and puffy as mine. I knew I had to keep my distance. I was about to get my ass handed to me, and I deserved it. Out of the corner of my eye, I could see everyone at our table staring out the window.

"You blindsided me at dinner. In front of everybody! Don't I mean more to you than that?" he said in a fury.

"I know. I was a coward. I am so sorry."

"Damn it, Stephanie, we are better than this."

"David, I am sorry. I'm going to miss you so much. Everything happened so fast. Please forgive me."

"I can't keep up with all your changes and surprises. It's nonstop and so secretive."

"David, I'm doing the best I can right now."

He hugged me, but I didn't feel his warmth. "I'll be back in ninety days," I whispered.

David was content with his community and a consistent life, as he put it. He wanted to help run Art Sake and produce Play de Luna every fall. He had a stable job and home he owned, just as he preferred. He knew I needed to go, and after his sadness dissipated somewhat, he believed in me enough for both of us—something I greatly needed. He put his hand on my back and we walked inside. Thankfully, after what they just witnessed, the others rallied, offering their full-fledged support for my endeavors.

• •

By the time I had locations, actors, props, and crew ready for filming, I was down to the wire. My friends came forward like an army ready for battle. They helped write the script and find filming locations, and all agreed to act in it. Even Yanira, who knew nothing about films, wanted to help.

We scheduled our "ninja filmmaking" for my last three days in Orlando. We had no time for anything to go wrong. So, when an actor I didn't know well showed up and decided he wanted his character to be homeless—even though the script said his role was "a put-together grandpa-like figure"—I had to roll with it. I started to feel like I was filming a promo for the circus. It didn't matter. I felt loved, supported, and immensely grateful for the committed and talented friends who surrounded me.

As we wrapped filming, I left the footage in the hands of the editor, who told me my film would be ready in July. I went home to finalize my packing. It was my last night in the apartment. Everything except my bed had been either sold or moved into the storage unit. I had two suitcases, a carry-on bag of faith, and a few hundred dollars ready to make the way to New York. As much as I had fallen down, and as foolish as I appeared, when I slowed my breathing, I was able to feel grateful and lucky for what was ahead.

Yanira, Angela, and David came over to say goodbye with a pizza in hand. Their farewell was cheerful and reassuring, which I needed. They didn't want my excitement to turn to tears, so they kept it brief and left me with my pizza, Charlie, and one small table lamp, now on the floor, lighting the empty living room.

• •

My eyes opened as soon as the sun started to rise. The sky was orange and red. *I can't remember the last time I saw the sunrise.* I slowly rose, savoring my last day in Orlando. My Art Sake friend, Jason, arrived to help me move my bed. He suggested that we do it wearing ski masks and see if the neighbors would call the police. His joke, while humorous, made me think of the burglary and how many things had changed since that day. As he slowly slid my mattress down the hall on a piece of plastic, with me lying on it, trying to keep it in a taco formation, I laughed harder than I had in ages. *This is a good day. Time to grab Charlie and head to my mom's. I am ready to go to New York.*

That afternoon, my mother drove us to say hello to my grandma at the nearby assisted living facility, where she gave us some time alone together. I sat down and could tell right away that Grandma Margherita had something up her sleeve.

"Esteffy, I gotta surprise. It's happy hour. In da fridgadaire. Vino. Shhhh! No tella anyone," she said with a finger over her lips.

I knew she couldn't drink with her meds, but I played along and crept to her tiny fridge. Opening it, I found Welch's grape juice and water and nothing more. "Granny, there isn't any wine in the fridge."

"The Welch-a-wine," she replied.

Smiling, I poured two glasses of grape juice and returned to her little sitting area. She had a mischievous look in her eye as if we were two kids who'd snuck liquor out of our parents' cabinet.

"I'm going to New York City, Grandma. To study. I'll be gone all summer. I will miss you."

"You be-a careful. No talka to strange-a-men."

"Grandma, I know you won't relax until I'm married. But I promise you, I'll be okay. Trust me." I grabbed her hand.

"I trusta you." She smiled.

"Remember how you helped me go to Italy? To see Zia and Zio?"

"Yes. You needa go to Italy more."

"Yes, Grandma. You are right. But you see, I like to go places. So, tomorrow I am going to New York City. Then I will think about taking another trip to Italy, okay?"

"Okay, Esteffy. You go. But first, pour me-a some more," she said, laughing.

Two rounds of grape juice later, my mom tapped on the door, indicating it was time to head out. I hugged my grandmother tightly and whispered, "Thank you for the wine. I love our happy hours, and I love you."

She grabbed my cheeks with both of her hands and kissed me, making a loud "muah!" with her voice.

As I got out of the car at the airport, my mom handed me twenty dollars. "I love you. I believe in you. But I also know you hate to fly. Go buy a glass of wine on me," she said, hugging me.

"I love you too, Mom. And thank you for taking care of Charlie."

After a brief cry in the airport bathroom, I made my way through security. The man waving people through the metal detector took one look at me and chuckled. "Let me guess, New York."

"What gave it away?" I asked.

"Everything, sweetheart." His words helped settle my nerves.

I took a seat at the Columbia restaurant bar and ordered the glass of wine my mom treated me to. I looked at pictures of Charlie on my phone, trying not to think of him shaking when I had to say goodbye this morning as if he knew it would be for a while. Guilt set in as a man sat down two stools away. "What are you looking at?" he asked. He was dressed as if he were ready to perform in a cover band at the local dive bar.

"Just pictures of my dog." I looked back down at my phone.

"Where you headed?"

"I'm going to study acting in New York City," I replied.

"I'm not surprised."

"Why is that?"

"You seem different," he said.

"That sounds like a horrible pickup line. You should work on that a bit," I replied, annoyed.

Laughing, he threw down some cash for both of our drinks and walked over to me. I wanted to be scared, but his facial expression was soft enough to disarm me.

"I was Prince's guitarist for many years. I don't need pickup lines. And I also know a badass when I see one. So, good luck to you, and keep going." He patted me on the shoulder and kept walking.

I had no idea if what he claimed was true, but the words *keep going* didn't feel like a coincidence. Nevertheless, once settled on the plane, I began to find my odd airport experience sweet. When mountain biking, the stronger riders would ride up behind those struggling, and give them a strong push on the back. When that happened to me, it was such a feeling of relief for my burning muscles. My day in the airport felt just like that push.

I pulled out my phone to tell my mom about it, and saw that she had sent a video. I almost saved it for when I landed, but quickly watched it before I had to put my phone away. It was my grandma. She was standing up holding her walker and looking straight into the lens. My heart melted as I heard her words.

"Esteffy. It's Gramma. You gonna make it. Keepa goin, Esteffy. Keepa goin. You gonna make it. Gramma knows."

CHAPTER 32

The taxi drove through the city streets toward the southern tip of Manhattan, a place I had never seen. I hung out the window like an excited dog, breathing it all in, straining to catch every detail on each building, the clothing the people were wearing, the names of all the stores and restaurants. To memorize every detail.

Celeste had instructed me to meet her at a place called The Dead Rabbit. I noticed her sitting at the bar and waved, then ran over with my two orange and gray suitcases in tow. She met my excitement with a stoic embrace, but her wide smile equaled mine.

"Is that a Bon Jovi shirt you have on?" she asked.

"Yeah, they're one of my faves," I said proudly, unsure of her tone.

The server set down the dirty martini Celeste had ordered for me.

"Cheers, welcome to New York!" she said as I took my first sip. My face puckered.

"Is something wrong?" she asked.

"I never had a dirty martini before. It tastes like the ocean."

"Never mind. I'll drink it. Excuse me, can you get her something fruity?"

"Actually, I'll take a glass of red wine, please."

I watched as Celeste made conversation with two men in suits sitting to her left. After a few minutes, she introduced me and I shook their hands, searching for a topic of small talk. "Looks like you just got off work. What do you gentlemen do?"

Celeste stiffened. "They work in finance," she said, then promptly steered the conversation back to the topic of her endeavors. The second they were out of earshot, she whispered, "In the city, it's considered rude to ask people what they do."

"Oh, I am so sorry," I said, beyond embarrassed.

Deciding it was safer to say as little as possible, I sipped my wine and smiled. Right as I was about to suggest that we head out, a man walked up and hugged Celeste. It was clear they were quite close.

"Stephanie, meet Rick. He owns the apartment we're staying in."

"So, you're Celeste's landlord, I take it?" I hoped the question was socially appropriate.

"No," Celeste said, "I don't live in the other apartment anymore. I told you that." She sounded annoyed.

No, she didn't tell me.

"Rick is letting us stay with him."

What the hell is going on?

Fifteen minutes later, I was standing in Rick's one-bedroom apartment on the thirtieth floor of a doorman building in downtown Manhattan. Celeste informed me the two of us would be sleeping on the futon in Rick's one-hundred-square-foot living room.

That night, unable to sleep, I stared at the wall. The heat from Celeste's body radiated on my back. I wanted to remove the covers and cool myself off, but didn't dare move lest I wake her. My thoughts raced.

I would never have come if I knew I'd be sleeping back-to-back on a futon in a stranger's apartment while he's still living here. But now that

I'm doing exactly that, I still would rather be here than give up. I didn't come this far to only get this far. I'll figure out a way forward. It's more so food I'm worried about. I can't just go cook in his kitchen or store stuff in his fridge. Eating out every day, my money will be gone in a week. Is this really the setup for the whole summer? It can't be. Maybe this is just temporary. Maybe she has a plan. Don't ask too many questions. Just get some sleep. Tomorrow will bring some clarity.

The minute I felt Celeste move at 7:00 a.m., I vacated the futon and asked permission to shower. She granted my request as if she'd been expecting it. Shortly after I was done, Celeste disappeared into the bathroom, and I seized the chance to reorganize my one suitcase so that I could easily live out of it. An hour later, she came back out with a towel on her head.

"Hey, I am in the thick of it with the conference. So, I can't spend time with you today."

"That's okay. I don't need a sitter."

"Have you done your presentation and curriculum?" she asked. "Just making sure you weren't writing it last minute on a napkin."

"Nope. It's all set." I chuckled. "I'm going to head out and spend the day getting my bearings. That way, you have your space."

"Thank you." She sat down in front of her computer with a cup of coffee, ending any further acknowledgment of my presence. I wanted so badly to partake in some coffee, but thought it best to just leave.

Undeterred, I felt secretly happy to have time alone to process everything. I rode the elevator to the lobby. As I reached for the door handle to exit the building, a man in uniform stopped me. "I'm sorry. Am I not allowed to be here?" I said anxiously.

The man grabbed the door handle for me. "Just doing my job," he said with a smile as he opened the door. "Have a great day, miss."

"You too, sir," I said, feeling stupid that I didn't know the basic duties of a doorman.

I turned north and started walking slowly up the West Side. I made it all the way to Central Park and found a spot to sit, enjoying how much cooler the weather was compared to Florida. Despite the tiny housing hiccup, I felt so good about life. This day was a perfect start in getting to know New York City. Stella Adler began in three days, and I couldn't be more excited.

While I was ordering some McDonald's fries for an early dinner, a man walked in wearing pink tights and a black leotard, then plugged in his CD player and began to practice ballet in the middle of the dining room. The entire place carried on as if he weren't there. I stared, mesmerized, feeling like this was my first true glimpse of New York City.

I headed back to find Celeste exactly as I had left her. "I don't want to bother you, but how can I help?" I asked.

"I got it. I just need some space."

"No problem. I'm here if you need me. Would it bother you if I read on the couch?" I asked.

She looked at me as if I were deliberately rubbing my free time in her face. Quickly I clarified. "I'm just asking in case you'd rather I leave. Again, I'm here to help."

"No. It's fine. Go ahead. Thanks for asking." She turned back to her computer.

I tried to read but couldn't help watching her pounding her keyboard and then putting her face right up to the screen as if she needed reading glasses. I leaned over, trying to get a glimpse without being obvious, but failed. *What on earth is she doing?*

The next morning played out the same as the previous day. I walked to Washington Square Park and sat, watching the dogs and their people everywhere, which made me miss Charlie. I thought about Celeste's weird behavior and couldn't escape the feeling that something was terribly wrong. I stood up and headed straight toward the apartment. Whatever it was, I was going to fix it.

"Hey," I said as I walked in to see her head down in her computer. "Can we talk for five minutes?"

"Sure." She turned around.

"What's going on? Talk to me. I know you don't want my help, but I can tell you are stressed about something."

She stared at me for a second, then coldly said, "I only sold two tickets to the conference."

I struggled to suppress both a panic attack and the strong urge to punch her lights out. The conference was scheduled for the following weekend.

"What can we do? Can we make flyers? Can I make some calls?" I was surprisingly calm.

"I just need to keep at what I'm doing," she said.

I was dying to ask what that entailed, but refrained. Instead I sat on the couch, taking deep breath after deep breath.

That night I didn't sleep a wink. Celeste, after three hours of pounding keys, sighing, cursing under her breath, and then clicking a million buttons with her mouse, had stood up and announced she was leaving to go on a date.

Oh my God, I need a job, and I need one fast.

The next morning, I didn't leave the apartment. After wasting my breath asking what I could do to help, I parked myself on the couch with my computer and spent the day looking at jobs and potential room rentals. In the late afternoon, I headed out to find something cheap to eat and popped into some restaurants, asking if they were hiring. As productive as I tried to be, I ended the day with no backup plan.

With forty hours of schooling a week, a day job was not an option. I still believed in working with Celeste, even if the first conference was going to be a flop. I didn't want to desert her; I just needed income. I tried not to feel angry, but staying positive was a struggle. *How could everything have lined up for me so perfectly, and then this happens? Am I being tested?*

The awkwardness of the situation and my growing anxiety made time crawl. A hundred years later, Monday morning finally arrived. My first day at Stella Adler.

"Hey," I told Celeste, "I get out early at one o'clock today. If you want, we can go pass out flyers or go to some businesses together. Just text me and let me know."

"Uh-huh," she answered automatically, barely looking up as I walked out the door.

• •

Even with six years of acting training under my belt, starting a new school in a major city felt daunting. *I need something to go right. Something to be positive.* Our first day lacked any kind of performance, but after meeting my ten teachers and sixteen classmates, I felt fantastic. One facet of my time in New York City was going to be successful, a lifeline I needed.

I got out of school promptly at one o'clock with no calls or texts from Celeste. I walked around the Midtown area, a bustling place to hand out flyers, in case she called. After an hour of not hearing from her, I eventually wandered into a shoe store, remembering the days when I could afford to shop for myself. My phone rang.

"Where are you?" Celeste asked coldly.

"I'm standing in a shoe store but am ready when you are."

"Oh, must be nice to be shopping."

"I've been waiting for you to call, Celeste."

"What, and you couldn't have called me? You don't really want to help. It's so rude and inconsiderate with all that I have done for you."

She hung up.

I stood, stunned. I wanted to call her back and try to explain, but I believed it best to back off and wait until it blew over.

I needed to sit. I walked toward our apartment building and found a park bench, a little off to the side of the main hustle, under a tree hanging over the bench like an umbrella. I lay down with my head on my book bag and stared up at the leaves. Closed my eyes. Tried to imagine being back on the ship, sitting on the deck watching the waves. Tried to imagine my Pop there with me. I bet he'd say, "Peanut, this is just an adventure in disguise." I drifted off.

Two hours later I woke up, shocked that I had passed out that long despite the city noises. I had missed a few texts from Celeste asking where I was, which frightened me. Quickly I returned to the apartment, where I was greeted by her ice-cold demeanor. She said nothing as I walked past her and sat on the futon. I wanted to clear up the misunderstanding, but I also had to be careful with my words. I believed one wrong step would set her off.

"Hey, Celeste, I think there has been a misunderstanding, and maybe if we both stepped back and shared our points of view, we'll understand things better, resolve this, and move forward," I said.

She sprang out of her seat so fast her chair fell over. I blinked to find her face three inches from mine. "There is no misunderstanding. You are selfish and inconsiderate. I haven't been able to function these last five days with your toxic energy," she screamed. Spit flew out of her mouth with each syllable, landing on my face.

Every time I opened my mouth, her hand came down over my face, touching my nose, stopping me so that she could continue. The forty-five seconds of her verbal assault felt like thirty minutes. When she finished she walked back, picked up the chair, and sat down at the table like nothing had happened, then resumed pounding her computer keys.

Incapable of forming a single thought, I sat there like a statue, staring at the dark TV screen, waiting for the saliva to dry.

CHAPTER 33

I arrived and checked into the hotel to find the room I was sharing with another speaker wasn't ready, so I made my way to their solarium and sunk into a cushiony couch. I didn't realize I had nodded off until I felt a sharp, painful nudge to my shoulder.

"Sleeping in the solarium, huh? I wish I could take a nap," Celeste said condescendingly.

"Celeste, why are you treating me like this?"

"Treating you how?" She gritted her teeth.

I tried to speak but only managed to utter the word "I" before she cut me off.

"Don't you dare say a word. You don't have the authority to speak to me," she yelled and then stormed off. On the verge of tears, I made my way to the rooftop, where I called David.

"Hey, is everything okay?" he asked.

"Am I a horrible, selfish person?"

David tried not to laugh, but couldn't help it, and his giggle was a soothing, welcome relief. While he loved me unconditionally,

I knew he would also shoot me straight. "Stephanie. You pander and placate to a fault. If anything, you need to be more selfish."

I gave him a rundown of the week's events. When I got to the part with Celeste spitting in my face, he couldn't contain his shock.

"What did you do?"

"Well, the next night, Nick, an old friend who lives an hour north of the city, came to take me out for a bite and welcome me to New York. I invited her as a peace offering and tried to apologize, but it just sparked more of an attack on her end. Well, that is, until Nick arrived. She became this sweet angel laughing at all my jokes as if nothing ever happened between us. I was stunned. I think she wanted me to put in a good word for her because she has been really nice to me all week, until just now. It's like a switch flips."

"What. A. Bitch," was all he could say.

I hung my head in disbelief. "David, it's as if all the critical friends I've gotten rid of have reemerged, morphing into one person," I concluded.

"You always figure out something. But don't put up with her. Deliver your end of the deal for this event, and then come up with a plan. Think outside of the box, Stephanie. You are good at that. You've got this. If you get stuck, call."

I was thankful for his support, but I'd also left out some vital information. David had no idea that I was out of money, or else he would have boarded a plane to New York to come rescue me.

For a while I sat on the roof, then decided that no matter what happened, I had a presentation on creativity to give, and I was going to put a smile on my face and make it happen. I would deliver my end of the deal, and then when the event was over, we could work out an agreement that would give me a little time to figure out a solution for myself.

Onstage I gave it my all in front of our two attendees, incorporating fun exercises to show how creativity is a form of yoga for the brain, teaching it to bend and breathe into possibilities and outcomes it wouldn't have come up with by itself. That creativity doesn't have to look sexy, be grandiose, or perfect; it simply has to move you.

My presentation was a success. I looked over at Celeste, thrilled to see her clapping with a broad smile. That night, I texted David to tell him how well the presentation had gone, but he didn't respond—which was odd. I checked his Instagram to see him out dancing at a club, so I texted him again saying to have fun and I would talk to him tomorrow.

After the departure brunch that Sunday morning, I gathered my things. My phone began to chime with messages, alerting me that there'd been a mass shooting at a nightclub in Orlando. *David.* I grabbed my phone. No answer. I called again right away, this time crying. He answered on the fourth ring, barely able to speak. He sounded so defeated. So fearful. So angry. But alive. He was alive.

"Your video of the nightclub. I thought you were there," I said, crying.

"No, I wasn't. But so many people are dead, Stephanie…people in our distant circles. The list is still coming out, but these people are dead." He began to sob. I stayed on the phone with him, listening for the next thirty minutes. Finally he asked, "Did everything go okay with the conference?"

"It did. I gave a great presentation." I tried to sound positive.

"Good," he said softly.

I gathered my bags before visiting with the other speakers in the lobby. Celeste arrived and went around our small group, hugging each of us and saying thank you—the only compensation we received for our part in the conference. When she got to me and we hugged, she softly whispered into my ear, "You aren't welcome to come back with me. You're on your own."

I nodded, pretending to be unperturbed. I had thirty-one dollars to my name and no room left on my credit cards. As I wondered who to call or what to do, I overheard her mention that she was now heading home to her parents in upstate New York.

I knew then and there that I'd never been welcome to stay with her the whole summer. She needed me only that week and would have discarded me no matter if I said and did all the right things. She'd used me and was now abandoning me with zero cares that I had nowhere to go.

Celeste drove me back to the apartment building to pick up my other suitcase. The whole way there, she smiled and rattled off fun facts about the unique buildings we passed while flying down the West Side Highway. I couldn't believe my ears, or her behavior. I tuned her out, obsessively thinking back to the hundred hours we'd spent on the phone designing websites, logos, creating content, doing webinars, planning out our partnership. It had all felt so legit, so real. *How did I miss the red flags?*

I couldn't exit her car fast enough. In an attempt to save face, I pretended to call a ride before discretely making my way back to the bench I'd napped on a few days prior. Shame poured over me like a wave. I tried to cry, but no tears came. I had nothing left in me.

In March, I stood on that stage in that fucking cape, proud of myself. I believed my heart. I followed the signs, the synchronicities with blind faith. And now I'm stranded on a park bench in need of someone to save me. Is this a fucking joke? I have single-handedly destroyed my life.

I've been reduced to nothing. A worthless bunch of nothing. I don't want to live anymore.

CHAPTER 34

I sat like a statue for most of the afternoon before gaining the mental energy to face matters. There was only one person to call. Yanira.

"Hey, Fef! What's up? How was the conference?"

"It went well, but I'm in a situation, and I need your help. My living arrangement fell through. I'm out of money. It's game over. I need you to do something for me."

"Oh my God, Fef, how…"

I cut her off. "I need you to buy me a plane ticket home. I need to live with you this summer. Just long enough to get a job and a place to live. Mom has my car, so I will have to figure that out, but I just need to do this on the sly. At the end of summer, when I am established, I will share what happened. But for now, I need money and I need a place to stay. Can you do that for me?"

"Fef. Of course. But what about Stella Adler?"

"I'm dropping out. And whatever you do to help me, I'll pay you back," I said without emotion.

"I don't care about the money. Fef, where are you right now?"

"Sitting on a park bench in Lower Manhattan."

"Can you get a hotel, and I'll fly you home tomorrow?"

"I'm dead broke. I'll sleep at the airport."

Yanira paused for a second. I could almost smell the smoke coming out of her ears.

"Hang on. I'll call you right back. Don't move."

I resumed my statue-like position until the phone rang. "You're going to a woman's house named Nora," she commanded.

"Who the hell is Nora? No. Yanira. Stop."

"Listen to me. I met her through a friend a few weeks ago. She lives just outside the city and recently divorced. She had mentioned she hated how empty her big house felt. She's only a few years older than you and really excited to have you."

"Yanira, there is no way I can go there."

"Fef. Listen to me. Toughen up. The Fef I know doesn't give up. I refuse to let you admit defeat. You got yourself into a bad situation, but you called me, and I have a solution. Don't you think that's a sign?"

"Nope, I am done with signs."

"I don't care. I'm sending you the address. If the Uber is too expensive, text me, and I'll send you one. Now, get your ass to her house. I love you, Fef. Text me when you get there."

I hung up and stared at my feet. Going to Nora's was a bigger decision than just staying in someone's guest room until I could make other plans. I needed strength to keep moving forward. Strength to focus in school. Strength to believe in my resilience. Strength I wasn't sure I had. I craved the feeling of relief I would have recreating a sense of security back home. But I wondered how long it would last before regret crept in. I imagined it to be like quitting a marathon at mile twenty and a year later thinking, "I could have kept going."

Curious, I pulled up the Uber app and looked at the price needed to get to the airport. I didn't have enough money. I typed in Nora's address from Yanira's text. It would cost twenty-seven dollars. I would have four dollars to spare.

Without my permission, my thumb pretended it wasn't attached to my body and pressed "confirm ride." A notification popped up stating my car was arriving. I loaded my stuff into the Uber, and as we drove to Nora's, I stared blankly out the window.

The car pulled up and a petite woman with huge black curly hair came running with her arms wide open—just like Yanira had when I'd arrived home from my big trip, making me leery and extremely hesitant at the level of affection she was showing a complete stranger. I slowly met her embrace.

"It's okay. You are going to be okay," she said, patting my back as if I were her child. "Come on, let's get you inside."

I carried up my bags and paused at the sight of a carpeted room with my own twin bed, a desk, and small dresser. *My own bed. My own space.* I took a moment to let it soak in, before heading downstairs to find Nora standing at her kitchen island, smiling at me, her new sidekick.

Nora urged me to change into something cute because we were heading to Dorsey's, her favorite local spot where I could meet all the other regulars. I explained I couldn't due to lack of money, but she insisted on treating me.

As if starving for a girlfriend, Nora went straight into all the details about her juicy dating life. I didn't mind. I welcomed the lighter topic after the day I'd had.

After hours of laughing like old friends over wine and food, I told her my story. She looked at me and grabbed both my hands. "I want you to stay through the summer with me, rent free."

"I can't do that," I said. "I just need ten days to get situated, figure out where I can get a job, and then I will leave. Or, if I stay, I will pay you rent. I insist."

"Stephanie, don't make me lecture you on how to receive help. And don't rush to get work. It will interfere with your studies. I'll totally feed you."

Her eyes were soft and sincere but also glassed over with tears, which I didn't fully understand. Not knowing who I could trust anymore, I felt hesitant to say yes in fear that the other shoe would drop. I took a deep breath and surrendered.

Holy crap. Okay. Here we go. I'm back in the game.

CHAPTER 35

Seven days into living with Nora was enough time to showcase what my new normal would look like for the remainder of the summer.

I'd wake up, make some instant coffee that she so kindly bought for me, and make my way into the city with her borrowed bus pass. I loved my time at Stella Adler and the ten teachers I studied with. They challenged me in new ways, especially my voice and speech teacher.

"You don't use your voice from a deeply-rooted place of power, instead, you strain it. You also hold your breath when your body feels fear. It's holding you back. But don't worry, with some exercises, we can get you there," he preached more times than I wished.

Thankfully, my critiques for my other classes—such as Scene Study, Shakespeare, Movement, Improv, and Script Analysis—while challenging, confirmed both my talents and Yvonne's teaching abilities. Every hour I spent there drastically enhanced my love for storytelling. If I could only learn to use my voice.

After class each day, I'd walk back to the bus station and make my way out of the city, starved for dinner. Nora didn't work, which left her days completely free. I would come home to find her dressed up, impatiently awaiting my arrival. I could always tell how much she day-drank by the eccentricity of her outfit. I would greet her, run up and change, and we would either head out to dinner or she would have food ready for us to eat on her back patio. Either way, it was dedicated girl time unless she—as pre-warned—had a date.

Spending time with Nora every night was the least I could do to express my gratitude before excusing myself to do homework. I gave her my full attention—listening to her rant about her ex-husband, helping her swipe on her dating apps, or reinforcing her attractiveness or any other insecurity she brought up. Being of service even in those minute ways made me feel good. Useful even. It was a weird dynamic, but it worked.

It was hard to believe that exactly one week before, I'd sat on a park bench, hopeless. Despite still having zero funds, I had come so far. To celebrate, I spent that first weekend peacefully walking around The Upper West Side. Every time I'd see a street of brownstones, I would stop and choose which one was mine. Halfway through my game of pretend, my phone rang. My mom's tone was sober, which caught me off guard. Then, she did the worst thing anyone could ever do over the phone. She asked me if I was sitting down.

I looked around and found church steps to my immediate right.

"I'm sitting, Mom, what's wrong?"

"Your grandma had a stroke this morning."

"Oh God, no. Please, no."

"At the moment, she is awake, but sweetheart, it's not looking good. You might want to come home and see her."

The world started to spin. I tried to make sense of my surroundings but couldn't. My mother kept talking, but I didn't know what she was saying. I put my head between my legs to try to catch my breath.

"Do you have the money for a ticket?" she asked.

Her question startled me. She didn't know my situation, and I had no intention of telling her. If I needed a ticket, Yanira would be the one I called.

"The ticket isn't the issue, Mom," I said as I tried to gather my thoughts. "But I'll be coming home for good because Stella Adler has a one-day absentee policy. So, I need to coordinate it all quickly."

"Are you sure?"

I can't handle these questions right now.

"Mom, it's Grandma. It's not even a question."

"Okay, honey," she said, sensing my irritation. "Let's just pause for a second." She was silent for a long moment. "Grandma would want you to stay."

"Mom, I can't even think about that right now, okay?"

"I know. So, let's see how she does overnight. She may recover and just have a long road of physical therapy ahead. I'll call you tomorrow, and you can decide then."

I hung up the phone and sobbed.

• •

When I arrived home, I found a note from Nora on the kitchen island. She was spending the night elsewhere. On autopilot, I opened the fridge to find the leftovers from Dorsey's the night before gone. With my discomfort in asking her to provide me breakfast or lunch, dinner was my daily feast. Tonight, it didn't matter. I don't know why I even looked; I couldn't bring myself to eat.

Mom's call came at ten o'clock that night while I sat in the corner of my room on the floor, motionless.

She was crying. "Honey, Grandma slipped into a coma. She isn't going to make it. You wouldn't have gotten here in time to see her awake anyway."

"I'm still coming. I'll fly home tomorrow, and then I'll go stay with Yanira for a while and get a job back in Orlando."

She didn't respond.

"Mom. I have to be by her side," I shouted while starting to sob.

"I know that. You two are so close, and I know she would want that. But I also know that she wouldn't want you to drop out. Honey, Grandma believes in you. You're her star. Honor her by staying and studying as hard as you can. One day, we will bring her ashes to Italy, together. For now, just make her proud."

All I wanted to do was hold my grandma's hand and rub her fingernails as she liked to do to mine. To let her know I was there. Her words from the last video mom sent on the day I left for New York haunted me. "Esteffy. It's Gramma. You gonna make it. Keepa goin', Esteffy. Keepa goin'. You gonna make it. Gramma knows."

When nothing was left to cry out, I crawled into bed and hugged my pillow. I would never see my grandmother again. Never hear her insisting I am too skinny or asking why I'm not married. Never hear her broken English. Never see her mischievous spirit shine through her eyes.

She was a warrior. She'd persevered through World War II, dressing up as an old woman in her Italian village and sneaking out to find extra food for her nine siblings. Immigrating to the U.S., leaving an abusive husband, and fighting her way to make it on her own as a seamstress before marrying Pop. I desperately needed one more day with her, drinking Welch's grape juice at our secret happy hours.

As much as it hurt my heart, I knew if she could talk, she would insist on me staying.

I will keep going in her honor.

• •

A week later, on June 27, I walked into my Film Auditions class, taught by a guy close to my age named Eddie. My first day in his class, he had asked me if I was a gymnast, noticing my stiff, upright posture, joking that I looked ready to take a punch, which I found rather hilarious.

But that day as I walked in, he immediately asked why my shoulders were hunched over in sadness.

"My grandmother died this morning, and I am hanging on by a thread."

"Let me buy you a drink after class, and let's talk about it." He saw a look on my face. "Professional. As two adults. I'm not hitting on you."

He'd misinterpreted my hesitation. Nora had been staying at a guy's place for the past two days, and I hadn't eaten except for a ton of instant coffee, a few Oreos I snuck from her pantry, and a free banana I managed to score from a smoothie truck. One drink would knock me over.

"No, I didn't think that at all," I clarified. "And sure. Let's go."

I sat opposite Eddie at a high-top table in a bar across from Madison Square Garden, nursing a beer and telling him about my grandmother.

"So, that's where you get your spunkiness from," he said.

"I don't feel much like her right now. I feel pretty beaten up," I admitted. "New York City is hard."

"It definitely is. But you deserve to be here. You deserve to be at this school. This might sound a little clichéd, but the city knocks everyone down. Those who get back up, get to stay."

"A little clichéd? Oh, it's very clichéd." We laughed, then Eddie gave me a sincere look.

"Listen, find a way to get a fire back in you. The one I saw when you walked in the first day of class. You were so excited to be here. I want to see her again. I'll help in any way I can." His warm smile felt soothing. I knew with zero hesitation that I had made a friend.

• •

It struck me that despite how heartbreaking and tragic life could be, it still oddly fit together like a puzzle. My voice teacher told us that Stella Adler had been a clothing factory back in the day, and that there were still needles in between the floorboards. My grandmother had been a seamstress who'd worked in the garment district. I had no idea whether she could have worked in the same building where I now studied acting, but the idea boggled me while comforting me at the same time.

My grandma's death pained me greatly, but it launched a surge of determination within. Nora's home was stable and safe. However, Grandma would faint if she saw how thin I had become. Walking around hungry was no longer an option, and it wasn't fair to expect Nora to feed me above and beyond the nights we had dinner.

Within days, I was contacted by a woman who'd attended Linda's conference, the one where I'd worn my Superwoman shirt and cape. She connected me to a company looking for someone to coach actors and put them on tape for their auditions. The hours were flexible and a perfect fit for me, and I loved the work. It took only a week to receive my first check; I had just enough money to get by—and it felt fantastic.

I received my film back from the editor. Despite my embarrassment in how makeshift it turned out, Nora loved it. She got the biggest kick out of my Photoshopped movie poster after finding out I'd shot the photos in her upstairs hallway. The day I sent it off to Lou, the woman who requested it, Nora cooked a celebratory dinner, telling me I needed to be more optimistic about it—something I refused to do at this point in my journey. Regardless of what happened with the film, and despite how obsessive Nora could be at times, I was grateful for the natural friendship that was beginning to blossom between us.

I dove into my studies with a fire that even Eddie noticed had returned. I put in extra hours rehearsing with my scene partner or working on my vocal exercises. I was committed to my growth, and it showed in my work during class.

Sometimes, on days when I missed my grandmother terribly, I would stay late, sitting on the floor of an empty studio, chatting on the phone with David, Yanira, or Angela while looking for old sewing needles between the floorboards.

CHAPTER 36

Ode to New York
You may have knocked me down but…
No longer do I feel the hunger pangs of someone struggling to eat.
No longer do I get lost on your now familiar streets.
No longer do your strange smells crinkle my nose.
No longer do your people come across as rude, or their eccentric behavior turn my head.
No longer does your intense chaotic energy intimidate me.
No longer do I feel like your guest. I have become one of your own. A New Yorker.
I can feel it.
I never imagined this.
An unexpected love affair.
Wait for my return. I'll be back.
XOXO

I graduated from Stella Adler with a new toolkit of knowledge I couldn't wait to use. New York had stretched me to the max, but I pulled through. In the mirror I saw a nourished, strong, and capable woman.

With one week left, what better way to celebrate than a gratitude dinner to thank Nora for her hospitality and friendship. I proudly saved up for this night so that I could pick up the bill, and told her to meet me at a Cuban place for tapas instead of the usual Dorsey's.

My excitement turned south the moment I arrived and found Nora had been there for quite some time, deep in sangria.

"No, serslee, babe, ahmso proud a'you," she slurred as we ordered our main dishes.

"Thank you. I couldn't have made it through school without you," I replied, annoyed.

Nora bowed her head and closed her eyes, staying there a little too long before her head popped up again. "Y'still have'n herback 'bout film?" she asked.

We have already discussed this.

"No, and I don't expect to. Lou was rather short with me in her email. Something changed. I suspect she didn't even send it anywhere. It's fine. The film was shit anyway."

Nora struggled to form a coherent thought, making it more enjoyable for me to ramble on and her to stay silent. "I might refilm it. It's a great concept and funny script. I just need to prioritize some other aspects of my life first. My life should be back to normal again by Christmas. After that, I might try to get an agent in Atlanta. I heard there's a ton of work there. So much to look forward to..." I smiled and took a sip of my sangria.

"I don't wan you t'leave. Who will hang out wid'me?" She started to sob.

"I will come visit. I promise."

Nora wiped her eyes, then leaned in and folded her hands together on the table. She tilted her head downward and then looked up at me while taking a deep breath. "Strap on'ya sea-belt, Steph-ny."

I leaned back in my chair and watched her put all the effort she had into getting this next sentence out.

"Ya'not goin'home."

"What are you talking about?"

"Stay here. You. Me. It'll be funnnn."

I drifted into thought before looking over to find her head in her hand, asleep. I canceled our order and asked for the check. *This night's over.*

• •

The next morning I awoke to the smell of pancakes. Nora was standing over the sink, cleaning her dish, and I made the mistake of asking how she was feeling. She looked shocked and unsure of what I could possibly be talking about. I microwaved some instant coffee in my travel mug and told her I was taking a walk and that I would see her later on.

As I put on my shoes downstairs, I heard her shout.

"I meant what I said last night. Stay with me through December for free. Get on your feet, and then if you want to stay with me after the New Year, it would be five hundred dollars a month rent."

"Nora, no. You've already done too much," I shouted back.

"I enjoy having you here. I'll be lonely if you aren't around."

"I'll think about it," I replied and headed out the door.

I found a park bench, marveling at how huge and fat the groundhogs were. Wanting food, they had no fear of approaching me. I stared at the city's skyline and began to count the hundreds of tall buildings, wondering what opportunities awaited me within them. *I'm not ready for "game over."*

I didn't like the terms and conditions, but I was thankful for the means to stay should I choose to. Even though Nora was erratic and very clingy, I believed she was harmless. Yes, she did drink excessively, and the men were on a rotating schedule, but neither made her a bad person.

I had to rebuild my life no matter where I happened to live. As I watched another oversized groundhog waddle by, I could hear my grandma. "Keep agoin', Esteffy, no stop, you-a gonna make it."

It would be hard being so far from my friends and Art Sake, not to mention delaying being with Charlie a bit until I established myself. I sensed the road would be a lonely one, but one I fully believed I needed to travel down. I had to see what I was made of. What I could truly accomplish. My heart told me my time here wasn't done, and I decided to listen. I stared at the skyline, knowing that life as I knew it was about to change. I agreed to give myself until the end of December to create a life up here. But not a day longer.

• •

I landed in Tampa, Florida feeling like I had just returned from boot camp. My mom and I had a good laugh when I asked her if I could borrow my own car. I needed to drive the two hours to my storage unit in Orlando and find whatever warm clothes I had for winter.

As I passed downtown Orlando, something came over me. Against my better judgment, I turned and drove straight to my old home. I hadn't seen her since leaving for my trip. I parked across the street and stared. The lawn needed work, and the trim around the roof needed cleaning. At least the hedges I had planted had finally grown high enough to offer privacy in the backyard.

A truck was parked in the driveway, making me feel territorial. *It's too soon.* I drove off.

I found a few sweaters I owned in my storage unit, then sat in my car realizing I was about to tell my tribe I was leaving for the third time—a scene I knew all too well. The first time had been riddled with excitement, promise, and adventure. The second, full of faith and some guilt. This time, for reasons I couldn't yet explain, it was all business. Yanira believed that Nora's offer was solid and a great chance for me to stay and see what I could make of myself. Angela agreed. They both were beyond supportive, just as I'd known they would be.

David's reaction surprised me, but at the same time it was rather poetic. I suspected he didn't remember what he'd told me upon hearing the news of my big trip. But all this time later, he had the exact same smile and the exact same words.

"I'm not surprised."

"I think everyone saw it coming but me, I guess."

"Stephanie, you seem to be on a mission. I don't even think you know what it is, but I am here for it. I am here for you. Always."

"I know," I said as he hugged me.

"Are you telling Yvonne today?"

"I am doing that in a few hours," I said as David erupted into laughter.

"That's going to be fun."

"Want to join?"

"Hell, no."

● ●

I walked into Art Sake studio, inhaling the familiar smell I had sorely missed. In two weeks, auditions for Play de Luna would take place, and I felt sad that I would be missing out. "It doesn't matter. Your home will always be here," I whispered.

Yvonne was shouting to me from the back office. I turned to head that way before stopping abruptly to stare at the wall of photos, adjusting my eyes to make sure I was seeing correctly. There were twenty-five pictures hung in uneven rows. My photo had hung there for years, signaling that I was a vital member of the theater. But now it wasn't there. Someone had removed it. *Who wants me gone? Did Yvonne do this? I don't understand.*

I was stung, but decided to keep quiet about it until we had settled in with our salmon and wine at Hillstone.

"Hey, did you know that my picture was taken off the wall in the lobby?" I asked.

"No. I had no idea. I'm never over there."

I stared at her, wondering if she simply didn't want to admit it. "Well, someone took it down."

"Let's get another one and hang it up. We could use the one of you that's in my office, but I'd like that one to stay there," she said.

Her suggestion reassured me, but the incident somehow made me feel better about my decision to move. The words flowed out of my mouth more easily than I had anticipated. "Well, no need to put it back up because I'm going to try to stay in New York for a bit," I said, looking directly into her eyes.

Yvonne didn't say much in response. Instead, she reached down into her bag, pulled out a deck of tarot cards, and began shuffling it.

Yvonne loved using the tarot. She was particular about only consulting them for birthdays. So, doing this today meant something special. It was her way of saying she missed me.

I kept laughing as she screamed with every card she put down. Everything referenced change, new beginnings, risks and leaps.

"See, even your cards say I have to continue moving onward. Maybe, one day, it will loop me back here."

Yvonne shrugged. Since we could read each other like a book, I knew she wanted to tell me I was strong, capable, and talented. But instead, she rolled her eyes and, smiling, called me delusional, showing me the bit of competitive jealousy which would occasionally surface. She didn't hide her imperfections; my need to be perfect made me notice it faster than most. Yvonne made me strive to remember I'm human, and I helped her take a risk every once in a while. We made a good pair. Silently, I understood her desire for me to stay, while she silently understood my need to go.

Before burying the topic of my leaving, I couldn't resist getting in one last jab. "Ya know, Yvonne, I have you to blame for all this. This monster right here is your creation." I pointed to myself.

She laughed her contagious guttural laugh before lighting a cigarette. "Fine," she said sternly. Her face softened into a smirk.

"But you must watch every single Play de Luna for the rest of your life. You can't NOT come."

"I wouldn't miss it for the world."

• •

I stayed a few extra days longer than planned to make sure my mom was okay. She struggled with my grandmother's passing. As much as I'd missed Charlie, he had his own purpose—caring for him was the perfect distraction for my mother. It also helped me to not feel so bad about delaying our reunion.

This departure process had become a bit systematic. A gut-wrenching goodbye to my dog. A car ride to the airport full of small talk. A brief cry in the airport bathroom before collecting myself and carrying on with my head held high. This time was no different.

I only prayed that no rock stars or TSA security guards would say anything to me like before; all I wanted was to board my plane in peace. I sat on the same stool at the same restaurant as last time, ordering my preflight glass of wine. Thinking back to that day, to that time in my life that felt like years ago despite it being just months, I couldn't help but remember how excited I'd been then. Perhaps even naïve. *It's insane how different the summer turned out. It's also insane that I'm going back—to be a New Yorker.*

CHAPTER 37

My dream for my life in New York was to work for myself while having the flexibility to pursue acting and directing. I desperately wanted to avoid spending a traditional eight-hour day in a place with muted gray walls and endless cubicles. I wanted to shift my path—from being an "operator," "manager," or "assembler" to that of "creator." And equally important to me was having Charlie at my side.

I spent my days locked up in my room at Nora's, trying to do three things at once: scouring the internet for a job, coming up with a business idea, and submitting myself for acting gigs. I left no idea unexplored and no potential opportunity on the table.

I tried to develop a comprehensive acting coaching program—only to find that my lack of a master's degree in fine arts was a deterrent. I devised a list of strategies and skills in sales training, culture training, and leadership training which I could teach to corporations—only to find that I had no credentials. I made a video for *The Today Show* as my application to become a guest host. I almost had a job as an assistant to a documentary filmmaker, but he chose someone who already had that kind of experience. I surrendered my list of preferences and applied to be a pharmaceutical sales rep, knowing how flexible and lucrative that job could be. Even with my great sales background, not once did I receive a request for an interview. I offered to photograph jewelry for jewelers in Midtown Manhattan. I became so desperate, I almost responded to a Craigslist ad looking to pay women with pretty feet to come be a part of an underground foot fetish club. *I'm working my ass off. Something's got to give.*

My brain started to spin by four o'clock each afternoon, which was about the time Nora became antsy to hang out and grab a bite. I began to envy those I saw on social media who seemingly could "bottle themselves up," package "it," and sell "it." *I just don't know how to be like them.*

The struggle became all too real. October arrived and I started to stress. One morning, I threw my hands in the air and hid on Nora's small side porch on a lawn chair, facedown, and cried the entire day. It was a grand-slam pity party. I was exhausted from trying to figure it all out. I needed to surrender and allow things to unfold as they were meant to, but in doing so, I felt like I was doing nothing.

One morning, lured in by the promise of an interview for a pharmaceutical sales job, I arrived at a hotel, took a seat, and began chatting with the nicest woman next to me with the coolest Jamaican accent. Minutes later, I learned we had been bait-and-switched into an industrial job fair. Annoyed, I stood to walk out, but the woman next to me put her hand on my shoulder as if we were longtime friends.

"Stay. What have you got to lose?" she said. Her eyes were so soft and sincere. For some reason, I couldn't bring myself to disappoint her.

The first company I interviewed with wanted me to buy into a franchise. *Hahaha. Right. I wish I had a printout of my bank balance of $170. That would turn them off in two seconds.*

The next company wanted me to carry fifty-pound bags of chemicals onto roofs throughout the city. *Yeah, not happening.*

I made it through five more interviews of nonsense before walking toward the elevator. Out of nowhere, that same woman appeared asking how it went.

"Why would you only go to five of the six interviews? Stay. See it through," she urged.

Why does she care so much! Is this woman even real, or have I imagined her? If this is one of my signs, I don't want it!

I told her goodbye and pressed the elevator button just as my name was called. With a sigh, I made my way into the final room—a company looking for someone to sell and engineer the installation of windows. *No way. Not for me.* I smiled, listened, and then anxiously headed home to regroup.

Back in my room, I opened my laptop to see a message that changed my entire day. I had to read it twice. *Julie and Kel are cruising on a ship that pulls into New York City the following week. They want to see me.*

"Book a place for dinner and then somewhere for drinks. The night is on us, so choose something we will remember," Kel's message instructed.

Their ship's arrival on Wednesday, November 19, couldn't come fast enough. I put on gray jeans, a black shirt, and black heels—all part of the few items I had kept from my cruise wardrobe. I wanted to look and feel the exact way I had when they last saw me.

I arrived late and could hear Julie's laughter as she saw me run down the street in heels to the port where we were meeting.

"Surrrrrreeee!" Kel shouted as we hugged.

"It's so good to see you. I am so happy you are here. Sorry for keeping you waiting."

"No worries at all, sweetheart," Julie said as I hailed a cab.

We piled in and headed to the Flatiron district to a Korean restaurant. Julie and Kel filled me in on their latest travels and how much they enjoyed their retired life, and I told them about the fun happenings on the cruise that took place after they disembarked.

We finished our dinner, keeping the conversation light before I took them to a rooftop bar overlooking the Empire State Building. After a round of drinks, I felt ready to say what I'd been wanting to say to Kel since the moment I hugged him.

"Kel, when we were having one of our many chats in The Crow's Nest, you said something to me. Something that changed everything. You told me, 'Don't be afraid to go broke.' "

Kel's face lit up. "I remember that."

"Well, I did go broke. Then, I took some chances in an effort to go big, and it didn't work out. Your words kept me going when I wanted to give up. Thank you from the bottom of my heart."

"Good," Kel said without pause. "I am glad you fell on your face. The best do. More than once if they're lucky."

For the first time, the events of the past year didn't feel so negative.

"It's the best way to learn," he said.

"That's one way to put it." I smiled.

"So, now that you have struck out, when are we going to see 'Stephanie Wilson' in lights?" he asked, using his hands to create a marquee.

"I'm not sure. But I'm working on it."

The night flew by too quickly. Reluctantly, I helped them hail a cab before hugging them both tightly, not wanting to let go.

Kel and Julie's visit recharged my battery and inspired me to find any solution, even if short-term. So, I met with a temp agency to see if there were any executive assistant positions available. I sat in the job coordinator's office as she looked over my résumé with a very concerned look on her face.

"Ms. Wilson, your resume is impressive. I see you have an MBA and studied abroad in South Korea."

"Yes, it was an amazing experience, and I cannot wait to bring the tools I learned into a company in New York City."

"This is all great, but tell me about your experience booking travel for other people."

I feel like she just asked if I knew how to tie my shoe.

"Other people? I haven't, but I have traveled extensively. I suspect it is like booking my own travel but using a different name." I didn't mean to be flippant, but I was shocked this was a serious question.

"Being an executive support system requires knowledge in these types of tasks, and you haven't done them in a professional setting. This issue will be a huge challenge for us to get you hired." I struggled to keep a straight face.

"What other duties are you referring to?" I asked.

"Scheduling meetings, booking hotels, restaurant reservations, and answering the phones." My eyes widened in disbelief. *Is this some kind of joke?*

She looked me in the eye with sympathy as if she were going to tell me I had three months to live. "Even if you did have experience with these tasks, you just moved here from Florida, and you need to prove that you are capable of doing them in New York City," she concluded, as if her mind was made up. I was at a loss for words.

The entire experience felt like a prank; somewhere there had to be a hidden camera. But then I heard similar comments from two other temp agencies. *How can I be rejected like this after everything I've accomplished?*

CHAPTER 38

Before long, the window company asked for a second interview at their office north of Manhattan. With no other opportunities on the horizon, I reluctantly said yes. One bus and two trains later, I exited the subway station catty-corner to the office, next to a rundown diner with decade-old chipped blue paint. I thought a zombie apocalypse must have occurred while I was underground because the people loitering just outside the restaurant were technically standing up but were also hunched over, asleep, with their arms dangling by their feet. Quickly I walked past them, hoping for the best, but also impressed with their superhuman ability.

Once inside the office, I was transported to a traditional bland setting with a sea of cubicles off in the distance. I asked the receptionist about the people outside sleeping while standing up.

"Oh, they're on meth," she said casually.

Before I could react, I was called into the main conference room by Shannon, the head of Human Resources, where Mike, the company's Vice President, was sitting with my résumé in his hand.

"Were we easy to find?" he asked after we'd greeted each other.

I feel like he is testing me to see if I mention the drug use just outside. "Oh yeah, super easy." I smiled back.

After a traditional interview session, in which I told him how I overcame obstacles, what my greatest weakness was, and how I would describe myself in three words, he asked me one final question. "Is there anything we have mentioned, or haven't mentioned, for that matter, that makes you feel like you aren't a good fit for the role?"

I let loose. "I know New York City is known for Murphy beds in offices and weekends spent working. But I will not be here at night or on the weekends. I believe in a healthy work-life balance," I said firmly.

"I'm fine with that." His tone dared me to say more.

"I act in my spare time, which is part of why I moved up here. If I need a day or two off because I booked a role on a show—"

"We will all watch it and be proud," he interrupted.

"Lastly, I would not come on board to sell windows long-term. It would be to learn the business so that I could be promoted into a leadership role."

"We're on the same page, Stephanie," Mike said with a smile.

The second part of the interview involved shadowing Paul, the VP of Sales and my potential new boss. Before he even said hello, Paul looked down at my feet and shouted, "How can you wear high heels on a job site?!"

"Relax, I have sneakers in my backpack," I said, matching his unprofessionalism with my own.

Unfortunately, the wrestling match between us continued throughout the rest of the interview.

Paul's smug demeanor became more apparent in the close proximity of his car. I did my best to look interested in the windows he described as we drove across Manhattan, but my heart wasn't in it.

We walked through one of their construction sites, and he started drawing engineering details.

"Can you read these?" he asked.

"No, sir, I cannot."

He rolled his eyes. "Well, you will have to learn."

I knew beyond a shadow of a doubt that my mind was not capable of learning such. *I need a few less failures in my life, and this is a failure waiting to happen.*

• •

A week later, they called and offered me the job. The pay was barely enough to get by if I rented an apartment with someone. I asked them for a few days to think on it. I had failed to find a way to stay on the terms I desired. Declining the offer would automatically mean returning home, unless of course, there was a last-minute miracle, which, ya-know, has happened before…

I wanted to remain positive and celebrate the victory of actually being offered a position in New York City, hoping the inertia would spark more opportunities. I texted Nora with the good news. She replied, ecstatic, and said to meet her at the Cuban restaurant for a celebratory lunch—the same place I'd taken her for her "thank you" dinner. She was leaving for Florida the next morning for two weeks, and it was a chance to connect before she left.

When I arrived, Nora was sitting at the bar, against the wall on the shorter side. Something was different about her. She felt distant and a bit off. I sat in one of the two empty stools next to her, finding a spread of tapas and a glass of sangria waiting for me.

"Congrats, babe!" she said as we clinked glasses.

"Thanks. But I haven't said yes yet. To be honest, I don't want to take the job."

"God gave you that job. You have to take it," she commanded with a look in her eye that scared me.

It was as if every obsessive and weird behavior she'd displayed all summer and fall added up right there in that moment. *Something's wrong.*

I took a deep breath, trying not to overreact while eating my appetizer. Silence consumed our meal until I finally looked over at her. "Nora, why are you crying?" I asked without sympathy.

"I don't want you to leave me," she said between sobs.

"Nora, nothing has been decided."

"I mean, if you don't take the job, you'll go home to Florida. If you do take the job, you'll move out into your own place."

She placed her head on my shoulder and continued crying. Reluctantly, I placed my arms loosely around her.

"Please don't leave me. I don't want to be left alone. Come January, I will only charge you five hundred dollars. Think of all the money you can save by paying so little," she begged.

Her obsessive plea made me even more uncomfortable. "Nora, we'll always be friends, no matter where I live," I lied. I knew that I needed to create some space between us.

The main dishes were set down on the bar, which helped me change the subject. As I loaded my first fajita, a guy sat down to my left, filling the last stool on our side of the bar. The rest of the bar area was empty, yet he'd chosen to annoyingly cramp our space.

"Hey," he said.

Nora responded, sparking a conversation between the two of them. I blatantly ignored him by scooting my chair back and hanging out on my phone to let them talk. The flirting became intense, so I got up to use the restroom, hoping that maybe he would move over while I was gone. Instead, I returned to find each of their arms resting on my chair.

"Hey, you! Sorry if we were ignoring you," Nora said.

"Oh, no. Don't worry about me. I was just answering some emails."

"Well, finish your drink 'cause we are all going somewhere else," Nora said.

"No thanks. I think I'll head home." I took my drink and finished it off.

That was the last thing I remembered before everything faded to black.

CHAPTER 39

I couldn't open my eyes. There were voices.

What are they saying? Hands are shaking me, but I can't move.

"Wake up, Stephanie, wake up. Open your eyes. Come on," the voice repeated, as if I had just come out of surgery.

My head hurts above my right eye. Where am I? A tingling sensation came over my nerves, and my eyes slowly opened. *Blur. Everything's blurry. Blinking helps.* I began to get my bearings.

I'm on a bed. Whose bed?

To my right there were arms. *Nora's arms? Yes.*

She was the one shaking me. *Naked. She's naked.*

"It's okay, Stephanie," she said. "Breathe, just breathe, hon."

My vision finally cleared, but my mind was slow to process what I was seeing.

"I'm into girls, Stephanie, so just relax. It's gonna be fun."

What is she trying to tell me?

"I'm not alone. Look." She pointed to my other side. My body was slow to move, but I turned my head. Hands were rubbing me over my clothes. A face came into focus. *It's the guy from the bar.*

My adrenaline surged to a level that overcame whatever was in my system, and I flung myself off the bed and stumbled several feet into my room. The second I locked the door, I succumbed once again to whatever had taken hold of my body, falling back onto the floor, lying with my left cheek pressed to the carpet.

I tried to keep my focus, but things began to blur again. I couldn't move, could barely see, but I could hear the sound of loud sex next door in Nora's bedroom. I felt drool slide down my face as I tried to relax and breathe…and then lost consciousness.

Sometime later I woke up to dead silence. I sat up, touched my throbbing head, and felt a huge lump. It took a few minutes to realize that what happened was not a bad dream. *It must be early the next morning. It's not even light out yet.*

I peeked out of my door. Nora's bedroom door was wide open. The house was completely dark. *No one is home.*

I looked out my bedroom window and saw Meghan's car in the driveway. She owned the house across the street. I walked over and knocked loudly. She opened the door dressed in her scrubs. I had no idea if it was early morning or late at night, and whether she had just returned from work or was heading out. This concerned her. She ushered me to the couch where I tried to tell her what happened.

"You're sure you weren't raped?" she asked.

"I'm sure."

"And it's still Thursday. So, this happened earlier today then."

"I guess so. I wasn't sure when I woke up."

We heard a car pull up in Nora's driveway, making us both pause. Meghan went to the window and peeked out the blinds. "Nora's back with some guy."

"Skinny white guy with a buzz cut?" I asked.

"No, someone different."

"I know she sometimes spirals out of control, but I had no idea she's like this."

"She hid it from you. You need to get out of there, hon."

"She leaves tomorrow morning for two weeks, so I'll be fine until then. I just need her to leave before I head back over."

"Yes, I know, you already told me twice. Stay here on the couch tonight. I want to monitor you. You're not talking normal."

Despite the knot on my upper temple, I woke the next morning with a clear head—and fierce determination. I looked up at the ceiling toward God, the universe…whatever was up there. With gritted teeth I whispered, "Enough is enough." Instead of waiting for Nora to leave, I stormed across the street and straight up to her room.

"What the fuck, Nora!" I yelled, demanding an explanation for the previous night's events.

"What do you mean?"

"What was in my drink? Tell me!"

She just stared.

"Answer me!" I screamed so hard spit flew out of my mouth.

"I don't remember anything. Maybe we were both drugged," she said.

"Stop lying! You were not drugged. You assaulted me. You and that piece of white trash." I slammed her door shut and went downstairs to look for my purse, hoping it hadn't been left at the restaurant.

My bag and shoes were on the couch, making me suspect I'd passed out there first. I looked back toward the stairs, wondering if I had hit my head while being carried up. *Or did they hit me with something? I'll never know.*

Nora came down the stairs.

"I really don't remember anything," she insisted.

"You liar!" I had her manipulative number down.

"Maybe we should both go get a rape kit," she suggested.

"Don't you dare play the victim. You know exactly what you did. What happened is not okay. I woke up with a man's hands rubbing me and you naked in the bed. How dare you think that is okay! You are sick. Absolutely sick. I heard you having sex while I was lying on the bedroom floor, unable to move, struggling to breathe. You didn't give two shits about my well-being. You better start praying I don't go to the police." I stormed out of the house.

I crossed the street and headed to a nearby bench, where I could wait for her to leave for the airport without her knowing I was watching. My thoughts quickly spiraled, running through scenarios of what could have happened. As angry as I was, I was thankful that it hadn't been worse. No matter how hard I tried to rid the thoughts and clear my mind, one thought kept surfacing over and over again. *I am back sitting on a park bench, feeling hopeless. This has to stop. This has to be my last bench.*

CHAPTER 40

Fifteen minutes after her car pulled away, I entered Nora's home on a mission. I needed to move swiftly. I sat at the kitchen table with my phone and computer, ready to attack.

I needed $3000 to afford first month's rent and security deposit if I could find a roommate. I retrieved the one business card in my purse and dialed the number.

"Hi, Shannon, this is Stephanie Wilson calling."

"Hello, Stephanie! Happy to hear from you. I know Mike is quite eager to have you come on board," she said. I chuckled at the unintentional ship reference.

"I would like to discuss a counter-offer."

"Oh?"

"I will accept all of your terms, but would also require an upfront three-thousand-dollar check for relocation expenses. If you agree, I can start immediately."

Shannon took no pause. "I normally would need to ask, but Mike figured you might want to negotiate your income, so I have just enough wiggle room to agree to this."

Done. Onto the next challenge.

••

Next, I found my sorority's alumnae Facebook page for Manhattan and posted a request for a roommate. A girl my age named Julie responded. Her last name looked familiar, so I clicked on her page to discover we'd gone to the same college, and she'd pledged our sorority the year after me. I wasted no time in asking her out for coffee to see if we were a good fit. She agreed to meet me in two hours.

I arrived in the city nervous, wondering how forthcoming I should be about whether I would get approved.

I sat down, and we began to talk about our college days. We knew all the same people and ran in the same circles. She seemed nice...and safe.

"So, what's your story?" I asked, eager to get down to business.

"My boyfriend and I just broke up, so I'm moving out. I'm game to live anywhere that's a quick train to Madison Square Garden. How about you?"

"I moved up from Florida. Been staying with a friend to get my bearings. I'm good with anything near the 1/2/3 or the 4/5/6 trains."

"How much furniture do you have?" she asked. "Because I have an entire kitchen and living room."

"My stuff is in Florida. I'll sell it all if you don't mind us using yours."

"Perfect."

"I'm leaving for Florida on the twenty-second and will be back for a January first move in. Does that work for you?"

"I have the same timeline. Sounds great."

"My only concern is that I just started my job, so I'm afraid I won't qualify," I said, trying to be honest without revealing too much.

"I have an established work history in the city and decent income. I think we'll be fine."

"You don't seem crazy, so I'm game to do this if you are," I said, which made her laugh as she nodded yes.

In one day I got a job and found a roommate. I made my way back to the bus station, feeling unstoppable.

• •

I woke up before my alarm on the first day of my new job and threw on an old pencil skirt and a sweater. Unfortunately, I didn't yet understand the art of wearing tights. By the time I arrived at work, my legs were frozen purple.

Paul took me to an empty cubicle with a computer, phone, and a coffee mug with the company logo on it. On the shelf was a binder that listed all of the company's products. Wanting to ask him a question, I turned around. He was already gone.

I sat down, not knowing what to do. *If I sit here any longer staring into space, I'll walk out.* I decided I would start reading the binder.

I hadn't packed a lunch thinking I would eat out with my new boss on my first day. One o'clock rolled around, and I was starving, so I made my way to his office to ask about nearby lunch places.

"There isn't much around here. Just go across the street."

"The rundown place?"

"Yes," he said without looking up from his computer. "Get the BLT," he shouted as I walked away.

I was certain that anything I ordered there would give me food poisoning, but I was too starved to skip lunch. Playing it safe, I ordered french fries.

When I returned to my cubicle, I couldn't bring myself to sit. I ran to the bathroom and full-on hyperventilated to the point of throwing up. I walked over to the sink and ran cold water on my wrists. I stared at my clammy face in the mirror and coldly whispered, "Get a grip."

Back at my desk, there was a note from a fellow salesman, Bill, asking me to come see him. His cubicle was so full of files, papers, and clutter I could barely breathe at the sight. He introduced himself and asked if I had eaten. I filled him in on my diner adventure, and he shook his head.

"No one knows why Paul eats there. He's obsessed with the BLT."

Bill grabbed his coat. "Come on, let's get you some food."

We walked a few blocks down the road to a proper restaurant where he treated me to a gorgeous lunch. We spent the entire afternoon sitting there, talking before he felt comfortable enough to share that the training efforts were lacking, and I would be mostly on my own. However, he would take me under his wing if in turn I helped him get organized. Happily I agreed.

• •

That week, Julie and I looked at apartments in Manhattan every day after work, with zero success. Any place we liked was taken before we could say we wanted it. I suggested we see what open houses were scheduled that weekend, and if we liked a place, we would take it on the spot. She agreed.

I found one on the Upper West Side that looked promising. Arriving an hour early, we were the first in line. As people lined up behind us, Julie gave them a dirty look that said, "Back up!"—which made me giggle despite the panic I felt deep within.

The second the agent opened the apartment door, we bolted inside like two lunatics. Within seconds I gave Julie a thumbs-up from across the living room, and she signaled her thumbs-up back and told the agent we'd take it. Two other couples echoed our decision. It was war.

"The first person to put a cashier's check in my hand for the deposit gets the place."

Julie and I took off running down three flights of stairs. We kept shouting at the cabbie to drive faster. At one point his tires squealed as he turned a corner, making me scream with laughter. I couldn't help but realize it was the first time I had laughed since the incident at Nora's.

Cashier's check in hand, I sprinted back up the stairs so fast I almost tackled the agent. I stood panting, drenched in sweat and in disbelief that we were officially the first in line to get the place.

The next day, the agent called me. "So, Stephanie," he said, "your half of the application has been challenging. I went to bat for you, and the owner will agree to have you. However, they are asking for an additional month's security deposit of three thousand dollars."

"Sir, I understand my credit cards went unpaid this past summer. But, my credit report has a mortgage that was never late, and it's also void of any rental collections. I will not let you down. But I can't ask my new roommate to put up more money just because I fell into a hard time. So, I will give you until ten o'clock tomorrow morning to decide if you can allow us to move forward with the apartment. If your answer is no, that's okay, but know then that we'll have to back out of the lease."

I went home to Nora's, and for the first time in a long while, I let go of everything. I felt at peace. I had fought so hard that week, taking charge of my situation, and I believed I'd done all I could. That's what mattered, not the result. I loved how that felt.

To celebrate, I bought a seven-dollar magnum of shitty white wine and invited Meghan, the neighbor whose couch I'd slept on, over for the evening. We drank, laughed, and danced in the living room. I had so much to celebrate. *If tomorrow means I'm going home, that's okay. Look what I accomplished! There is no defeat. No reason to hang my head. And on the flip side, if I get to stay, then what a great reason to put my whole self into my new job, despite it being the last thing I wanted.*

The next morning, even a small headache from the cheap wine couldn't stop me from smiling at the freedom I had felt dancing like a crazed woman the night before. It was 9:45. I sat at my desk, studying engineering drawings, refusing to lose faith. Still, I shook my head in disbelief when the phone rang at ten o'clock on the dot. It was the agent. If his answer was no, then I would fly home. If his answer was yes, then I had done it. I had made it through the fire. Either way, I felt at peace.

"I'm sorry it took so long, but I did speak to the owner, and they agreed to the original terms. You'll only need a one-month deposit and the first month's rent to move in. I can send over the paperwork today to sign."

HELL, YEAH! THIS IS INSANE!!! Okay. Calm down. He's still on the phone. "Great, thank you." I hung up and ran to the bathroom. I started laughing, but tears were flowing down my cheeks. *I did it. I flippin' did it! I have an apartment!!!*

The lease appeared in my email an hour later. We would be granted access January 1. A new year, a new home, and a new beginning. It was perfect! Absolutely perfect.

I thought about how hard it was asking for what I needed. Asking the window company for a relocation bonus and asking the real estate agent for help hadn't been easy. Both moments bruised my ego. But thanks to my bravery, I had gotten myself out of a bad situation and into an apartment on the Upper West Side of New York City.

CHAPTER 41

Nora returned the following Monday. I was leaving that coming Thursday for Florida. Despite what happened, I wanted our relationship to remain civil enough for me to stay there for the next three days, and then pick up my stuff when I returned. She had texted that she was sorry and asked to have dinner after I got off work that Monday. I agreed.

When I got to Dorsey's, she was already having a drink. I sat down and ordered chamomile tea, which surprised her.

Nora told me about her trip to Florida with the latest guy she was dating, acting as if nothing had happened, which I found shocking and very disturbing. I hoped this mood of hers would last until Thursday morning.

The minute I told her I was moving out, my voice shaking, I knew I should have waited until after leaving to break the news.

"Life in the city is too expensive. You'll be back sitting on a park bench before you know it," Nora mumbled.

"Is it okay if I stay until Thursday and then pick up my stuff when I return?" I asked, ignoring her insult and clutching my tea with a death grip.

"Yeah, that's fine. What are you getting for dinner? I was thinking the carbonara."

Two more days. Just two more. I've got this.

Tuesday came and went without a peep from her. I spent the night organizing my stuff so that it would be easy to grab when I returned in January.

Wednesday was the last full day of living with Nora. One day left of living in fear and eleven more days until the official start of my new life. I had made it. And, since I'd invested in a nice pair of tights, not even the frigid temps could bring me down that day. I boarded the subway, smiling as a text came in from Nora.

You owe me rent for the last six months. Then another text. *How did you manage to stay here past the summer? You were supposed to move out in August. Been trying to get you to leave.*

I stood frozen in shock. Chills raced through my body. I knew I was in danger.

I want December's rent today. I mean it.

I reread the text sequence. Fear enveloped me, causing me to get on the wrong train. At the next stop I got off and boarded another wrong train. I kept going in the wrong direction, feeling like a zombie. I made my way back above ground, knowing I needed to just stop and breathe. I had to act fast but wasn't capable of functioning.

After calling in sick, I instinctually phoned Eddie, my friend and former teacher from Stella Adler. The minute he heard me say his name, he knew I was in trouble. He gave me his address and told me to come straight over.

He sat me down on the couch while his partner Shannon made me some tea.

"It's my fault for staying. I was trying to save my money," I said after explaining the situation.

"None of this is your fault. Listen, we're going to rent a car and go get your belongings and then figure it out from there, okay?"

I nodded. I looked at my bank account. I had $580 and prayed it was enough to get me through this ordeal.

At the car rental place we ran into a snag. The company required a credit card, and neither of us had one. I kept asking the young man behind the counter to reconsider, but he was loyal to the company's policy. Taking a cab or Uber would have been horribly expensive and I had too much stuff for the bus. We needed this rental car.

Then Eddie started to talk, delivering a monologue I never dreamed someone would give on my behalf.

"Please, sir. She's in danger, and I have to get her belongings out today so that she doesn't get hurt again. Can you make an exception, please? Help me help her."

I wanted to close my eyes and hang my head in shame, but I refused. I looked up at both Eddie and the young guy with a look of determination and power.

I realized there's a difference between hitting rock bottom and getting to the point where you cannot take anymore. I had now experienced both. After hearing Eddie's plea, the guy at the counter not only made an exception, but also gave us a 50 percent discount. I wanted to express my gratitude, but his compassionate nod told me I didn't need to say anything.

As Eddie drove out of the city, my nerves resurfaced. *Please don't be home, please don't be home.* I was terrified.

We made a quick stop at a drug store and Eddie bought a box of black garbage bags. "Don't worry about being neat. Just throw stuff in these as fast as you can. Half full so they are easy to carry, okay?"

Though having a plan felt good, I was still frightened. We pulled up to the house and I knew Nora was home, because her latest boyfriend's car was in the driveway.

"Stephanie, it's going to be okay."

We made our way up to my bedroom. Nora was down the hall in hers, lying in bed with her boyfriend. Seeing I was not alone, she came running out, screaming, "How dare you bring a strange man into this house!"

If I weren't so scared, I'd laugh at the irony.

Eddie put his hands in the air like he had a gun pointed at him. Nora had a look of rage in her eyes that would petrify anyone.

"Nora, I'm moving out today. Thank you for giving me a place to live these past months. You asked for December's pay. Here is a check for three hundred thirty-eight dollars, which is the prorated amount through today, the twenty-first. I will be out of your way shortly," I said with as much authority and confidence as I could produce.

I started grabbing everything I could and shoving it into garbage bags, handing them to Eddie so he could go load them into the car.

A muffled conversation took place in Nora's bedroom, then she stormed back out. Eddie was downstairs. Proactively I fired at her. "If you dare touch me or my stuff, I will call the police, so step back and let me pack."

Shocked by my roar, she stormed out of my room, returned to hers, and slammed the door. *Go, go, go. Faster.*

I packed my things in a record-breaking ten minutes. As I went to grab my last garbage bag, Nora returned and stood in the doorway.

"I need my key, right now," she demanded.

I walked over to the dresser and grabbed her butterfly key chain. With shaking hands, I started to remove my mother's spare key. Nora leaned in and screamed, "And don't you dare try to keep my key chain."

Thinking she was going to hit me I covered my face, then removed the key, handed her the rest, and raced down the stairs. Halfway down, I shouted to Eddie that I would be right back. *I can't leave the place a mess.* I ran back up and grabbed the vacuum in the hallway closet and quickly ran it over the carpet. I took a rag and wiped down the dresser and ran to my hallway bathroom and made sure it looked clean before running as fast as I could back downstairs. Eddie was waiting with the car running. He took off down the road as calmly as he could for my benefit. Then it hit me. *It's over. I am never going to have to go back there again. I have a job and an apartment, with no one other than myself to rely on. I am safe.*

I glanced to my left. Eddie was fighting tears. It was hard for him to fully learn of the struggles I had endured from the minute I'd landed in the city. He helped me on a day when I desperately needed a true friend—someone who I am bonded with forever.

While we unloaded garbage bag after garbage bag into the unit, we must have looked like two criminals hiding evidence. I remembered Jason helping me move my stuff in Orlando and suggesting we do it wearing ski masks, and I laughed and told Eddie the story. When we finished, we sat on the floor, bewildered, with one suitcase left—the one I had conveniently packed the night before to take home with me to Florida.

"Stay on our couch. Shannon has chili in the slow cooker."

"That is so sweet to offer. You have already done too much, and I think I need to be alone tonight."

I was able to find a decent hotel with the money I had left. I hugged Eddie and got in the driver's seat of the Toyota Camry. I opened the windows, blasted the rock station at top volume, and took off like a bat out of hell down Columbus Avenue.

CHAPTER 42

I pulled up to my parents' home with a U-Haul full of the belongings I had stored in Orlando, so they could all be sold in the coming weekend's garage sale.

That Saturday I sat in a lawn chair, struggling as people relentlessly bargained for my stuff as if it meant nothing to them. All of my things were gorgeous, barely used, and all bought after the cruise. Now they looked like abandoned orphans out in the driveway.

I pushed back successfully, meeting people in the middle. I had it under control. Until an elderly woman with a heavy Japanese accent arrived, who wouldn't give up her determination to pretty much own my former apartment's contents for pennies on the dollar. As we haggled, I got louder and louder, and her accent got heavier and heavier. She kept yelling "One dollar" for everything she picked up. I was moments away from throwing her over my shoulder and carrying her off the property.

"One dollar?"

"No."

"One dollar?"

"No!"

"ONE DOLLAR!"

"I SAID, NO!"

By the time our faces were inches apart, Jim came running out, grabbed my arm, and brought me inside the house. "Hey honey, what's going on?" he said. Jim, who had been in sales for twenty years, was confused about why negotiating prices made me lose my patience.

"I just can't do this. I had Yanira last time. I had mimosas and a firepit. She set the prices. I had no idea what they were, but I do know that my stuff is worth way more than a dollar. How dare she take advantage of me. I'd rather throw it out than sell it for a dollar."

"Sweetheart, I'll help you. Go take a break. I've got this." He strutted outside, wearing his best salesman grin.

I made my way to the bathroom. I sat on the floor hyperventilating and crying at the same time, which made me sound like a puppy trying to find its bark. As insignificant as a garage sale seemed, I was getting rid of almost everything I owned for the third time.

The first time had been exciting. Since my new Italian-themed house didn't match the modern apartment I was moving from, instead of selling my things, I donated them all to charity with a heart full of gratitude.

The second time came with mixed feelings. I had combined my excitement of the world cruise with an undying faith that somehow I would be able to pull it off. Getting rid of so much stuff was more of a dare to the universe than anything else.

This time was downright painful. It hung on the coattails of so much pain, loss, and lack. If I could afford to bring my stuff to New York, I would have. I longed for something to hold onto. I stood up and walked straight outside to my chandelier, then dragged the box back into the garage. I was going to keep it and somehow get it to New York one day.

The decision made me feel slightly better. I was still a mess, but the woman had left, which made me feel like I could re-engage. With Jim by my side, I held it together until the last item I owned was loaded into the trunk of a gray, two-door Honda Civic.

• •

My mother could sense that I was carrying the weight of the world on my shoulders. She just didn't know why. I still wasn't over what happened with Nora, but couldn't tell her. Instead, she assumed I was sad over leaving Charlie. As a result, she spent the entire week telling me over and over how well she took care of him and how much he enjoyed staying with her, while hyping up Christmas and how Santa was coming—something Amie couldn't wait for.

On Christmas morning, I sat watching Amie tear through the wrapping paper on her presents like a tornado, wondering what this past year would have been like for me if I had her childlike sense of wonder and worry-free joy. I was alive and unharmed, yet there had been times when I questioned if that would be the outcome. Now that I knew it would end well, I wished I could go back and do it again without the worry, taking time to breathe a little more. But maybe that wasn't the purpose of it all. Maybe the point was for me to feel, to fear, and above all, to surrender.

• •

After the holiday, I borrowed my former car and drove to Orlando to see my tribe. I met Yanira, David, and Angela at a local restaurant.

"My Feffy!" Yanira shouted as I walked in. "Did you sell everything?"

"Yes, thanks to Jim. It was hard, but it feels good now. The Band-Aid is ripped off, and I'm ready for New York."

"You learning a lot about windows?" David asked.

"I will never look at them the same again," I said as the two of us exchanged a smirk that really felt like a twenty-minute long conversation. Our drinks arrived and everyone raised their glass to toast me.

"You are indestructible, Stephanie. Cheers!" David said as Angela and Yanira agreed. My heart exploded.

"I couldn't have done this without you. Now, stop acting like I am moving to the South Pole. You are required to visit twice a year. So, start planning," I said as we all clinked glasses.

• •

Yvonne, true to her style, wanted alone time with me, so we gathered at our tried-and-true place. This time, my stint working at Hillstone felt so distant that I was able to bask in our old oasis, which I had so missed.

As always, Yvonne skipped pleasantries and went straight to the heart of the matter. "I know I give you a hard time about coming home, but we support you, me included. I hope you feel that."

"I do," I said, piling smoked salmon onto a toast point.

"Well, then, what's weighing on you?"

"Nothing. I just need to gain my footing in New York."

"Ohhh-kayyy," she said in a tone that meant "bullshit!" followed by a look that said, "out with it, missy."

"I know I have you guys. I'm grateful for my tribe, but it took me a decade of living in Orlando to find you all. My people. When I went on the ship, I found that same feeling immediately with my dinner table. I know I'm a bit of a loner at times, but it helps to have a group of people who I know have my back, no matter what. In New York, I made a friend or two, even a teacher who helped me out of a tight spot. But, I feel like I'm swimming in the middle of a sea of predators. I don't think I'll find anyone like you all up there. Then again, maybe I'm not meant to…"

My thoughts were interrupted by a seaplane coming in for a landing on the lake. It pulled into the dock, and a couple exited and came up to eat. The event caused quite a stir among the other guests, who lined up to take photos in front of the banked plane. For Yvonne and me, it was the perfect comic relief.

As we waited for our cars from the valet, Yvonne leaned in and whispered, "You'll find your people. It may look different, but they're there." She hugged me.

It was our last moment alone together. Afterward, we went to her end-of-year awards party, where Yvonne was like a celebrity, adored by her students, current and former, who came to celebrate the "kiddies," as she called her new students. *I remember when I was that new to the craft. Excited, vulnerable, and unsure of my abilities. It seems like a hundred years ago and yesterday at the same time.*

I thought about what she taught, and why she was such a magnet. It wasn't just acting and directing. Yvonne taught me how to prepare for a scene—and then to get onstage and abandon expectations. "You don't know what your scene partner will bring to the table. Take the focus off yourself. Pay attention to them. Respond to them. Work with them, and together look for the small moments that guide the scene forward."

Those same teachings carried over into life. They taught me to be nimble and open during the past year. To notice the way forward by abandoning what I thought it had to look like. To feel the pain, but not let it stop me. "Feel the emotions, but don't let them tank you. Harness them. Use them," she would say. I did just that. I took in all the sadness and pain and transmuted it into the strength I needed to persevere.

• •

Every one of my close Art Sake friends had come to the awards party, to see me and partake in the post-awards karaoke showdown. I was so elated to see every single person I had missed those past months.

As I watched one of them badly sing Journey's "Don't Stop Believin'," a performance dedicated to me, I smiled. The love, support, and encouragement showered on me the entire night was uplifting. I felt accepted and embraced despite my choice to leave.

After chatting for most of the night, I later found myself tucked away in a corner, watching everyone laugh and enjoy themselves. It felt like my first night off the ship, when all my friends were in a fishbowl swimming around while I was on the outside looking in. But this time, it didn't come with a feeling of detachment. This time, I had put them in there, myself. To keep them safe and cherished in my heart. To carry them with me to New York.

CHAPTER 43

With a 7:00 a.m. New Year's Day flight, I went to bed well before the ball dropped. *Good night and go screw yourself, 2016.*

I dragged my two heavy suitcases out of the back of the car at the airport before hugging Jim goodbye. I gave my documents to the curbside agent, who informed me that since the flight was so early on a holiday, a first-class upgrade was only fifty dollars, cheaper than the checked bag fees in coach. I instantly perked up from my early-morning grogginess. *2017, it's hours into your arrival, and boy, do you know how to flirt!*

Sitting in first class, I felt quite sophisticated. With the trials I'd been through, even thinking I would sit in first class had felt so far off my personal radar. It was weird and wonderful at the same time.

"Coffee or juice for you, Miss?" the flight attendant asked.

"Pinot grigio, please," I replied.

"I like your style. Let me go grab that."

• •

I walked into my new apartment building, taking in the preserved, original, mint-green and wood finishes that complimented the

rose-colored granite steps—which I'd never noticed the last time Julie
and I were there, sprinting to claim the apartment. In the corner of
the lobby, a box as tall as me stood with my name on it. *My compressed
mattress arrived. Thank God.*

An hour later, after deadlifting the hundred-pound box
step-by-step to the fourth floor, I sat soaked in sweat in the hallway,
catching my breath. When I finally opened the door, a gritty reality
greeted me. The place was dirty, the door lock broken, there was
no hot water, and the toilet didn't work. My annoyance with the
management company's negligence helped contain the flood of
happiness, but it didn't diminish it. I saw the apartment's potential. I
saw *my* kitchen, *my* living room, *my* bedroom. I placed my hand on
the wooden kitchen counter and smiled.

I ran out to buy some cleaning products and to TJ Maxx to find
bedding and sheets and other basic necessities, then treated myself to
an Uber, since deadlifting my mattress just about killed my ability to
lift anything over ten pounds for more than thirty seconds. As the
driver pulled up to my building, I took in the street for the first time.
Above it were branches of trees that, come spring, would cascade like
umbrellas over the five-story brick buildings. It was perfect.

Standing in front of the apartment building were two guys. They
appeared to be in their fifties, born-and-bred New Yorkers. One
was tall, very tan, and built. The other was short, had pitch black
hair, a receding hairline, and facial features I guessed were probably
Hispanic. I had no idea how to behave. After all, I was on their turf.
So I kept my head down, pulled out my keys, and tried to walk
straight through them to the front door. I didn't get very far.

"Hey, you live here now or somethin'?" the dark-haired one said.

I smiled and said yeah while continuing to the front door.

He shouted, "Hey, Vince, get ova here and meet the new girl."

I cringed. Vince turned around from talking to the barbershop
owner, whose business was two basements over. He looked me up

and down, tossed his cigarette, and came to shake my hand. "Which apartment are you in?" Vince asked.

I hesitated.

"Oh, come on," the other guy said. "I live in the building. Gonna find out sooner or later."

"4RE," I replied.

"I live next door. I'm Armando. That's my friend, Vince. Welcome to the building."

"Thanks," I said, turning to open the door.

"Here, let us help you with your bags," Vince said.

"Nah, I got it. Thanks, though," I said quickly as I ducked inside. The door closed behind me.

Mildly upset that my apartment door lock was broken, I distracted myself by cleaning while my decompressed mattress expanded to its normal size. As soon as it did, I took out my new, unwashed sheets and comforter. Nap time.

An hour later, I awoke to a knock at the door. I sat up and stared down the hallway. My heart raced. I crept quietly toward the door as the knock repeated, harder. I noticed a white box where the peephole should have been. It had a lever on the right side, so I pushed it down, hoping to see who was there before pretending not to be home. The lever had different plans. It squeaked so loudly, it echoed. I cringed.

"Ya don't have to use the peephole. Not gonna kill ya. It's just me, Armando, ya'neighbor. Open up."

Embarrassed, I complied, and as I did, he took the opportunity to look through the small opening of the door to see that I had zero furniture.

"Yeah, I guessed you had nuthin'. It's New Year's Day, so no moovas."

"My roommate, Julie, and her furniture are coming tomorrow. I'm just getting the place cleaned in preparation."

"Well, Vince is cookin' sausage and gravy over ziti. Wanna come ova for a gatherin' next door at four o'clock? We figured ya had nuthin' to eat and nuthin' to cook with. Besides, like it or not, we're neighbors. We wanna get to know ya."

In a city that seemed so cold, unforgiving, and challenging, his invitation was the first hint of a different kind of New York City. "I have some stuff to run out and do. If I'm back by four, I'll come by," I said, giving myself an out in case I changed my mind.

Showing up empty-handed was out of the question; my grandma would come back alive and kill me. Despite my apprehensions, I stopped and bought an inexpensive bottle of red wine before getting some baby wipes from a drugstore, since we had no running water.

I sat on the stairs on the first floor of our building as the chatter and laughter drifted down from Armando's apartment. The sounds reminded me of my table. In just a few days, the 2017 Grand Voyage would set sail with only Ken on board. The rest of us weren't able to keep our promise.

By 4:45, I decided to bite the bullet and proceeded upstairs, dropped off my bags, washed my armpits with baby wipes, and headed next door with my bottle of wine.

"What? Ya didn't have to bring dat. Dat's so kind of you," Armando said as he opened the door. Vince was busy in the kitchen making magic—or so I was told by the other guests who bragged about his cooking skills. In the living room were two friends, Elena and Keith. I sat down, and Keith offered me what was left of the appetizers sitting on various TV trays. Closest to me was a plate of bread and some anchovy dip. I politely took some bread, skipped the dip, and snagged a few pieces of cheese while thanking him for offering.

"Ya sure ya don't wanna try Vince's famous anchovy dip? It's addictin'," Armando said.

His comment reminded me of pretending to like snails to earn Sally's approval. I smiled at the memory.

"I hate anchovies, but thanks," I said confidently, popping a piece of cheese in my mouth.

I learned they all had been friends for three decades. Their deep connection was evident by an unmistakable in-sync rhythm that I noticed in their words and actions. Like long-time married couples, they completed each other's sentences. Everyone had their well-practiced part to play in these shared meals. They knew exactly who would do what.

I looked around and noticed that Armando's apartment had never been renovated. "Armando, I love the original woodwork in here and how you kept it all intact."

"Thanks. Ya gotta see this claw tub I have in the bathroom. I was born here. Lived here fifty years. My apartment is rent-controlled, so it'll never be renovated. I don't pay enough rent." "He pays one-sixth what you pay, and his place is twice as big," shouted Vince from the kitchen.

"Oh wow. So you never, ever lived anywhere else." I was shocked. "I could never do that."

"Yeah, but you could never pay what I pay for rent."

"Very true, Armando." I smiled.

"But listen, this isn't the me-show. You're the new girl here."

As if I were right back at the singles' event on the ship, I braved the same inquisition.

"Yes, I am single."

"No, I have never married."

"No, I don't have any kids."

"No, I'm not twenty-nine, but wow, thanks for thinking I am."

"I came to New York after circling the globe on a ship."

Silence.

"You what?" Armando asked.

"I sold my house and took a one-hundred-fifteen-day cruise around the world."

"You have to tell us more," Keith said.

Clearly, I had a captive audience. So, I told them about the fun times. My table at dinner. The places we stopped, the crazy things that happened to me like the Tongan exfoliation scrub and being asked to be someone's second wife—two stories that always worked a crowd.

My stories opened them up to tell their own. By the time dinner was ready, we all felt comfortable with each other. Genuinely connected.

Armando's kitchen was ten feet by ten feet with antiquated appliances, exactly what I would expect for his place. His square table barely fit against the side wall, but Vince put in the leaf so I could fit—which made the table too big for the kitchen. It now sat on a diagonal, forcing whoever sat on the far side to crawl under to get to their seat.

Vince placed a huge pot of sausage and gravy on the table, and we crammed around it, ready to dive in.

"So, Stephanie, we do this often. You better come!" Vince said.

"Absolutely. I love dinners like these. If you want, I can cook next time."

Everyone threw up their hands in protest. "Don't get all carried away now. Vince is the cook. No one tops his gravy," Armando said.

I laughed. "Fine, I'll just bring wine."

They cheered.

"Oh, we also stoop on Sundays. Ya gotta join," Armando said.

"I don't know that is," I replied.

"Ya don't know what stoopin' is?" Vince asked.

"It's the stairs in the front," Keith said, "The stoop. We hang out there. Drink and people-watch." He was a doctor, so his explanations were rather concise.

"Oh. I didn't know what a stoop was. I don't think we have those in Florida," I said as more laughter erupted. "Wait. Today is Sunday. That's what you were doing down there? I thought you were loitering. You were stooping?"

"Loitering? She thought we were loitering. Get outta here!" Vince said.

"Leave her alone. She's new," Armando said. "But now ya gotta join us."

"Okay, okay. I'll join you on the stoop."

They all cheered and shouted. Armando raised his glass of wine. "Thank you all for being here. Stephanie, ya gave us such a welcome surprise today. Welcome to the family, kid. Happy New Year's, everyone," he said as we all clinked glasses.

CHAPTER 44

A YEAR AND A HALF LATER

N ew York City knocks you down. Those who get back up get to stay."

Eddie's words to me the day my grandma died couldn't have rung truer.

I've grown to believe that New York City holds up a veil for those it hasn't yet welcomed. That veil gives the city an appearance of a busy, cold, merciless place that is better enjoyed from the comforts of a weekend visit to the tourist traps.

But once the city accepts you as one of its own, that veil lifts and everything looks and feels different. The city softens, becomes more personal, even a bit quieter, which charmed the hell out of me. I fell in love with New York City, and like a gecko against its backdrop, my colors began to change. I noticed more and more how well I blended in with my dark clothes, strategic shoes, and insanely fast walk through the now memorized subway tunnels.

As if it were an unexpected form of icing on the cake, selling windows allowed me to stand in the most unbelievable apartments and see views I would never have otherwise seen. To learn about a building's history, its artistic designs. I got to see New York City from the inside out—a rare gift for a newcomer.

• •

I sat comfortably in my brown leather reading chair as an electrician stood on a ladder, hanging up my chandelier which I had managed to dismantle and fit into a suitcase on my last trip home. It was the perfect final addition in my newly rented studio apartment, located directly across the street from where Julie and I had lived for the past year. I sipped coffee while admiring the perfect view across the apartment and out the front window. I noticed how the leaves were in full pre-summer bloom and no one walking by needed a jacket. If I leaned my head far enough, I could see the stoop from my old building where I still hung out with Vince and Armando, standing around like I was one of the locals born and raised on the block.

It had taken only a year to earn a promotion working directly for Mike, which greatly enhanced my financial situation and afforded me the freedom to live on my own. I felt extremely grateful for the opportunity, but never stopped applying to more creative jobs or working on my artistic endeavors. Through a contact of Eddie's, I took on the role of resident producer at a theater in Long Island City, hoping to learn more about the business side of things and eventually earn my way onto their stage.

While I couldn't say I had reached a mountaintop, the climb has felt less steep. Less risky. Despite my continued efforts, I felt more grounded. More at peace. But above all, I took pride in the life I had created.

After the electrician left, I stood underneath the chandelier. I placed my hand on it, happy to be touching something once attached to my old home. As if it were a time machine, I closed my eyes and transported back to a time before the robbery, standing in my old bedroom where it once hung as Charlie played with his favorite toy on the bed. Those days had been so simple. I had my dog, my friends, Art Sake. Blissfully existing, fully numb to how unfulfilled I was in life. But most importantly, there were no painful goodbyes to endure.

I opened my eyes and wiped the tears before grabbing one of my orange and silver suitcases. It was time to pack for my flight the next morning. Another quick trip home to visit Yvonne.

• •

The plane was rather empty for a Thursday morning in May. I had a row to myself, grateful for the space to breathe. As much as I tried to process everything, I still couldn't shake the sight of walking into the studio last December to see an angry, tearful, yet determined Yvonne packing her office like a madwoman, filling box after box with twenty years of paperwork. Art Sake Acting Studio, as we knew it, was over.

Yvonne insisted that only the six of us closest to her know the facts "until the dust settled," as she liked to say with her twisted sense of humor. Despite my disagreement, anytime she called and asked me to secretly fly in for the day to help her with real estate matters, or to just grab lunch, I couldn't say no. I would have done anything for her.

I cursed the jarring May Florida heat and blasted the air conditioning in my rental car. Driving past the downtown area, I noticed the handful of buildings that served as its skyline. The past years in New York made the once-exciting downtown of Orlando now look barren.

Despite my protests, Yvonne and I were not meeting at Hillstone. Instead, she had chosen a small grill close to her house. I pulled in and spotted her sitting outside, sipping an iced tea. I waved and her big, brown doe-eyes lit up as she waved back.

I ran out of the car and hugged her.

"Thanks for coming on such short notice," she said.

"Of course!"

"I ordered you an iced tea. Is that OK?

"That's perfect."

"Sit. I want to hear all about New York."

"Well, my job is going well since my promotion. It's a lot of work, but it's a good, stable job."

"That's great," she said flatly as she began to look over the menu.

"I think it is. Between that and finishing decorating my new place—it feels good to be settled."

"I was hoping for some juicy story about a hot man, or men, even. Instead I get an update on your job," she said wryly.

"Yvonne, you know I refuse to go out and look for love. Don't roll your eyes at me. He will show up when he is meant to. Until then, I have things to do."

"Don't get too used to being alone."

"I'm not!"

Yvonne rolled her eyes again. I took my straw and flung iced tea at her.

She eyed my black jeans and olive tank top. "Well, you look very New York."

I looked at her intently, happy to see a tinge of the old jealous Yvonne back in action.

"Funny you should say that; I almost wore the same outfit I wore to my first day of class with you."

"Oh, God," she snorted as she laughed. "Those red heels."

"I was trying to look like an artist."

We both laughed. She shook her head, savoring the memory before changing the subject. "Any acting or directing work?"

"Well, I attend casting director workshops and submit myself to auditions. I am also working with someone to rebrand my image with new headshots and whatnot. Nothing has come of it yet. But in all fairness, I had to put finances on the front burner. So, I couldn't go at it full force. But I'm still producing plays at that theater I told you about."

Yvonne shrugged her shoulders in disappointment. I understood. I was disappointed too.

"Producing isn't the same."

"I know, Yvonne. Trust me, after a day in an office, the last thing I want to do is the business side of making other people's art. But, if I put in the time, let them get to know me better, I'm hoping I can get a shot at directing something, or even acting in a production."

"If you're tired of being asked to be the producer, then stop walking into a room like you are the boss."

"Oh, is that my problem?"

"Might be." She smiled an evil grin, then put her hands together. I could see her thinking carefully about her next words. "Don't give up on your art. If I were to put my money on someone, it's you."

My stomach clenched in shock over her words.

"Yvonne, I…"

"No. Don't respond. Accept the compliment. I know exactly what you were going to say, and I don't want to hear it."

She was right. I was about to tell her what she meant to me. How she'd changed my life. But I knew better. I regrouped. "Actually, I was going to say that I'm shocked that you're not telling me to come home again."

Yvonne laughed, but only softly this time. "I'm just happy you still call this place home."

I remained silent.

"Don't get me wrong. I still want you to come home. It's my dying wish."

"That's not funny," I said.

She giggled at her own dark humor.

I couldn't put off the question any longer. "So, how's chemo going?"

"Well, the tumor markers are still going down, but I hate the treatments."

"But it's working!"

"No, no. Don't you do that too," she warned.

"Do what?" I asked.

"Be hopeful."

"I'm sorry."

"The drugs and treatments are only buying me a little extra time. I have at most six months. I need to come to terms with this. Hope is making it harder for me." Her eyes filled with tears.

"It's just that you are so loved, Yves."

"I am dying, and I need people to honor that and prepare."

I understood, but also found her words a little hypocritical. Yvonne had told only a handful of us, and so when her last day came, hundreds of people were going to be shocked. I looked at her wiping her tears and saw a tired version of the same Yvonne I knew. How could it be that inside her a terminal cancer was spreading, waiting to take its victory lap?

"You're right. But it's hard not to be hopeful. If your treatment only gives you to us for a few extra months, I will happily take it."

"I'm just thankful it's given me and the hubby time to have a beach weekend now that it's hot."

"I'm glad. You and Simon love the beach." I tried to change the mood. "Remember when we got a hotel for a long weekend, and you were mad at how skinny I was? You insisted on sitting ten feet away from me on the beach so no one could compare our figures as they walked by. Remember that? I wanted to slap you."

Yvonne laughed. "I'd kill to go back in time and visit that day." More softly, she said, "I also wish I could see snow one more time."

"You will! I will Facetime you at our first snow. Sometimes it snows as early as October, so you never know!" Then, remembering her wish, I added, "And if not, I promise to enjoy it for you."

She smiled, but said nothing.

We talked for a few hours, falling into a rhythm that felt like old times at Hillstone. I missed those days already and silently made it my mission to get us back there one more time before it was too late. As we joked and laughed, I couldn't ignore my desperate need to know that Art Sake would live on.

"I know Christy has been teaching for you. What did you tell the students?"

"That I had stomach surgery."

"Okay. That's pretty believable."

"I decided I'm going to have Christy take over Art Sake permanently. She knows my curriculum. David can help run things as well. They'll do great together." Christy was her best friend and well-trained. It was the perfect solution for Art Sake, but one that made me feel far away and helpless.

"If they need me, know that I'll be here as much and as often as needed," I assured her.

"Thank you for that, and for today."

I could tell by her heavy eyes that she had grown tired.

"You ready to get outta here?" I asked.

She nodded.

"Where did you park?"

"I got a ride. I'm too tired to be driving and didn't want to make you pick me up," she said stubbornly.

"YVONNE!" I shouted. She laughed and got into the back seat of my car as if I were driving "Miss Daisy."

"Let's do this again soon," I said, pulling up to her house. I watched her slowly walk up her driveway, memorizing every detail I could.

CHAPTER 45

David called at the end of August with news. "Yvonne's cancer has spread to her brain, and she is bedridden and barely able to talk. She can make noises, but when she does get a word out, it isn't the right word," he said quietly.

"I should have known when she told me to hold off on visiting. Her mind was not right all summer."

"We all noticed. She didn't tell us. Simon finally called and told me last night."

"How long, David?"

"Not long. She's down to eighty-five pounds and fading fast. This it, Stephanie."

"I'll be there this weekend. God, I don't know how I'm going to do this."

"It's okay if you can't."

"I have to," I whispered.

"Then I'll be there for you when you're done."

I hung up and sat down to process his words. My visions of planning one last sunset with Yvonne over smoked salmon at Hillstone faded to gray as I searched for the strength to say goodbye.

Sunday morning, after Yanira force-fed me breakfast, she hugged me while I cried on her shoulder in the driveway. "Fef. Be strong. Not for you, but for her. I love you. I'll be here when you get home." She kissed my cheek.

Yvonne's best friend Christy, who had been with her almost daily, spent the morning preparing me for what I was about to see. David sat next to me, holding my hand as I listened to her instructions. "You won't have long with her with all her pain meds. She'll try to speak a word, but it won't be the right one. Simon and her sister are there. Just go spend some time with her. Remember, the last thing Yvonne wants is sobbing or some outpouring of gratitude." Christy smiled slightly. "She's a captive audience, so don't torture her."

I needed a script. I was petrified to accidentally say something that would make her sad or angry about having to "shed her earthly coil," as she often put it. I hated that I had no amazing updates to share. I wanted her to be proud of me. I wanted nothing more than to tell her I was directing or acting. *But I'm not doing either of those things. I'm afraid I failed her…that she wasted her bet on me.*

The worst part was that no matter what I decided to say to her, she wouldn't be able to respond.

From the front door of Yvonne's home, I could see directly into the her bedroom. Yvonne was lying in bed with the news on. She was the size of a ten-year-old; her hair was unevenly cut short. As I came closer, I realized she resembled a skeleton more than a child. Instantly thankful for Christy's warning, I tried to contain my shock.

I climbed into bed with her and talked about anything I could think of, trying my best to ask questions that she could reply to with either "ah-hah" or "uh-uh." Between my stories of life in New York, Yvonne tried to lift her head to say something, but then stopped, exhaled, and lay back down again. I wanted so much to know what she was trying to say, and watching her struggle made it hard to keep my composure.

"Water," she finally said, slurring the word quite heavily.

"Water? I can get you some." I pointed to the glass on her table. She shook her head.

"Waddder," she repeated.

"Do I want water? I'm good. But thank you for asking."

"No," she said again, pointing to the table.

I saw only two things: a glass of water and a lamp.

"Do you want me to turn on the light?"

"Ah-hah, waddder," she said.

I walked around the bed to her lamp and switched it on. She smiled widely and made a cooing sound like a baby.

I caved. All the strength I had borrowed to bring me to this point now deserted me. I did something I never in a million years thought I would do. I got back in bed and looked into her eyes.

"Yvonne. I have some great news for you! I'm moving home to be with our tribe," I announced.

Her face lit up like a Christmas tree—which instantly changed into a shadow of sadness. I couldn't tell if she knew I was not telling the truth, or if despite her comments, she never really wanted me to give up. Maybe she was sad that she wouldn't be here for my return. It didn't matter. I lied. I lied to my dear friend on her deathbed. Like a coward. Heavily disappointed in myself, I decided to undo it.

Before I could gather the strength to come clean, her discomfort took over like a tidal wave. Simon suggested it was time to let her rest. I didn't know what to do. I couldn't say the word goodbye. I got up and slowly walked to her side of the bed. Hugged her softly. Whispered, "I guess it's time to circle up, bitches." I saw a gleam in her eye followed by a half smile.

When I walked out of her bedroom, I looked back one last time. Yvonne waved weakly. I waved back, then closed the front door behind me knowing I would never see her again.

I got into my car and headed straight to Christy's. Thank God she lived only a few blocks away because I don't remember driving there. I fell into her embrace, crying, drenched with guilt.

"Oh, God, Christy. Oh, God. I lied to her. I told her I was moving home," I said, sobbing in her arms.

"Sit down. Let it out. It's okay. Look at me, Stephanie. It's okay."

"No, it's not okay. I'm a horrible person. Why the hell did I say that?"

She grabbed my hands. "Let me ask you something. If David and I struggled with the fate of Art Sake, and we called you and asked you to move home and help run it, would you?"

"In a heartbeat."

"Okay. That's what matters. If needed, you WILL come home."

"I will. I swear."

"Despite the shit Yvonne always gave you, she wants you to fly. She left David and me in charge—not you—for a reason. Now, if you were living here, she would have included you, but you aren't. So, do what you're meant to do up there. If we need you, we'll have you come home. In the meantime, find a way of honoring her. Think of something, and then do it—for her."

"Okay. I promise," I said, having no idea what "that" would be. But I vowed to find out.

CHAPTER 46

In mid-November, and only forty-nine days after Yvonne's death, our first winter snowstorm blasted into New York City. I took the day off, made some coffee, and went outside to sit on the stoop. I'd poured my coffee into a champagne flute that Yvonne had given me as a gift when I was her assistant director for the very first time. She'd had it engraved with the play's title, *Misfortune*.

I was underdressed for the bitter cold but liked the sharp, stinging feeling of snow on my bare arms. The fast-falling, thick flakes would have been visible enough for Yvonne to see through video chat. Instead, I took it in for her just as I had promised, marveling at how my picturesque Upper West Side street slowly turned into a clean canvas of pure white.

Beginning to shiver, I moved my viewing party indoors. I put on a Dave Matthews vinyl and sat in my reading chair, enjoying the snow out the window of my thoughtfully decorated apartment. With its red velvet couch, brick wallpaper, huge chandelier, and mixture of bohemian and retro décor, it was a place she would have loved as much as I did.

I could feel Yvonne there with me. I could see her rolling her eyes. I could hear her loud laugh and her words, asking me when I'm coming home. I knew I couldn't go through with my lie. But on this day of staying home in a crazy snowstorm, her words spoke to me differently than they had before.

Maybe "coming home" didn't have to entail returning to Florida, as she had wanted. Maybe it meant coming home to myself. To refrain from the desire to shape-shift and morph into what I thought I needed to be to gain a certain desired outcome. To be authentic— despite fears of unworthiness, the unknown, and rejection; despite society's expectations. Whatever it meant, one thing was for certain—I had found the first feelings of home the day I walked into her studio in my obnoxious red heels. That simple day changed everything.

I realized my efforts to be seen and chosen by those with artistic opportunities had put a strain on the heartbeat I had been desperately trying to keep alive, while all along, its vitality was in my hands. I now knew what I needed to do for not only myself, but also to honor Yvonne.

I recalled every one-act play we had done at Play de Luna, and one I had directed stood out in my mind. *Role Playing Night*, about a woman who thinks her partner wants to spice up their sex life by role-playing, while he is asking her to role-play in a game of Dungeons and Dragons with his two best friends.

Coincidentally, the theater company where I helped produce was having a one-act festival. I checked the submission deadline and saw that it wasn't too late to enter. I emailed the script to Eddie. He called me immediately.

"Oh, Stephanie. This play is hilarious. I want to direct this."

"Good, 'cause I directed it already at my theater back home. I want to be the female lead."

I could almost hear his wheels begin to spin. The creative energy stirred up from our brief phone call already felt just like it did back at Art Sake. I stood up to get more coffee. Walking into my kitchen, I realized I'd left a cabinet door open. My eyes were pulled toward the top shelf, where a custom-designed aluminum water bottle was pushed so far forward it was about to fall. As I pushed it back, the bottle rotated and the image of the cast from when I directed *Role Playing Night* for Play de Luna stared straight at me. A gift given to me by one of the actors. I stood motionless, staring at it staring back at me. A huge smile stretched across my face. "YVONNE!"

• •

The first few rehearsals were tough, as I had to dust off my actor skill set. But as I settled into my craft again, my joy carried over, making every aspect of my life more colorful. I wasn't super close to the other actors, and the theater space wasn't Art Sake, but the energy I felt from expectation-free creative expression was the same. For my role, at the end of our play, I had to wear a Princess Leia slave costume that looked more like a bikini than an outfit. This pushed me to return to the elliptical again, which greatly helped me work through Yvonne's passing.

One day, after rehearsal, Eddie asked me to stay to chat about something. We sat in the theater's lobby with coffee as I watched him prepare his words while also trying to keep his excitement from exploding out of his body.

"I have a crazy idea to sell you on," he began.

"Okay, go for it," I said enthusiastically, remembering how vulnerable I had felt whenever sharing my big ideas over the years.

"I want to make this short play into a short film with you all as the cast. The topic is perfect, and the writing brilliant. I think that if we raised enough money and did a high-quality job, we could get it into Comic Con."

Eddie spoke at length about all the opportunities and potential success that could come of our project. I observed his nervous energy, his excitement. His eyes widened with possibility and a tinge of delusion. I smiled. Watching him was like watching myself talk about Tina Fey and my film for her sequel. It made me want to support him even more. I promised to help him any way I could.

• •

Forty short plays entered the January 2019 festival, which would be narrowed down to the top ten through audience voting over a period of two weeks. Advancing into the finals confirmed for Eddie that our play should be made into a film, and I was thrilled that I gained one more week of acting.

The day before our final performance, Eddie called me at eight in the morning, which was alarming.

"The playwright decided not to sign over the film rights," he said. "Something about family health issues. He didn't explain further."

"Could be serious, Eddie."

"I tried to tell him that no one else will want to make something of his script. A director from New York City wants to try and take his script to Comic Con, and he refuses?" he said, his ego flaring. Eddie went on and on about how to change the playwright's mind, insisting that we needed to find a way to make the film happen.

I know how Eddie feels...all too well.

I honored that fight inside of him, but also wanted to tell him not to attach himself to his endeavors. To let go and trust that it isn't meant for him. But when I was in his shoes, that's the last thing I wanted to hear.

I was tempted to fix the situation by calling the playwright and trying to change his mind, but I knew better. Instead, I told Eddie to meet me for brunch. There was something I wanted to share with him.

CHAPTER 47

After two hours of listening to my entire story, Eddie stared at me speechless.

He sat back and pushed the Bloody Mary I made him order aside. "I have so many questions to ask you. First, I HAVE to know what happened to everyone from the ship. Kiki, your table, Julie and Kel…"

"I still talk to Julie and Kel. They love to phone me, all tipsy when Australia rings in the New Year."

"How fun," Eddie said.

"I know, right? I just love them. They're still waiting for 'Stephanie in lights,' as they say. Um, Kiki is great. Her ship pulls into New York every once in a while, which gives us a few hours to hang out. I haven't kept in touch with Sally and Don. They aren't on social media, but Detta, Pete, and Ken are, and we chat online. Pete just moved into an assisted living facility last month, so he's hard to reach."

"He isn't okay, is he?"

"Knowing how stubborn Pete is, he wouldn't go to a facility unless he really needed help. I'm not sure I'll ever hear from him again."

"It's obvious how much they all mean to you. How much the entire trip meant to you."

Words failed me. I had no response. I could only nod.

"Are you still close with everyone from Art Sake?"

"Yes. I mean, more people left Orlando, some married and had kids. Life moved on for many of us, but we make an effort to remain close. A huge group of us just went on a cruise together. We see each other twice a year or so. I make it a priority. And I'll never miss a Play de Luna like promised."

"Charlie too? You get to see him?"

"Oh, yes. I go home every other month or so to visit him for the weekend. He's about ten or eleven now, or so we think. He is my little old man. I never told anyone, but I moved him here right after I got promoted."

"No way. What happened?"

"He really struggled with the shock of the city…the noise and such. After ten stressful days, I knew in my heart he needed to go back to my mom and stepdad. I ugly-cried the whole way back on the plane."

"Oh, hon, I am so, so sorry."

"Yeah. It's tough. I feel like I didn't make him a priority, and I hate myself for that sometimes."

"You did what was best for him. He needs a stable, low-key environment. To me, you making that sacrifice tells me you are a great mom to him."

"Thanks. I needed to hear that."

Eddie stared off in the distance.

"Actually, there is something I don't get," he finally said.

"What?"

"Every time you walked into the theater to produce or whenever we met up, you always looked so poised, professional, and like a boss. I thought you loved that lifestyle. It boggles me to hear how you really feel about your career. After you got on your feet, why did you stay there?"

"Well, nothing ever panned out. I never stopped trying to think of a business idea or researching other companies. Even artistically, I never stopped trying, but I no longer lean on it so desperately. I learned to take what I love and find a way to insert it into any environment...even a window company." I smirked. "I use my artistic training there way more than my MBA. And they have no idea."

"Like hiding vegetables in the mashed potatoes?"

I laughed. "Exactly."

"That can't be enough, though. Can it?"

"For me, it's not about it being enough. It's to help me enjoy my time there while I wait for the next pull forward."

"I'm bewildered, Stephanie. I really am. I would have never left Florida. And I certainly would have gone home that day on the park bench. Hell, both days on the park bench. Why on God's green earth did you stay?"

"I have asked myself that same thing, many times. The answer was always the same. In those moments of despair, I would think of going back and recreating a steady life and it would feel amazing, in an instant relief sort of way. But, at the same time, the thought felt physically painful. Like my soul was shriveling up, if that makes any sense."

"It does," he whispered.

"I can't go live a life where I always wonder what I am really made of all while pining over one hundred fifteen days I'll never recreate because I gave up and played it safe. Here, no matter how long it takes, I feel like my soul has plans. I just don't know them.

And being here is my way of holding out hope that I could feel the way I did on that ship again in some new capacity."

"You are a hopeless romantic, you know that?"

"Nah." I blushed.

"And you never shared this with anyone."

"The people involved knew pieces, but I never told the entire thing at once."

"So, why did you decide to tell me today?"

"It felt like the right thing to do. Your being upset over the film made me realize that the only stories we truly have to work with are our own. Don't lean into this film too far, Eddie. You have so many stories inside of you. Harness those. Let this all go."

"You are right, but it's just such a good idea! I can't help it," he said, and we both laughed.

Underneath my laughter, the words I had just spoken created a ping, a pull as strong as the day I drew lines on a map. A burning sensation in my core consumed me. I knew what I had to do, but I was reluctant. It's one thing to go on an adventure, a leap of faith, or test one's resilience. It's another to feel called to do something you believe you're bad at. My insecurities and vulnerabilities overwhelmed me.

"Hon, are you okay?"

I wasn't. I needed to process.

Eddie snapped his fingers in front of my face and I barely moved to meet his gaze. Like a dam breaking, the words poured out of me.

"I need to try and write my story," I said softly.

"You totally should."

Eddie took a long pause, staring at what I assumed to be the fear I sat drenched in.

"Here, try this. After we wrap the play tomorrow, get a good night's sleep. Then wake up and begin scouting out places that inspire you. Bring your laptop. Write a few pages of whatever comes into your heart. Go there and do that every day. Just a suggestion."

It wasn't a suggestion. He had delivered me the instructions for my first step forward.

"Just. Get. It. Out. Of. You," he yelled as everyone turned and looked.

"Shh," I said, embarrassed. But Eddie didn't care.

I put my hands through my hair and exhaled sharply.

"I just don't know if I am capable," I admitted.

"Oh, hon, that's the fun part!" he said as we clinked our watered-down Bloody Marys.

• •

The next evening, Eddie and I walked into the theater alongside the three other actors in our production. Eddie seemed more calm, relaxed, and excited to watch our final performance. As he was about to break the news to the cast about no longer making a film, I excused myself and headed into the dressing room to be with my thoughts and prepare myself to perform.

When the time came for the play to begin, I turned my mind and body toward the stage I was about to enter. I inhaled deeply, feeling that beloved heartbeat exude out of my chest. I exhaled slowly as the lights dimmed, and the audience fell silent. It was time to go and enjoy the comedy of a well-told story of high hopes and misunderstandings. To lose myself in this final performance to a play that came from my theater, written by someone in my tribe. To honor Yvonne, Art Sake, and the inner artist within who only ever craved a safe space to freely and authentically express herself. To honor every person, place, and moment that brought my body and mind to this very stage.

In the end, standing half-naked to a standing ovation, I took my bow.

EPILOGUE

After relentlessly walking in and out of more than ten places on Amsterdam Avenue, Olma, a bar on the corner of my street, was my final choice. It seemed friendly and quiet, but most importantly, its bar had the exact same granite I'd had installed in the kitchen of my old home. I sat down and slid my hand across the familiar pattern, then exhaled as a fair-skinned, blond server walked up.

"What can I get you?" he asked.

"I need a place to write. I just want a glass of seltzer, but I'll tip you as if I'm ordering beers. Would that be okay with you?"

"Absolutely. What are you writing?"

"A book," I replied, trying to appear self-assured.

"I write too. But I do more stand-up and sketch writing."

"That's awesome! I came to the right place."

A couple at the end of the bar chimed in. "You are a writer?" the woman asked.

"Yes, I am," I said, playing into the situation.

"What books have you published?"

"This is my first one."

"Wow, congratulations!" she said as her partner nodded. "What is it about?"

"It's a true story. My story."

"Wow, what happened?"

"Actually, I'm up against a huge deadline with my editor. I need to get to work."

"Oh, yes. Go ahead, dear. We won't bother you," she said.

I lied. I had no deadline. I had no editor. I hadn't written one word, and no one in my life other than Eddie knew I was going to even try. Today wasn't about telling a stranger my story. I needed to tell it to myself, first.

I could see out of the corner of my eye two people joining the couple at the far end. I could faintly hear the word "book" come out of the woman's mouth. I saw them all staring at me with intrigue. Mission accomplished; I had the external accountability I needed to force me inward.

I put ten dollars down on the bar to let the bartender know I was serious about tipping him for the use of the space while encouraging him to keep my seltzer full. From my bag I pulled out my Dave Matthews Band drumstick and set it next to my laptop. I closed my eyes and took a deep breath.

Okay, time to begin. Time to tell the truth. To share my story of how I awakened my soul while traveling around the world in all its splendor. But to also release the shame and embarrassment I've secretly held onto from the aftermath. I'm not done rebuilding all that was destroyed in my life, especially financially. I look pretty horrible on paper, and that is hard to admit. And some of my decisions, like listening to that healer…? I've always been afraid of being judged if others knew of my idiocy. Sharing my story would be for me—and for the people who deserve to fully see me, including my shame. An act of freedom my soul is calling for so that I can say goodbye to it all, or perhaps to somehow say hello. I don't know.

Though I must confess: my feelings toward what happened after the cruise waffle between gratitude and anger. I proved myself to myself, and I am thankful for my sense of self-rising, but will never fully understand the cost.

Some days, I look back and feel strong, capable, and fortified. Proud of the courage I had to embrace life and its adventures, and equally proud of my bruises and scars. I look in the mirror and see an essence of authenticity I didn't possess before. I walk to the subway feeling like no matter what the day brings, if my world turns upside down, I am capable enough to survive it. My time spent down and out on a few park benches freed me of that fear. Like a warrior who won a battle, I have respect for my story and myself.

Then, sometimes I feel hopeless. I wake up ungrateful and nostalgic. I think of only the good parts of my past, romanticizing and missing them. My loneliness wraps around me like an uninsulated coat, and I head out into the day with only one goal: to force a smile.

Once upon a time, my solution to these struggles would have been to obsessively seek out success and money to fill those holes of sadness, shame, and unworthiness. To use that superficial sizzle to make me feel lovable. Or even to lean too far into my artistic passions, expecting them to save me. But I know now that doing so only built a false foundation—one that inevitably imploded—multiple times.

Today I am making a different choice. No running, no hiding from people's perceptions, no masking or self-soothing. Instead, I will sit fully in it. With every word I am about to write, I aim to free myself from the need to fill those holes and hopefully lessen the days when I cast a negative light on my journey.

I want to say that I was a fool at times for trusting my inner compass, that indescribable force that pulled me forward. But, I can't. If my future struggles had been magically foretold, I still would have gone. I was destined to sail on the MS *Amsterdam* and those cherished 115 days will forever be worth it.

I will admit, my steadfast optimism and unwavering determination has now been slightly tamed, or rather matured for the sake of peace—a peace that came once I stopped craving and pushing toward a life I desired, but didn't have.

Still, I will continue onward. As tempting as it is to play it safe and declare, "Absolutely not. That's insane. There is no way I am doing that," the truth is, the minute I'm pulled forward again, into the whirlwind of the unknown, I'll go.

But for now, my journey forward is actually a journey backward. As I sit here at a bar on the corner of my street, being observed by random patrons who think I am some big fancy author, I now need to stop writing my feelings and start telling my story. A story that brought me around the world and a story that took me down. Two tales. Two adventures. But I believe—one purpose.

Where on earth do I begin? Start your story where everything changed, they say. Some will say it was with a bad dream, a robbery, getting fired, and PTSD. But I know deep in my soul that those events were merely the aftermath. A necessary destruction resulting from the courageous first steps I took on the path of my personal destiny: a journey home to myself.

IN LOVING MEMORY

Andrè "Pop" Lampert
1/27/1915 – 12/19/2003

• •

I hope I've made you proud, Pop.

Margherita "Gramma" Fiorillo Lampert
1/1/1922 – 6/27/2016

• •

I feel you with me every day.

Yvonne Suhor
11/29/1966 – 9/27/2018

• •

My mentor, my teacher, my friend.

Elmer "Pete" Thompson
4/17/1933 – 6/27/2019

• •

Until we sail again.

Charlie Wilson
? – 12/8/2021

• •

I will forever be sorry we didn't have more time together.
I miss you, my baby boy.

Until we see them.

ACKNOWLEDGMENTS

First off, I want to thank each and every one of you who took the time to read my story. Your support means the world to me. If you loved the book, a shout-out on social media, or even just telling one friend would help me greatly. Thank you!

TO MY EDITORS:

Kathy Szaj – Thank you for teaching me the basics. For supporting me when I was clueless about writing a book. Yes, you are a wonderful editor, but it's your guidance that I will forever cherish.

Jake Manning – You have such a raw talent for developmental editing. You protected my voice and called me out when I got whiney or long-winded. Thank you for your dedication to helping my story come to life. I can't wait to see what life has in store for you!

Magda Bartkowska – Wow. Just wow. I am in awe of your talents. You brought my storytelling skills to a new level. And your editing is mind-blowing. Thank you for bringing this book to the finish line.

TO MY PRODUCTION TEAM:

Paula Sadok – You are not only a friend who has quickly become family, but your blurb blew me away. I still can't believe you wrote it in an hour. I am sorry I had to take out the word "simulacrum." I genuinely had no idea what it meant. In all, you amaze me.

Matt Scott – Thank you for capturing me so authentically for my author photo. You are so gifted.

Gertrudis Achecar – Thank you for keeping my mindset on point and giving me a hand-up when I needed it the most. You are an amazing coach.

Lydia Hubbell – Thank you for being the book's final set of eyes.

SPECIAL MENTIONS:

Yanira Santiago, David Meneses, Angela Doman and Amber Watson – There are no words. None. You all were the wind in my sails during those trying years. So enjoy your cheesy pun and know that my life is so much better for having you in it. I love you.

Maritza Parks – Thank you for braving the storm and reading my first draft. Looking back now, seven drafts later, I wouldn't wish that on my worst enemy. Thank you, my dear friend.

Olivia Freeland – If I had a nickel for every time I asked you to reread parts of my book for notes, I'd be rich. That says so much about your devotion as my friend. Thank you, thank you, thank you!

Brian Marsh – Thank you for getting me through the dark parts of the book-writing process. You came along so randomly, but now I can't imagine my life without you in it.

Kel Martin – You were one of those pivotal people in my life. After just meeting me out in the middle of the ocean, you saw something in me I didn't. I am so proud to show this to you. Everyone who read the book early is dying to meet you. You might just be the star of my book.

My table (Sally, Don, Pete, Ken, and Detta) – What I wouldn't give for another dinner with you. If I wrote about every fond memory we shared, the book would be a thousand pages long. I miss you all so terribly and hope that those of us left can one day sail together again.

My book club ladies: Diana Chen, Emily Hertz, Carolyn Kaleh, and Vaneta Qendro – I will never forget showing up to book club as an author to listen to you talk about my work. It was so surreal. A memory I will forever cherish. Thank you all so much for supporting my efforts.

My beta readers: Matt Einhorn, Lydia Hubbell, Lindsi Jeter, Aaron Sherry and Amber Watson. Your notes challenged me in the best of ways. Thank you for giving me so much of your time on those long zoom calls.

TO MY FAMILY:

Mom, Jim, my three siblings, niece and nephews, my family in Italy, and everyone I adopted as family – Thank you for supporting me when at times all you could understandably do was worry. I am sorry for all the gray hair I have given some of you. Thank you for loving me. I hope I have made you proud.

TO MY DEAREST FRIENDS:

There are so many of you (not mentioned) that I want to thank for giving me the gift of your friendship. I am so very blessed to have you in my life. The below are a few of you that knew of my book and were actively present while I wrote it.

Gertrudis Achecar, Alberto Bonilla, Steve Borkowski, Jennifer Brenner, Angela Doman, Matt Doman, Courtney Davis, Julissa Deleon, Daryl Edelstein, Matt Einhorn, Olivia Freeland, Lydia Hubbell, Lindsi Jeter, Greg Magana, Brian Marsh, David Meneses, Mike Millett, Betty Monroe, Maritza Parks, Yanira Santiago, Aaron Sherry, Julie Sopko, Kathy Szaj, Maggie Tierney, Amber Watson, Laura Zamora and the "Stoop Crew." – Your presence has made my life richer. Your feedback challenged me to be better. Your words of encouragement when I felt scared and alone kept me going. Your problem-solving skills helped me navigate road bumps. Your calls, texts, check-ins, flights to NYC, and long walks reminded me how loved I am. I am so thankful for the time you gave me to help me make this book fly. I love you all.

My Art Sakers – You all are always and forever my tribe.

Lastly, to all those whose actions challenged me to grow stronger and wiser – Thank you.

ABOUT THE AUTHOR

STEPHANIE WILSON believes storytelling can save lives. Her MBA and over a decade of artistic training both help her live out that passion. Born in New Jersey, but raised in Florida, she lives to laugh and is a lover of animals. As a kid, Stephanie dreamed of being the first female president, but always added the disclaimer that if she couldn't make that happen, she just wanted her life to be a good story. In her eyes, she definitely got her wish. Stephanie resides in New York City's Upper West Side with her scruffy Puerto Rican street dog, Luna.

Photo & Video Collection

A chapter by chapter visual collection accompanies this book.
If you would like to follow along during (or after) the read,
you may do so here:

Book's Instagram:
@BigWavesWoodenBenches

Facebook:
Facebook.com/BigWavesWoodenBenches

Or on my personal website:
www.TheStephanieWilson.com

www.ingramcontent.com/pod-product-compliance
Lightning Source LLC
Chambersburg PA
CBHW050853150626
46549CB00013B/1454